LUKE

LUKE

Storyteller, Interpreter, Evangelist

MIKEAL C. PARSONS

BAYLOR UNIVERSITY PRESS

Cover Design by Pamela Poll

Library of Congress Cataloging-in-Publication Data

Parsons, Mikeal Carl, 1957–
  Luke : storyteller, interpreter, evangelist / Mikeal C. Parsons.
  252 pages cm
  Includes bibliographical references and index.
  ISBN 978-1-4813-0068-1 (pbk. : alk. paper)
1. Luke, Saint. I. Title.
  BS2465.P37 2014
  226.4'06—dc23
                        2014015572

For Heidi

Contents

Part Three: Luke the Evangelist

Preface

A book devoted to the examination of the composition and reception of Luke's writings deserves a brief compositional history of its own. About a decade and a half ago, when Patrick Alexander was still at Hendrickson Publishers, he, in his famously irresistible way, recruited me to write a manuscript on Luke's writings. At first, the agreement was oral and conceptual in nature. Over time, it took the shape of a companion volume to Warren Carter's *Matthew: Storyteller, Interpreter, Evangelist*. Eventually, Patrick left Hendrickson, and I was adopted by James Ernest, who promptly began breathing new life into the plan for a volume on Luke and also recruited writers for the other Gospels (including a repeat performance by Warren Carter). Not long after, James, too, left for other professional opportunities, and I was inherited by Sara Scott, who, thankfully, stayed around to see the completion of this volume. I could never have guessed at the outset that the gestational period of the book would extend through three editors, and that those seemingly insurmountable production problems would have real advantages, as all three editors contributed their own unique and considerable skills to the final form of the book.

The post-publication life of the volume has been no less adventurous! *Luke: Storyteller, Interpreter, Evangelist* was one of the titles (along with the others in the series) purchased from Hendrickson by Baker Academic in 2010. After two years, Baker Academic decided to let the book go out of print. Thankfully, Carey Newman and Baylor

University Press saw fit to keep the book in circulation. For their work on this current iteration of the volume, I am deeply grateful!

Early on I was intrigued by the nomenclature of Warren Carter's original book in the series—"Storyteller, Interpreter, Evangelist"— and though Carter himself did not use these as organizing principles, I determined from the beginning that I would organize my book around those concepts. Over the next several years, as I was invited to contribute to various collections or *Festschriften*, I took each occasion as the opportunity to write an essay related to one of the three themes: Luke as Storyteller, Interpreter, or Evangelist. As a result, much of this book has appeared already in print, scattered in various books and journals, some more obscure than others. And I gratefully acknowledge all those publishers who subsequently granted permission to reproduce various portions of those previously published essays (see "Acknowledgments"). But this book is not simply a collection of essays, since each essay from the beginning was planned to be an essential component of this project. Whether the volume "hangs together" in its various concerns will be a matter for its own reception history.

Dr. William H. Bellinger Jr. (Baylor Religion Chair) and Dr. J. Randall O'Brien (then Baylor Provost, now President at Carson-Newman College) were instrumental in providing resources for the original publication. Parts of two of the chapters (4 and 6) were originally cowritten with students, Justin R. Howell (now pursuing doctoral studies at the University of Chicago) and Pamela Hedrick (now on faculty at St. Joseph's College, Maine). Appreciation is expressed for their willingness to include this material in the present volume. Finally, for the love and support of my family, and especially my wife, Heidi, I am grateful beyond words. Despite her own pressing duties as scholar, teacher, and mother, she shouldered additional responsibilities at crucial times both in the production and in the reprint of this book. I (once again) dedicate this volume to her in love and gratitude.

Mikeal C. Parsons
Baylor University
April 2014

Foreword

Perhaps it is best to begin by stating what this book is *not*. This book is not a commentary on the Lukan writings; it does not attempt to provide a sequential, passage-by-passage interpretation of the text. Nonetheless, one will find plenty of exegesis of specific passages throughout the book. Nor is this book a monograph proper; that is to say, the book does not argue a sustained thesis from beginning to end about some particular Lukan theme(s) or purpose(s). The book is not an introduction to Luke-Acts, either, though the reader of this text will indeed have been introduced to many of the central issues involved in interpreting the Lukan corpus. Finally, this book is not focused on the history of Lukan research, though as one can tell from the nearly 400 notes in the text, Lukan scholarship is hardly neglected.

Rather, this book represents a series of forays into the Lukan terrain from three different angles—Luke as storyteller, Luke as interpreter, and Luke as evangelist.[1] Since the book is organized around these rubrics, a brief explanation of what each of these terms represents is in order.

Following a survey of the traditions surrounding the author of Luke and Acts, known as "Luke" at least since the second century, we turn, in the first major section, to the first rubric. Luke as Storyteller suggests taking seriously the rhetorical and theological artistry of the Third Evangelist. Recent studies in narrative criticism have certainly highlighted Luke's storytelling abilities, but as we shall see, the recognition of Luke's rhetorical skills is an ancient one. Rather than present a narrative-critical study of Luke and/or Acts,[2] I have decided to explore various aspects of Luke as storyteller within the context of ancient rhetorical criticism as practiced in the Hellenistic world and as represented by the Hellenistic rhetorical tradition, especially the progymnasmata. This section contains two chapters, one in which I explore, in a preliminary way, the texts of Luke and Acts in light of Theon's progymnasmata for examples of how the rhetorical tradition influenced "how" Luke said what he said. In the second, I take one specific passage, the Lukan prologue (Luke 1:1-4) and try to show how that knowledge of rhetorical conventions might shed light on Luke's opening argument.

Luke as Interpreter presents the opportunity to explore the author's treatment of traditional materials and social conventions. In three chapters, I explore Luke as an interpreter of pagan, Jewish, and Christian traditions. In each case, I have tried to pursue "a path less traveled by" in order to offer some fresh insight into this otherwise very familiar territory. In the chapter on pagan traditions, I explore the relatively uncharted territories of ancient physiognomy and friendship, seeking to show how knowledge of these larger Greco-Roman thought patterns and customs illuminates certain aspects of Luke and Acts. In the chapter on Jewish traditions, rather than a global analysis of the well-worn question of Luke's use of the Jewish Scriptures, I have chosen to compare Luke's view of Jerusalem with the place the holy city held in first-century Jewish thought, followed by an exploration of the much-disputed use by Luke of the suffering servant image of Isaiah 53 in Acts. In the chapter on Luke's interpretation of Christian tradition, I have, for the most part, eschewed the typical redaction-critical wanderings in the labyrinth of the Synoptic Problem in favor of looking at how Luke may have dealt with a preexisting "L" parables collection and what that collection may tell us about the overall emphasis of the journey narrative in which those parables are set. The second half of that chapter explores how Luke's characterization of Paul in Acts would have been heard by an audience already familiar with the "Paul of the letters." The conclusion reached there, going against Philipp Vielhauer and scholars with similar views, is that there is remarkable coherence between these two portraits.

In the final section, Luke as Evangelist, I explore Luke's view of the Jesus event as a light for revelation to the Gentiles and for the glory of the people of Israel (see Luke 2:32). One specific text, the conversion of Cornelius (and Peter; Acts 10–11), allows us to examine Luke's view of the inclusion of Jew and Gentile in the eschatological community of God. In all these cases, the attempt is to be illustrative not exhaustive, providing some models of how one might approach these or similar questions.

Notes

1. In its earlier version, *Luke: Storyteller, Interpreter, Evangelist* was part of a series that included Warren Carter, *Matthew: Storyteller, Interpreter, Evangelist* (Peabody, Mass.: Hendrickson, 1996); Francis Moloney, *Mark: Storyteller, Interpreter, Evangelist* (Peabody, Mass.: Hendrickson, 2003), and Warren Carter, *John: Storyteller, Interpreter, Evangelist* (Peabody, Mass.: Hendrickson, 2006).

2. There are numerous studies already that analyze Luke's writings from the perspective of modern narrative criticism, beginning with Robert Tannehill's two-volume work, *The Narrative Unity of Luke-Acts* (Philadelphia: Fortress, 1986, 1991). My own attempt at this kind of work, focusing especially on narrative beginnings and endings, may be found in my book, *The Departure of Jesus in Luke-Acts: The Ascension Narratives in Context* (JSNTSup 21; Sheffield: JSOT Press, 1987).

Acknowledgements

The author and Hendrickson Publishers are grateful to the following publishers:

Bible Review for kind permission to reprint, in revised form, the original version of chapter one, "The Life of a Legend: The Making of 'Luke,'" originally published as "Who Wrote the Gospel of Luke?" in *Bible Review* 17.2 (April, 2001): 12–21, 54–55.

Scholars Press for kind permission to reprint, in revised form, the original version of chapter two, "Luke and the Progymnasmata: A Preliminary Investigation into the Preliminary Exercises" in Todd Penner and Caroline Vander Stichele, eds., *Contextualizing Acts: Lukan Narrative and Greco-Roman Discourse* (SBLSymS Volume 20; Atlanta: Scholars Press, 2003), 43–63.

Baker Academic for kind permission to reprint on pages 64–71 another version of material originally published as chapter six, "His Ankles and Feet Were Made Strong: Signs of Character in the Man Lame from Birth," in *Body and Character in Luke and Acts: The Subversion of Physiognomy in Early Christianity* (Grand Rapids: Baker, 2006), 109–22.

Mercer University Press for kind permission to reprint, in revised form, the original version of part of chapter five, "Interpreting Jewish Traditions," originally published as "The Place of Jerusalem on the Lukan Landscape: An Exercise in Theological Cartography," in Richard P. Thompson and Thomas E. Phillips, eds., *Literary Studies in Luke-Acts: Essays in Honor of Joseph B. Tyson* (Macon, Ga.: Mercer University Press, 1998), 155–72.

Trinity Press International for kind permission to reprint, in revised
form, the original version of part of chapter five, "Interpreting Jewish
Traditions," originally published as "Isaiah 53 in Acts 8: A Reply to
Morna Hooker," in William Bellinger, Bruce Corley, and William Farmer,
eds., *Isaiah 53 and Christian Origins* (Valley Forge, Pa.: Trinity, 1998),
104–19.

Southwest Journal of Theology for kind permission to reprint, in revised
form, the original version of part of chapter 6, "Landmarks along the
Way: The Function of the 'L' Parables in the Lukan Travel Narrative," in
SwJT 40 (1997): 33–47.

Polebridge Press for kind permission to reproduce two charts from
Robert W. Funk, *The Poetics of Biblical Narrative* (Sonoma, Calif.:
Polebridge, 1988), 83f.

Abbreviations

General

B.C.E.	Before the Common Era
C.E.	Common Era
ch(s).	chapter(s)
cod.	Codex
col.	column
diss.	dissertation
frag.	fragment
NIV	New International Version
NT	New Testament
OT	Old Testament
v(v).	verse(s)

Ancient Sources

Apocrypha
    Sir   Sirach
Achilles Tatius
    Leuc. Clit.   *The Adventures of Leucippe and Cleitophon*
Alexander
    Fig.   *De figuris*
Ambrose
    Off.   *De officiis ministrorum*
Aristophanes
    Th.   *Thesmophoriazusae*

Aristotle
 Eth. Nic. *Nichomachean Ethics*
Basil
 Lit.   *Litterae*
Cicero
 Inv.   *De inventione rhetorica*
 Off.   *De officiis*
Clement of Alexandria
 Paed.   *Christ the Educator*
Demetrius
 Elec.   *Style*
Demosthenes
 Or.   *Orations*
Dio Chrysostom
 Or.   *Orations*
Dionysius of Halicarnassos
 Gell. An.
Epiphanius
 Pan.   *Panarion*
Eusebius
 Hist. eccl. *Ecclesiastical History*
Hesiod
 Op.   *Works and Days*
Herodotus
 Hist.   *Histories*
Homer
 Il.   *Iliad*
 Od.   *Odyssey*
Iamblichus
 VP   Lives of the Pythagoreans
Irenaeus
 Haer.   *Against Heresies*
Jerome
 Vir. ill.   *De viris illustribus*
John Chrysostom
 Hom. Act. *Homiliae in Acta apostolorum*
Josephus
 Ag. Ap. *Against Apion*
 Ant.   *Jewish Antiquities*
 J.W.   *Jewish Wars*
New Testament Apocrypha
 Gos. Thom. *Gospel of Thomas*

Philo of Alexandria
    Spec. Laws   On the Special Laws
Pliny [the Elder]
    Hist. Nat.   Natural History
Plutarch
    Tim.   Timoleon and Aemilius
Polemo of Laodicea
    Adam.   Epitome Adamantiana
    Phys.   On Physiognomy
    Anon. Lat.   Anonyme Latin
Pseudepigrapha
    Ass. Mos.   Assumption of Moses
    2 Bar.   2 Baruch
    1 En.   1 Enoch
    Sib. Or.   Sibylline Oracles
Pseudo-Aristotle
    Phsyiogn.   Phsyiognomica
Pseudo-Polemo
    Epitom. Matr. Epitome Matrido (Madrid Epitome)
Rabbinic Literature
    b.   Babylonian Talmud (followed by tractate name)
Seneca the Younger
    Brev. vit.   De brevitatae vitae
    Ep. ad Luc. Epistulae morales ad Lucilium
Suetonius
    Aug.   Lives of the Caesars: Divus Augustus
Tertullian
    An.   The Soul
    Cult. fem.   The Apparel of Women
Xenophon
    Hell.   Hellenica

Bible Versions

LXX	Septuagint
NIV	New International Version
NJB	New Jerusalem Bible
NRSV	New Revised Standard Version
RSV	Revised Standard Version

Modern Literature

AB	Anchor Bible
ABD	Anchor Bible Dictionary. Edited by D. N. Freedman. 6 vols. New York: Doubleday, 1992
AnBib	Analecta Biblica
ANRW	Aufstieg und Niedergang der römischen Welt: Geschichte und Kultur Roms im Spiegel der neuren Forschung. Edited by H. Temporini and W. Haase. Berlin: De Gruyter, 1972
ANTC	Abingdon New Testament Commenaries
ASNU	Acta seminarii neotestamentici upsaliensis
BBR	Bulletin for Biblical Research
BDAG	Bauer, W., F. W. Danker, W. F. Arndt, and F. W. Gingrich. Greek-English Lexicon of the New Testament and Other Early Christian Literature. 3rd. ed. Chicago: The University of Chicago Press, 2000.
BDF	Blass, F., A. Debrunner, and R. W. Funk. A Greek Grammar of the New Testament and Other Early Christian Literature. Chicago: The University of Chicago Press, 1961
BETL	Bibliotheca ephemeridum theologicarum lovaniensium
Bib	Biblica
BZ	Biblische Zeitschrift
BZNW	Beihefte zur Zeitschrift für die neutestamentliche Wissenschaft
CBQ	Catholic Biblical Quarterly
ETL	Ephemerides theologicae lovanienses
ETR	Etudes théologiques et religieuses
EvQ	Evangelical Quarterly
EvT	Evangelische Theologie
FFNT	Foundations and Facets: New Testament
GBS	Guides to Biblical Scholarship
HTKNT	Herders theologischer Kommentar zum Neuen Testament
HTR	Harvard Theological Review
HTS	Harvard Theological Studies
HUT	Hermeneutische Untersuchungen zur Theologie
ICC	International Critical Commentary
Int	Interpretation

JAOS	*Journal of the American Oriental Society*
JBL	*Journal of Biblical Literature*
JETS	*Journal of the Evangelical Theological Society*
JSNTSup	Journal for the Study of the New Testament: Supplement Series
JSP	*Journal for the Study of the Pseudepigrapha*
JSPSup	Journal for the Study of the Pseudepigrapha: Supplement Series
JTS	*Journal of Theological Studies*
LCL	Loeb Classical Library
NIB	*The New Interpreter's Bible*
NICNT	New International Commentary on the New Testament
NIGTC	New International Greek Testament Commentary
NovT	*Novum Testamentum*
NovTSup	Novum Testamentum Supplements
NTS	*New Testament Studies*
OBT	Overture to Biblical Theology
ÖTK	Ökumensicher Taschenbuch-Kommentar
OTP	*Old Testament Pseudepigrapha.* Edited by J. H. Charlesworth. 2 vols. New York: Doubleday, 1983.
PG	Patrologia graeca. Edited by J.-P. Migne. 162 vols. Paris: 1857–1866.
PL	Patrologia Latina. Edited by J.-P. Migne. 217 vols. Paris: 1844–1864
PRSt	*Perspectives in Religious Studies*
RelSRev	*Religious Studies Review*
RevExp	*Review and Expositor*
SBLDS	Society of Biblical Literature Symposium Series
SBLSP	*Society of Biblical Literature Seminar Papers*
SBLSymS	Society of Biblical Literature Symposium Series
SBLMS	Society of Biblical Literature Monograph Series
SBLRBS	Society of Biblical Literature Resources for Biblical Study
SBLTT	Society of Biblical Literature Texts and Translations
SBT	Studies in Biblical Theology
SEG	Supplementum epigraphicum graecum. Germantown, Md.: Sijthoff & Noordhoff
SJLA	Studies in Judaism in Late Antiquity
SNTSMS	Society for New Testament Studies Monograph Series
SP	Sacra pagina

SwJT	*Southwestern Journal of Theology*
TAPA	*Transactions of the American Philological Society*
TBei	*Theologische Beiträge*
TDNT	*Theological Dictionary of the New Testament.* Edited by Gerhard Kittel and Georg Firiedrich. Translated by G. W. Bromiley. 10 vols. Grand Rapids: Eerdmans, 1964–1976
TLG	*Thesaurus Linguae Graecae. TLG Digital Library.* CD-ROM. Version E. Irvine, Cal.: University of California, Irvine, 1999
VT	*Vetus Testamentum*
WBC	Word Biblical Commentary
WUNT	Wissenschaftliche Untersuchungen zum Neuen Testament
ZNW	*Zeitschrift für die neutestamentliche Wissenschaft und die Kunde der älteren Kirche*
ZTK	*Zeitschrift für Theologie und Kirche*

CHAPTER 1

The Life of a Legend: The Making of "Luke"

If the Third Gospel were attributed to a person named Luke very soon after its publication, then it is reasonable to assume that the first audiences of this Gospel were already associating this document with the Luke known to be a participant in the Pauline mission.[1] This chapter attempts to trace the traditions regarding the identity of the writer; hence, the making of Luke.[2] Understanding something about these traditions associating "Luke" with these writings is a necessary prerequisite to considering the writer as a storyteller, interpreter, and evangelist.

Luke was, according to tradition, a physician and a friend of Paul, and he is described as a Gentile writing for a Gentile audience. He is also credited with writing the canonical Acts of the Apostles, the earliest account of the first followers of Jesus. The textual evidence suggests that these stories are very early, dating to as early as the second century. By the fourth century, these traditions were well enough established to be summarized by the historian Eusebius in his *Ecclesiastical History* (312–324 C.E.):

> Luke, being by birth one of the people of Antioch, by profession a physician, having been with Paul a good deal, and having associated intimately with the rest of the apostles, has left us examples of the art of curing souls that he obtained from them in two divinely inspired books,—the Gospel, which he testifies that he wrote out even as they delivered to him who from the beginning were eyewitnesses and ministers of the word, all of whom [or all of which facts?] he says he had followed even from the beginning, and the Acts of the

Apostles, which he composed, receiving his information with his own eyes, no longer by hearsay. (3.4)

But how have these traditions withstood both the test of time and the critical eye of modern biblical scholarship? Before exploring the identity of the writer, we might begin by querying the extent of that which was written. In the opening lines of his Gospel, Luke offers his own explanation of why he began to write:

Since many have undertaken to set down an orderly account of the events that have been fulfilled among us, just as they were handed on to us by those who from the beginning were eyewitnesses and servants of the word, I too decided, after investigating everything carefully from the very first, to write an orderly account for you, most excellent Theophilus, so that you may know the truth concerning the things about which you have been instructed. (Luke 1:1–4)

The "events" to be described are, of course, the life, death, and resurrection of Jesus. Note that the Gospel writer does not count himself among the eyewitnesses to Jesus' life. And he describes himself as only one of many who have set out to write Jesus' story. The author dedicates his text to Theophilus, who is not mentioned again in Luke's Gospel.

Theophilus's name does appear once more in the New Testament, however—in the introduction to the book of Acts. This is our first clue regarding an assertion that is commonly made about the author of the Third Gospel: He is also responsible for writing Acts.

The book of Acts begins:

In the former treatise, Theophilus, I wrote about all that Jesus did and taught from the beginning until the day when he was taken up to heaven, after giving instructions through the Holy Spirit to the apostles whom he had chosen. (Acts 1:1–2)

The book of Acts is thus presented as the Third Gospel's sequel. In it, Luke will continue to relate the events that transpired among the earliest Christians, from shortly after Jesus' death until just before Paul's.

The extrabiblical evidence that these two books are by the same hand dates as early as the last third of the second century, when both the Muratorian Canon (the earliest known list of writings deemed canonical by the church)[3] and the early church father Irenaeus, bishop of Lyons, identify Luke as the author of both the Third Gospel and the book of Acts.[4]

Of all the assertions traditionally made about Luke, this one has fared the best in modern scholarship. Today, however, the attribution of Luke and Acts to a single author is based primarily on shared literary and thematic elements.[5] For example, both texts include travel narratives in which the hero—Jesus or Paul—journeys to Jerusalem and is arrested on false charges (Luke 9:51–19:28; Acts 19:21–21:36). The miracles performed by Peter and Paul in Acts mirror those of Jesus in the Gospel of Luke. All three figures heal lame men with the instructions: "Stand up and walk" (Acts 3:1–10, 14:8–11; Luke 5:17–26); and all three resurrect the dead, with Peter and Jesus employing the same command: "Get up" (Acts 9:36–40, 20:7–12; Luke 8:40–56).

In Luke, the Holy Spirit descends upon Jesus while he is at prayer before 40 days of "testing" and before he begins his public ministry (Luke 3:21–22). So it is in Acts, when the Holy Spirit falls upon his disciples on the Feast of Pentecost while they are at prayer after 40 days of instruction but before they begin their public ministry (Acts 2:1–4). Furthermore, the account of the first Christian martyr, Stephen, who is tried before the high priest and then stoned to death (Acts 6:8–15, 7:54–60), reflects the trial and death of Jesus (Luke 22–23). Jesus, at his trial, predicts that "the Son of Man will be seated at the right hand of the power of God" (Luke 22:69); Stephen, standing before the high priest, exclaims that he "[sees] the heavens opened and the Son of Man standing at the right hand of God" (Acts 7:56). When Jesus dies, he cries out: "Father, into your hands I commend my spirit" (Luke 23:46); Stephen makes a similar plea during his martyrdom: "Lord Jesus, receive my spirit" (Acts 7:59).

Luke and Acts also share an overarching geographical plan that has Jerusalem at its center.[6] In Luke, events move toward Jerusalem, with the gospel beginning and ending in the temple. In Acts, Paul and others alternately journey outwards from Jerusalem (to Judea and Samaria, Asia Minor, Europe, and ultimately Rome) and back again (see Acts 12:25, 15:2, 18:22, 19:21, 20:16, 21:13, 25:1). Both books also see salvation history as falling into three periods: the period of Israel, the period of Jesus, and the period of the church. Both books demonstrate an interest in the same themes: Christology, the Holy Spirit, eschatology, and discipleship. Finally, both employ the same vocabulary and exhibit a strikingly similar writing style. Together, these features have led to a widespread consensus among scholars regarding the common authorship of Luke and Acts, underscored by the widespread use of the phrase "Luke-Acts" ever since it was coined by the American biblical scholar Henry Cadbury in 1927.[7]

The separation of Luke from Acts in the canon of Scripture is usually explained by the limitations of the scroll, the presumed medium of communication in the first-century Mediterranean world. Luke and Acts were simply too long to fit on one scroll, this theory goes, and thus were divided prior to "publication."[8] Or, some scholars have suggested, the two treatises may have been separated when they were taken into the canon (John's Gospel now separating Luke from Acts), with Luke being subsumed under the rubric of the "four-fold gospel" and Acts serving as a bridge between the gospel collection and the letters. There is, of course, neither any manuscript evidence that these two documents were ever circulated as one nor any canonical list that in placing the texts together might provide a clue to a pre-canonical unified form.[9] Still, it is reasonable to assume that the two writings came from the same hand, one (Acts) functioning as a sequel to the other (Luke). The next question, of course, is from whose hand?

The Gospel title—"εὐαγγέλιον κατὰ Λουκᾶν" (*euangelion kata Loukan*, the Gospel According to Luke)—appears at the end of the oldest extant manuscript of the Gospel of Luke, a papyrus known as 𝔓[75], now in the Bodmer Library in Geneva. But this fragmentary manuscript dates only to about 175 to 225 C.E., or 100 to 125 [100 to 150?] years after the Gospel is thought to have been written. The title probably reflects the oldest tradition, linking an author named Luke to the writing of the Third Gospel. Though the title does not specify Luke as a physician, since there were no other early Christians known to us by that name from the first century, this is a logical inference.

What else do we know about the author? In the prologue to the Gospel (Luke 1:1–4), the author seems to identify himself as a second-generation Christian relying on others' eyewitness testimony. He cannot therefore be counted among the apostles. Furthermore, throughout the book of Acts, when describing Paul's activities the narrator occasionally shifts from the third- to the first-person plural "we" (Acts 16:10–17, 20:5–15, 21:1–18, 27:1–28:16). For example, of Paul's final trip to Jerusalem, he writes: "When we found a ship bound for Phoenicia, we went on board and set sail. We came in sight of Cyprus; and leaving it on our left, we sailed to Syria and landed at Tyre, because the ship was to unload its cargo there. We looked up the disciples and stayed there for seven days. Through the Spirit they told Paul not to go into Jerusalem" (Acts 21:2–4). While it is safe to say modern scholars are deeply divided regarding the significance of the "we" passages in Acts,[10] there can be little debate that the early church took them to indicate the author of Acts (and Luke) was a companion of the Apostle Paul.

The church father Irenaeus was one of the first to interpret these "we" passages as evidence that Luke was a companion of Paul: "But that this Luke was inseparable from Paul and was his fellow-worker in the gospel he himself makes clear, not boasting of it, but compelled to do so by truth itself."[11] Refuting especially the followers of Marcion and Valentinus, Irenaeus argues on the basis of the common authorship of Luke and Acts that the veracity of the two works must stand or fall together. For Irenaeus, the book of Acts is the glue which holds together the two major portions of the New Testament, the "Gospel" and the "Apostle," as they were called by early Christian writers.

The book of Acts is not the only potential source of information about the relation between Paul and Luke, however. The name Luke appears three times in letters attributed to Paul. Unfortunately, this Luke is never identified as the Gospel writer. Of course, that has not stopped speculation, from the time of Irenaeus on.

In a letter to Philemon, a Christian living in Colossae in Asia Minor, Paul lists a man named Luke as one of his "fellow workers" (Phlm 24); and in an open letter to the Christian community of Colossae, the writer, identified as Paul, sends greetings from "Luke, the beloved physician" (Col 4:14). Finally, the author of the Pastoral Epistles, most likely one of Paul's followers who writes in Paul's voice, inserts these words in 2 Timothy: "Do your best to come to me soon, for Demas, in love with this present world, has deserted me and gone to Thessalonica; Crescens has gone to Galatia, Titus to Dalmatia. *Only Luke is with me* [emphasis added]. Get Mark and bring him with you, for he is useful in my ministry" (2 Tim 4:9–11). These scant references have augmented—or simply reflect—Luke's reputation as one of Paul's most faithful companions.

If Luke is the author of Luke and Acts, then it is a small move to claim that he was a physician, an identification suggested by Col 4:14. This, too, is repeated in the writings of Irenaeus and in the Muratorian Canon, and this point was picked up in the literature of the early and medieval church where it was asserted that in his writings, Luke the physician had provided "medicine for the soul." Jacobus de Varogine's comments in the *Golden Legend* are typical:

[Luke's] Gospel is replete with benefits; whence he that wrote it was a physician, to signify that he has set before us a most healthful medicine. This medicine is of three kinds. There is the medicine that cures diseases, namely penance, which cures all spiritual ills. There is the medicine which improves one's well-being, namely the observance of the counsels which makes man better and more perfect. There is the medicine which preserves one from sickness, namely the avoidance of sinful occasions and of evil associations. And Luke shows us in his Gospel that the heavenly Physician set all these medicines before us.[12]

The view that Luke was a physician has received mixed reviews in recent scholarship. Late in the nineteenth century, Irish physician and scholar William K. Hobart searched the healing stories in Luke for what he believed were medical terms, such as "crippled," "pregnant," or "abscess," or ordinary words used in a "medical" sense. From this "internal evidence" Hobart concluded that Luke and Acts were written by the same person, and that the writer was a medical man.[13] But Henry Cadbury soon dismantled this argument by demonstrating that the terms on Hobart's lists occur in the Septuagint, Josephus, Plutarch, and Lucian, all non-medical writings. Cadbury concluded, "The style of Luke bears no more evidence of medical training and interest than does the language of other writers who were not physicians."[14] In a tongue-in-cheek lexical note entitled "Luke and the Horse-Doctors," Cadbury later showed that Luke's vocabulary shows a remarkable similarity with the corpus of writings of ancient veterinarians![15] His refutation was so effective that he virtually eliminated this special pleading to a so-called medical vocabulary.[16] His students used to jest that Cadbury earned his doctorate by taking Luke's away. Still, we should not claim more for Cadbury's evidence than does Cadbury himself. Cadbury is careful to say that the so-called medical language cannot be used to prove that the author of the Third Gospel was a physician, but neither, he asserts, should Cadbury's own analysis be used to "prove" that he was not. Subsequent critical scholarship has often heard the first caveat but not the second.

The modern period has also witnessed a sharp attack on the traditional identification of Luke as a Gentile writing for a Gentile audience. This long-dominant view may have roots that reach back as far as the second century to an extrabiblical text, *Prologue to the Gospels.* This text, also known as the "*Anti-Marcionite*" *Prologue,* contained a description of Luke that church father Eusebius, among others, followed: "Luke was a Syrian of Antioch, by profession a physician, the disciple of the apostles, and later a follower of Paul."[17] In Luke's day, Antioch was a prominent early Christian center. According to Acts 11:26, "It was in Antioch that the disciples were first called 'Christians.'" All of Paul's missionary journeys departed from and returned to this city. Connected to the view that Luke was not Jewish is the widely held assumption that Luke's Gospel is the "Gentile Gospel," written for a predominantly, if not exclusively, Gentile audience. It includes Simeon's prophecy over the infant Jesus that he would be a "light for revelation to the Gentiles" (Luke 2:32), the healing of the Gentile centurion's slave (Luke 7:1–10), and the commission by the risen Christ to the disciples to preach "forgiveness of sins to all nations" (Luke 24:47),[18] all of which foreshadow the interest in the Gentile mission that occupies much of Acts.

Recently, however, a small but vocal minority has raised the possibility that Luke was in fact Jewish, or at least deeply interested in Judaism. They assume that the Luke referred to in Colossians was either a "God-fearer" with deep Jewish interests or not the same person as the author of the Gospel. This view also has ancient roots. In the fourth century, Bishop Epiphanius of Cyprus suggested that Luke was one of the 70 disciples sent out by Jesus (Luke 10) and was thus presumably Jewish.[19]

Some have assumed that if Luke were from such a well-known Greco-Roman city as Antioch, he must have been a Gentile. The first-century C.E. Jewish historian Flavius Josephus gives evidence that a Jew from Antioch could have been called an "Antiochene." Thus, even the tradition that Luke was from Antioch, an "Antiochene," does not preclude his being Jewish.[20] Antioch did have a Jewish community: Josephus notes that the first Seleucid king, Seleucus Nicator (c. 358–281 B.C.E.), who made Antioch his capital, granted the local Jews citizenship in gratitude for their having fought with the Greek armies.[21] And according to John Chrysostom, who served as deacon of Antioch in the late fourth century C.E., the city had several synagogues. The archaeological evidence of the Jewish community is limited, however, to a small stone fragment of a menorah and a lead curse tablet referring to the biblical God Yahweh.

The narrative of Acts can also be read as supporting the view that Luke was a Jew or at least deeply interested in Judaism. Acts clearly presents the "Christian" movement as one Jewish sect among several. This perspective is shared by Christian, Jewish, and Roman characters in Acts, as well as the narrator himself: Twice, the Christian Paul in Acts makes the claim, "I am a Jew" (Acts 21:39, 22:3). Later in Acts, he states that he has "belonged to the strictest sect of our religion and lived as a Pharisee" (Acts 26:5, see also Acts 24:14). Tertullus, the Jewish advocate for the high priest before Felix, states: "We have, in fact, found this man a pestilent fellow, an agitator among all the Jews throughout the world, and a ringleader of the sect of the Nazarenes" (Acts 24:5). Further, the Jews in Rome say to Paul: "But we would like to hear from you what you think, for with regard to this sect we know that everywhere it is spoken against" (Acts 28:22). The Roman procurator Festus reports to King Agrippa about Paul: "His [Jewish] accusers . . . brought no charge in his case of such evils as I supposed, but they had certain points of dispute with him about their own superstition" (Acts 25:18–19).[22] Finally, the gospel narrator states: "But some believers [in Jesus] who belonged to the sect of the Pharisees stood up and said, 'It is necessary for them to be circumcised and ordered to keep the law of Moses'" (Acts 15:5). Such evidence has led Lukan scholars like David Tiede to conclude that "the polemics, scriptural arguments, and 'proofs' which are rehearsed in Luke-Acts are part of an intra-family struggle [among Jews] that, in the wake of the destruction of the temple, is deteriorating into a fight over who is really the faithful 'Israel.'"[23]

Physician, Gentile or Jew, companion of Paul, writer of the Third Gospel and Acts: what one thinks about the identity of Luke rests in large part on one's assessment of these traditions. Did the early church have information about the identity of the author of Luke and Acts that is no longer available to us? Or did someone looking to identify the otherwise anonymous author simply deduce Luke's identity from the text of the New Testament?

Presumably the Gospel's prologue, where the author seems to identify himself as a second-generation Christian, excludes identifying the author as an apostle (and thus making the choice of a "lesser" figure almost inevitable). The "we" sections in Acts demand someone who was a companion of Paul, and Luke the beloved physician emerges as a likely—though, importantly, not the only—candidate.

On the other hand, we must consider the stability of the tradition that identifies Luke as the author. Strictly speaking, the Third Gospel is an anonymous document, making no claims about its authorship. That all testimony agrees in identifying the author as a relatively obscure man named Luke is no trivial matter. Regardless of his identity, the author of Luke and Acts has left for us works that remain two of the most significant contributions by an early Christian to our understanding of the founder of Christianity and its first followers. In the pages that follow, we attempt to explore these writings in terms of Luke's abilities as a storyteller in the context of ancient rhetoric, as an interpreter of pagan, Jewish, and Christian traditions, and as an evangelist whose stories of the elder brother (Luke 15) and Cornelius (Acts 10–11) serve as paradigms for the inclusion of Jews and Gentiles into the people of God. And so the life of this legend continues!

Notes

1. The title of this chapter echoes the work of R. Alan Culpepper, *John, Son of Zebedee: The Life of a Legend* (Columbia: University of South Carolina Press, 1994), in which he collects the various traditions regarding the Apostle John

from the second century to the present. Students of the Lukan writings will also notice in the subtitle an allusion to *The Making of Luke-Acts* (London: SPCK, 1958; repr., Peabody, Mass.: Hendrickson, 1999) by the American "doyen of Lukan studies," Henry Cadbury.

2. I am here concerned with the traditions regarding Luke the physician as the author of Luke and Acts. No less interesting, but surely less well known, are those later traditions that identify Luke first as a painter of icons (especially of the Virgin and Child) and later as the patron saint of the painters' guild. I have treated these traditions in the first chapter ("Luke: Physician, Painter, Patron Saint") in a work co-authored with Heidi J. Hornik, *Illuminating Luke: The Infancy Narrative in Italian Renaissance Painting* (Harrisburg, Pa.: Trinity, 2003).

3. For arguments for a fourth century date for the fragments, see A. C. Sundberg, "Canon Muratori: A Fourth-Century List," *HTR* 66 (1973): 1–41; for a response and defense of the traditional second-century dating, see Harry Gamble, *The New Testament Canon: Its Making and Meaning* (GBS; Philadelphia: Fortress, 1985).

4. Irenaeus, *Haer.* 3.14.1.

5. See esp. Charles H. Talbert, *Literary Patterns, Theological Themes, and the Genre of Luke-Acts* (SBLMS 20; Missoula, Mont.: Scholars Press, 1974); I. Howard Marshall, "Acts and the 'Former Treatise,'" in *The Book of Acts in Its Ancient Literary Setting* (ed. by Bruce W. Winter and Andrew D. Clarke; Grand Rapids: Eerdmans, 1993), 163–82.

6. A feature noted by many, including Luke Timothy Johnson in *Luke* (SP 3; Collegeville, Minn.: Liturgical, 1991). See chapter 5 in this volume for another reading of the role of Jerusalem in the Lukan narratives.

7. See n. 1 on Cadbury. There have been challenges to the assertion of common authorship, largely on the grounds of vocabulary and style. Most notable is Albert C. Clark (*The Acts of the Apostles: A Critical Edition with Introduction and Notes on Selected Passages* [Oxford: Clarendon Press, 1933], 394), who, after a detailed study of the syntax and style of Luke and Acts, concluded "that the differences between Lk. and Acts were of such a kind that they could not be the work of the same author." Wilfred L. Knox countered Clark's arguments in a carefully constructed rebuttal, however. Like Clark, Knox deals with the use of particles, prepositions, conjunctions, and other small parts of speech. Knox reasoned: "It may seem that to discuss such matters is to waste time over minute trivialities; but a man can be hanged for a fingerprint" (*The Acts of the Apostles* [Cambridge: Cambridge University Press, 1948], 3; also 4–15, 100–109).

Other interesting linguistic dissimilarities between Luke and Acts have been more recently observed by Stephen H. Levinsohn, *Textual Connections in Acts* (SBLMS 31; Atlanta: Scholars Press, 1987), who incidentally is not primarily interested in the authorship question.

Modern scholars generally affirm the position of common authorship held by the early church, though the implications of that common authorship are not always clearly distinguished. See, e.g, Mikeal C. Parsons and Richard I. Pervo (*Rethinking the Unity of Luke and Acts* [Minneapolis: Fortress, 1993]), who suggest that we must distinguish among various kinds of unity (e.g., narrative, generic, theological) when speaking of the unity of the Lukan writings and also allow for the possibility that some elements of discontinuity between the two writings might arise from time to time.

8. This argument is made, among others, by Donald Juel in *Luke-Acts: The Promise of History* (Atlanta: John Knox Press, 1983).

9. For more on the canonical shape of Luke and Acts, see Parsons and Pervo, "Introduction," *Rethinking the Unity of Luke and Acts,* 8–13.

10. See Vernon K. Robbins, "Prefaces in Greco-Roman biography and Luke-Acts," *PRSt* 6 (1979): 94–108; Susan Marie Praeder, "The Problem of First Person Narration in Acts," *NovT* 29 (1987): 193–218; Joseph A. Fitzmyer, *Luke the Theologian: Aspects of His Teaching* (New York: Paulist, 1989), 16–22.

11. Irenaeus, *Haer.,* 3.14.1.

12. Jacobus de Voragine, *The Golden Legend* (trans. Granger Ryan and Helmut Ripperger; New York: Longmans, Green, 1941), 626.

13. The quotation is taken from Hobart's cumbersome subtitle to *The Medical Language of St. Luke: A Proof from Internal Evidence that "The Gospel according to St. Luke" and "The Acts of the Apostles" Were Written by the Same Person, and that the Writer was a Medical Man* (1882; repr., Grand Rapids: Baker, 1954). Hobart's thesis was supported by the eminent scholar Adolf von Harnack (*Luke the Physician* [trans. J. R. Wilkinson; New York: Putnam, 1909]).

14. Henry J. Cadbury, *The Style and Literary Method of Luke* (Cambridge: Harvard University Press, 1920), 50.

15. Cadbury, "Luke and the Horse-Doctors," *JBL* 52 (1933): 55–65.

16. That is not to say that defenders of the tradition no longer exist, only that appeals to medical terminology rarely appear in their arguments. See esp. Joseph Fitzmyer, *The Gospel according to Luke: Introduction, Translation, and Notes* (AB 28; Garden City, N.Y.: Doubleday, 1981), 35–59; and *Luke the Theologian: Aspects of His Teaching* (Mahwah, N.J.: Paulist, 1989), 1–26. Fitzmyer offers a carefully and critically nuanced defense of the tradition: Luke the physician was an uncircumcised Semite and sometime companion of Paul.

17. The view that Luke was a Gentile does not rest solely on the tradition that he was an Antiochene, however. Rather, some accept Col 4:14 as identifying Luke as a Gentile. In the preceding verses of this letter, Paul lists a number of Jews who work with him: "Aristarchus my fellow prisoner greets you, as does Mark the cousin of Barnabas, concerning whom you have received instructions—if he comes to you, welcome him. And Jesus who is called Justus greets you. *These are the only ones of the circumcision among my co-workers for the kingdom of God,* and they have been a comfort to me [emphasis added]" (Col 4:10–11). Paul then goes on to list a handful of other workers who, many readers presume, must not be Jews, but "Greeks." He includes "Luke, the beloved physician" in this latter list (Col 4:14).

18. The Greek word ἔθνος (*ethnos*), like *goy* in Hebrew, can mean both "Gentile" and "nation" (a point often noted in discussions of Matt 28:16–20). In Luke 2:32 ἔθνος is translated as "Gentile" but the same word, which also occurs in Luke 24:47, is almost always translated as "nations." Although the Lukan Jesus clearly has Gentiles primarily in mind, Jews are not excluded: " . . . and that repentance and forgiveness of sins is to be proclaimed in his name to all nations, beginning from Jerusalem."

19. Epiphanius, *Pan.* 51.110. A variant reading in the fifth-century manuscript Codex Bezae inserts the phrase: "And there was much rejoicing, and when we were gathered together" at the beginning of Acts 11:28, which makes this verse another "we" passage set in Antioch. This variant reading almost certainly derives from the tradition associating Luke with Antioch.

20. Josephus, *Ag. Ap.* 2:39.

21. Josephus, *Ant.* 12.119.

22. See also the letter of Claudius Lysas in Acts 24:29.

23. David Tiede, *Promise and History in Luke-Acts* (Philadelphia: Fortress, 1980), 7; see also Jacob Jervell, *Luke and the People of God* (Minneapolis: Augsburg, 1972).

PART ONE

LUKE THE STORYTELLER

Luke and the Progymnasmata: A Preliminary Investigation into the Preliminary Exercises

Introduction

Regardless of the "true identity" of the author of Luke and Acts, whom we have traditionally called Luke, this writer's achievements as a storyteller among the NT writers have been widely recognized.[1] Long before the emergence of the literary study of biblical narrative in critical studies, B. H. Streeter referred to Luke as the "consummate literary artist."[2] Ernst Haenchen recognized that Luke was not only a historian and a theologian but also an accomplished writer.[3] Haenchen attributes to Luke the "gift of enlivening bare facts."[4] Slightly modifying Haenchen's rubric, Mark Allen Powell speaks of Luke as "Historian, Theologian, Artist."[5] The swell of interest in the literary aspects of the Third Gospel and Acts, acknowledged by Powell's chapter title, has only increased the references to Luke's literary artistry.[6] In *The Narrative Unity of Luke-Acts,* one of the first literary-critical treatments of Luke, Robert Tannehill called Luke, "an author of literary skill and rich imagination."

But this appreciation for Luke's storytelling abilities reaches into the patristic and medieval periods. Jerome comments several times on the quality of Luke's writing style. In his *Commentary on Isaiah,* he asserts that Luke's "language in the Gospel, as well as in the Acts of the Apostles, that is, in both volumes is more elegant, and smacks of secular eloquence."[7] Elsewhere he notes that Luke "was the most learned in the Greek language among all the evangelists."[8] In light of these passages, when Jerome claims that Luke is the anonymous believer who "wrote the Gospel, of which the same Paul says, 'We have sent together with him the brother whose praise is in the gospel through all the churches,'"[9] that praise must also include Luke's literary ability to write elegantly in Greek.

John Chrysostom, in the first of a series of sermons on Acts that he preached in 401 as the newly appointed bishop of Constantinople, inquired concerning the reason for Luke's two volumes: "And why did he not make one book of it, to send to one man Theophilus, but has divided it into two subjects? For clearness, and to give the brother a pause for rest. Besides, the two treatises are distinct in their subject-matter."[10] This view of Luke's literary prowess continued right through the Middle Ages and the Renaissance. In the thirteenth-century *The Golden Legend*, Jacobus de Voragine remarks that "Luke was well ordered in relation to his appointed task, that of writing his gospel. This is shown by the fact that his gospel is permeated by much truth, filled with much usefulness *adorned with much charm*, and confirmed by many authorities" (emphasis mine).[11] Later, Voragine expands this third point, that Luke's writing is "adorned with much charm":

> His style and manner of speaking are indeed charming and decorous. If someone wants what he says or writes to have grace and charm, then, as Augustine says, it must be pleasing, clear, and touching. If his words are to please, they should be eloquent; to be clear, they should be easy to follow; to touch hearers, they should be fervent. Luke had these three qualities in his writing and in his preaching.[12]

In ancient rhetorical traditions, clarity combined with vividness was celebrated as virtue in the ancient rhetorical handbook tradition. Quintilian says: "It is a great gift to be able to set forth the facts on which we are speaking clearly and vividly. For oratory fails of its full effect . . . if its appeal is merely to the hearing . . . and not displayed in their living truth to the eyes of the mind."[13] Later Quintilian lauds those rhetors who were able to represent facts "in such vivid language that they appeal to the eye rather than the ear."[14] Likewise, the anonymous author of *Ad Herennium* defines vividness in terms of clarity: "Vivid description is the name for the figure which contains a clear, lucid, and impressive exposition of the consequences of an act."[15] Also noteworthy is the fact that the handbooks at times make comparisons between styles of oratory and styles of painting. Quintilian says: "The question of the 'kind of style' to be adopted remains to be discussed. This was described in my original division of my subject . . . for I promised that I would speak of the art, the artist and the work. But since oratory is the work both of rhetoric and of the orator, and since it has many forms, as I shall show, the art and the artist are involved in the consideration of all these forms."[16]

These comments on vividness, clarity, and style were not limited to orators. Not only do the rhetorical handbooks draw examples from a wide variety of literature, but the authors of the so-called *progymnasmata*, (rhetorical exercises for schoolboys) celebrated the rhetorical skills of both the accomplished speaker and writer. The first-century C.E. author, Aelius Theon, devotes an entire chapter to a discussion of *ekphrasis*, which he defines as "descriptive speech, bringing what is portrayed clearly before the sight."[17] Theon also combines clarity and vividness when he asserts that the "virtues of an *ekphrasis* are as follows: most of all, clarity and a vivid impression of all-but-seeing what is described."[18] Theon also compares the training of the novice orator with that of the aspiring artist: "Just as it is of no advantage for those who want to be painters to look at the works of Apelles, Protogenes, and Antiphilus unless they themselves also attempt to paint, so also for those who are going to be orators."[19]

These comments from patristic and medieval writers are particularly instructive. In this chapter, I will argue that when these "premodern" writers used the language of the rhetorical tradition to describe Luke's writing as "elegant," "learned," and especially "clear," they were acknowledging Luke's rhetorical skills as a writer. In order to appreciate Luke's abilities to tell the story of Jesus in an elegant, learned, and clear manner, we must place him squarely in the rhetorical tradition, a tradition he apparently was intimately familiar with, and to which his audience would have responded.[20]

Luke and the Rhetorical Tradition

Since George Kennedy's brief chapter on Acts in his *New Testament Interpretation through Rhetorical Criticism*, a flurry of rhetorical analyses of the speeches in Acts have appeared.[21] Though these works differ markedly in detail, the cumulative effect of these studies has been to demonstrate that the author of Acts was familiar with the devices and strategies of ancient rhetoric as practiced during the Hellenistic period.[22]

Nonetheless, scholars, with some notable exceptions, have been reluctant to apply these insights to the Gospel of Luke and the narrative portions of Acts, refusing in effect to follow the pioneering work of R. O. P. Taylor, *Groundwork for the Gospels*, published in 1946.[23] One reason for hesitation has been the recognition that the rhetorical handbook tradition represented by Cicero, Quintilian, and others, is aimed at training orators for declamation; that is, their focus is on delivering oral speeches, not on writing narratives. This reading of the handbooks, of course, misses the point that Quintilian, Cicero, and the others generously quote examples from various Greek and Latin epics, histories, poetry, etc. Still, the reluctance is understandable.

If, however, these other studies of the speeches in Acts do show that Luke was more than competent in the handbook tradition, then it would be fair to conclude also that he would have cut his rhetorical teeth on the *progymnasmata* tradition. The *progymnasmata* were "handbooks that outlined 'preliminary exercises' designed to introduce students who had completed basic grammar and literary studies to the fundamentals of rhetoric that they would then put to use in composing speeches and prose."[24] As such, these graded series of exercises were probably intended to facilitate the transition from grammar school to the more advanced study of rhetoric.[25] Four of these *progymnasmata* from the first to fifth centuries, C.E., have survived.[26] What is important about these writings is that some of the exercises in the *progymnasmata* are clearly intended to embrace both written and oral forms of communication. For example, in his chapter "On the Education of Young Students," Aelius Theon remarks:

> So then, I have presented these things, not thinking that they are all suitable for all beginners, but in order that we might know that training in the exercises is absolutely necessary, not only for those who are going to be orators, but also if anyone wishes to practice the art of poets or prose-writers (λογοποιῶν, *logopoiōn*), or any other writers. These things are, in effect, the foundation of every form of discourse (70.24–30; Patillon, 15).[27]

Thus, the rhetorical handbooks and the *progymnasmata* often address the same topics. The *progymnasmata*, intended as they are to equip young students with the building blocks of both written and oral communication, serve to filter out of the handbooks what comments might be more appropriate for written communication.

Furthermore, George Kennedy has commented:

The curriculum described in these works, featuring a series of set exercises of increasing difficulty, was the source of facility in written and oral expression for many persons and training for speech in public life . . . Not only the secular literature of the Greeks and Romans, but *the writings of early Christians beginning with the gospels* and continuing through the patristic age, and of some Jewish writers as well, *were molded by the habits of thinking and writing learned in schools* (emphasis added).[28]

If the last part of Kennedy's comment is true and if Luke at least, among the Gospel writers, was familiar with the rhetorical exercises similar to those discussed by Theon and others, then we should thoroughly investigate Luke's rhetorical conventions.[29]

I am also interested in the way the "authorial audience" *hears* the rhetoric of Luke and Acts.[30] By "authorial audience," I mean the audience Luke had in mind when he wrote Luke and Acts, that is a general Christian audience, living in the Roman empire near the end of the first century.[31] Given the "rhetoric in the air" of antiquity, Luke's authorial audience, while probably unable themselves to reproduce these rhetorical devices in composition, were nevertheless able to respond to their effects. Since Luke's authorial audience presumably knew how to respond appropriately (if unconsciously) to persuasive rhetoric, we should determine then how that same authorial audience would have understood his rhetorical strategies and literary conventions.

My arguments about Luke's knowledge of the rhetorical devices preserved in the *progymnasmata* tradition are drawn primarily from the *progymnasmata* of Aelius Theon of Alexandria (ca. A.D. 50–100), the only textbook roughly contemporary to Luke. I am not suggesting any kind of literary dependence between Luke and Theon, but rather that Theon's text conveniently represents the kind of rhetorical exercises practiced in the first century, many of which had been practiced as early as the first or second centuries, B.C.E.[32] Thus, I assume that most (but not all) of what Theon says about these rhetorical exercises was not unique to Theon.

The extant Greek manuscripts of Theon preserve twelve chapters; the Armenian versions add another five. The first two chapters consist of a brief preface, summarizing the contents which follow, and a philosophy on "On the Education of the Young" from which we have already cited. Theon's presentation is unique among the extant *progymnasmata* in that it is addressed to the teacher and not the students and in its order and number of the exercises. Table 1 conveniently summarizes the differences:[33]

Table 1. Order of Treatment of *Progymnasmata* in Extant Treatises

Exercise	Theon (1st C.E.)	Hermogenes (2d C.E.)	Aphthonius (4th C.E.)	Nicolaus (5th C.E.)
Fable	2	1	1	1
Narrative	3	2	2	2
Chreia	1	3	3	3
Maxim	1[34]	4	4	4
Refutation	3	5	5	5
Confirmation	3[35]	5	6	5
Common-Place	4	6	7	6
Encomium	7	7	8	7
Invective	7	-	9	7
Comparison	8	8	10	8
Speech-in-character	6	9	11	9
Ekphrasis	5	10	12	10
Thesis	9	11	13	11
Law	10	12	14	12

While not totally ignoring the other subjects, I will deal more extensively with the first three of Theon's topics: *chreia*, fable, and narrative, paying most attention to the third topic, narrative. I will make brief comments also about Theon's remaining *topoi*. Finally, I will make some observations about the exegetical implications of the rudimentary exercise of grammatical inflection, which Theon commends for practice on *chreia*, fable, and narrative. The intention here is not to be exhaustive, but rather to demonstrate the virtues of the study of the *progymnasmata* both for themselves and for their contribution to our understanding of Luke the storyteller.

On Chreia

Theon defines the *chreia* as "a brief assertion or an action revealing shrewdness" (96.19–20; Patillon, 18) that can, in the exercise, be expanded or compressed (101.4–5; Patillon, 24). After discussing the general categories of *chreia* (verbal, descriptive of an action, or mixed—97.11–99.12; Patillon, 18–21), Theon lists the species of a *chreia*. Of these, the most significant for our purposes is the enthymeme. Theon illustrates the enthymeme with the following example: "Socrates the philosopher, when a certain Apollodorus, said that the Athenians had condemned him to death unjustly, laughed and said, 'Do you wish that they had done so justly?' It is necessary for us to add a proposition that it is better to be condemned unjustly than justly, which seems to have been omitted in the *chreia*, but is potentially clear" (99.34–100.3;

Patillon, 22). Theon's example reflects the general view that an enthymeme is an assertion, expressed as a syllogism in which one of the premises or rationales is omitted.

The *chreia* or anecdote has surely received the most attention from biblical scholars.[36] Earlier works tended to limit their discussion to an isolated *chreia* and its elaboration through expansion or compression in the narrative immediately following the anecdote.[37] Vernon Robbins, who has explored the *progymnasmata* in relation to the NT perhaps more than any other biblical scholar,[38] has recently moved the discussion to a new level in his examination of Luke 11:1–13, and especially the Lord's Prayer in vv. 2–4, from the perspective of the progymnasmatic elaboration of the *chreia*.[39] Robbins gives a careful and richly textured discussion of Luke 11:4 within what he calls the "enthymemic network of reasoning" related to Jesus' earlier saying, "Forgive, and you will be forgiven" (Luke 6:37–38). Robbins demonstrates how Luke 11:5–8 and 9–10 further elaborate the theme of forgiveness in the Lord's Prayer.

Furthermore, Robbins notes both similarities and differences between Luke and the *progymnasmata*, demonstrating that there was no compulsion for writers to follow the exercises slavishly. For example, rather than having a well-articulated rationale follow the *chreia* as the Hermorgenean Progymnasmata suggests, Robbins points out that the Lord's Prayer, treated by Robbins as an abbreviated (rather than expanded) *chreia*, itself contains a supporting premise, "Forgive us our sins; for we ourselves forgive every one indebted to us." The enthymemic network reaches its conclusion in v. 13, which defines the topic as "the heavenly Father's giving of the Holy Spirit in contexts where people pray the prayer Jesus taught his disciples."[40] While it is impossible to do justice in a few brief sentences to Robbins's complex argument, let me assert that his work here (and elsewhere) demonstrates the fruitfulness of looking to the *progymnasmata* for clues to the rhetorical strategies Luke employed in communicating his story—a story whose rhetorical subtleties would have been easily understood by his audience.

On Fables

If the *chreia* tradition is a well-furrowed field in biblical studies, the second topic of the *progymnasmata*, the fable, is relatively untouched. This is somewhat surprising given the fact that Theon's definition of the fable as "a fictitious story which depicts or images truth" (72.28; Patillon, 30) sounds like a typical, rough-and-ready definition many would use to describe Jesus' parables. To be sure, studies, like those of Mary Ann Beavis, have quite effectively explored some of Jesus' parables in light of Aesop's fables,[41] but no one has given more than a cursory look at the *progymnasmata* in this light. However, if the authorial audience of Luke might have heard Jesus' stories also as fictitious stories imaging truth, then comparing the parables to the preliminary exercises might prove worthwhile. I cite one example.

At one point Theon notes, "It may be possible for one fable to have several conclusions (or morals), if we take a start from each of the matters in the fable" (75.28–31). When read in light of this comment, the parable of the Dishonest Steward in Luke 16 takes on new dimensions. The relation of the parable proper, 16:1–8a, to the material that immediately follows, 16:8b–13, has long vexed interpreters. C. H. Dodd called vv. 8–13 "notes for three separate sermons on the parable as text."[42] Joseph Fitzmyer concludes that the applications of the parable found in 8–9, 10–12, and 13 "undoubtedly stem from different settings."[43] On the contrary, if Luke and his audience were accustomed to a fable or parable having more than one conclusion or interpretation or "moral," then it is very unlikely that anything about the literary shape of this parable would have given the authorial audience any reason to question its rhetorical unity.[44] Far from a clear sign of redactional disruption and separate social settings, a conclusion with multiple interpretations or applications, according to the *progymnasmata*, was a conventional and acceptable way to end a fictitious story depicting a basic human truth.[45]

On Narrative

Theon's comments about narrative are the most intriguing in their potential for understanding Luke's rhetorical strategies.[46] In his chapter, "On the Narrative," Theon defines a "narrative" (here διήγημα, *diēgēma*) as "an explanatory account of matters, which have occurred or as if they have occurred" (78.16–17; Patillon, 38). In his first reference to the topic, Theon used the term διήγησις (*diēgēsis*) to describe the elementary exercise of narration: "For the one who has expressed well and in varied ways a narrative or a fable will also compose a history well" (60.3–4; Patillon, 2).[47]

He further asserts: "The virtues of a narrative are three in number: clarity, conciseness, and plausibility (or persuasiveness); above all, if it is possible, the narrative should have all the desirable qualities" (79.20–22; Patillon 40). Let us look briefly at these virtues in light of Luke's writing.[48]

Conciseness

Theon states: "Likewise the narrative is concise in its content and its style. For conciseness is communication that signifies that which is the most essential of the matters, neither adding that which is not necessary nor taking away that which is necessary according to the content and the style" (83.15–19; Patillon, 45).[49] Theon advises the avoidance of synonyms (since they make the sentence needlessly long), the use of words instead of phrases where appropriate (say "he died" rather than "he departed from this life"), simple words rather than compound ones, and shorter rather than longer words (84.5–17; Patillon 46). Three further comments are necessary. First, Theon clearly warns against sacrificing clarity for conciseness and credibility in expression (79.21–24; Patillon, 40; 84.17–18, Patillon, 46). Second, Theon concedes that writing history (here he uses the term ἱστορία, historia)[50] may of necessity take longer than speaking a narrative, since in writing one may need to narrate the protagonist's ancestry, prior events, etc. (see 83.25–64.10; Patillon, 45–46). Finally, what Theon says here about conciseness has to be balanced with his rather extensive treatment in his introduction about the virtues of the paraphrase, saying the same thing well a second or more times (see 62.10–64.25; Patillon, 4–7; see also ch. 15 on "Paraphrases" in the Armenian versions; Patillon, 107–108).[51]

With these caveats in mind, we turn to Luke.[52] We begin by acknowledging that the Third Gospel rivals the First for the longest text. Surely Luke was no slavish follower of the progymnasmata's call for conciseness! With a closer examination, however, some interesting points emerge. In his chapter on "Length" in Tendencies in the Synoptic Tradition, E. P. Sanders examines the phenomenon of relative length among the Synoptics.[53] Sanders concludes that these developments cannot be charted dogmatically in such a way as to fix the flow of information (and thus definitively solve the Synoptic Problem), since developments flow in both directions (the pericopae become both longer and shorter, more and less detailed, more and less Semitic). Nonetheless he finds that when Mark and Luke are compared, Luke is shorter than Mark more times than Mark is shorter than Luke.[54] This finding is rather remarkable given the fact that the whole of Luke is approximately 50 percent longer than the whole of Mark.

Thus while Luke has the tendency in Acts to repeat material (Jesus' ascension, the conversion of Cornelius, Paul's Damascus Road experience), in Luke there is a tendency toward conciseness. Given the Third Gospel's overall length is a bit surprising. This observation was made long ago by Cadbury, who after detailing repetition as one the tendencies of Lukan style (especially in Acts), observed:

> In contrast to this prolixity in Acts [repetition], the apparent tendency in Luke to avoid parallel scenes must be mentioned. The Gospel, if we may assume that it used Mark, not only omits the second of Mark's accounts of the feeding the multitude, but appears to cancel his account of Jesus in his home town (Mark 1:6), and of his anointing by a woman (Mark 14:39), and perhaps other sayings or scenes in Mark by introducing, before he came to these scenes, independent versions (Luke 4:16–30; 7:36–50, etc.). Matthew, on the contrary appears to repeat passages from Mark a second time.[55]

Not only does Luke eliminate whole scenes from Mark (e.g., the second feeding story, Mark 8:2–9), at times he will eliminate seemingly unnecessary phrases (see Theon above). For example, Luke has replaced Mark's temporal introduction in 1:32 ("When evening came, when the sun set") with the more concise phrase "When the sun was setting" (Luke 4:40). E. P. Sanders concludes, "In the case of Matthew, I think the title of abbreviator is unjustified, although it may be applied to Luke with more justice."[56]

Plausibility/Persuasiveness

According to Theon, "for the narrative to be credible/plausible, one must use words that are suitable for the persons and the subject matters and the places and the occasions/contexts; in the case of the subject matters those that are plausible and naturally follow from one another. One should briefly add the causes of things to the narration and say what is unbelievable in a believable way" (84.19–24; Patillon, 46).[57] Let's consider Luke 5:1–11, the call of the first disciples and the miraculous draught of fish in light of these comments[58] and in relationship to Mark's version of the call of the first disciples (1:16–20). A number of commentators have argued that inserting the miraculous catch of fish just before the call of the disciples provides a "psychologically plausible" account of why these fishermen would have left Jesus to follow everything.[59] Rather than seek a psychological reason for the change, however, the *progymnasmata*, along with the rhetorical handbooks (Quintilian, 4.2.32; *Rhetorica ad Alexandrum*, 30.143b.1–4; Cicero, *Inv.* 1.21.29–30), may provide the context for understanding the Lukan version as an example of "rhetorical plausibility."

In the Markan version of the story, Jesus has hardly begun his ministry when he sees two pairs of brothers fishing. He calls these presumably complete strangers, who inexplicably follow without hearing his teaching or witnessing his miraculous power. The rendering of the story sounds somewhat far-fetched, and perhaps Mark intends it so. Nonetheless, Luke makes changes in the story to "tell the unbelievable in a believable way." Among the healings that precede the call of Simon is the healing of Simon's mother-in-law (Luke 4:38–39). The audience is led to believe Simon knows of her miraculous recovery. This fact makes more understandable Simon's willingness to allow Jesus on board his boat and to teach from it. Simon, in Luke, is not welcoming a stranger on board, but acknowledging the holy man who had already healed a family member.

While we may view Luke's redaction as a distortion of Mark's rhetoric, no longer does it seem implausible in the Lukan account that these fishermen would leave everything and follow Jesus. The audience would have little difficulty in believing that the fishermen follow Jesus. In a sense, this scene also provides the plausibility for the call of Levi, later in this same chapter, which, following Mark very closely, has Levi follow immediately and presumably without any prior relationship with Jesus. Theon's comments on plausibility suggest that the audience would have conceived of this plausibility in rhetorical terms, however much those of us living in the early twenty-first century might wish to speak of this plausibility in psychological terms. Finally, I would contend that mining the comments on narrative in the *progymnasmata* might give exegetical assistance at other points in understanding the literary conventions employed elsewhere in the Lukan narratives.

On the Other Rhetorical Exercises

Below is a brief description of six of the remaining eight chapters (omitting the last two on Thesis and Law)[60] in Theon's Progymnasmata and various works that have already related these rhetorical topics to Luke-Acts and/or suggestions for further study. The chapter number corresponds to Theon's order (see Table 1).

Chapter 3. Refutation and Confirmation

While later writers treat refutation and confirmation as separate topics,[61] Theon includes them in his discussion of narrative. One of the most complex of the rhetorical exercises, refutation and confirmation demand that the student not only be able to recite an argument but to evaluate it as well. While little work has been done in examining the rhetorical character of Luke-Acts in these terms, there are some striking linguistic and conceptual similarities between Theon's comments and Luke's stated purpose to provide Theophilus with "confirmation" (ἀσφάλειαν, *asfaleian*, a term, along with its cognates, that also appears in Theon, ἀσφαλής—124.9; 126.21; ἀσφαλέια—122.8) of the "things that have been fulfilled among us" (Luke 1:1–4).

Chapter 4. Commonplace

Alan Culpepper has labeled the Lukan version of the Parable of the Ten Pounds (Luke 19:11–27) as a "cultural type scene" about evil tyrants.[62] While Culpepper is right in placing this story in its larger cultural context, it might be better to view the story in light of the discussion of the "Commonplace" in the *progymnasmata* tradition. According to Theon, a *topos* "is speech amplifying something that is acknowledged to be either a fault or a brave deed; it is of two kinds; one is an attack on those who have done evil deeds, for example, a tyrant (!), traitor, murderer, profligate; the other in favor of those who have done something good, for example, a tyrannicide, a hero, a lawgiver" (Theon, 106.1). Apthonius even gives as his examples of commonplace a speech against evil tyrants (18R–21R; Kennedy, 82–84).

As a commonplace against tyrants, the actions in Luke of the evil tyrant, who orders the execution of those who object to his unjust treatment of the third servant, are not to be seen as reflecting the impending eschatological judgments of a righteous God.[63] Rather, the parable in Luke 19 sets the stage for Luke to depict Jesus in the following story, the Triumphal Entry, as a benevolent ruler ("Blessed is the King who comes in the name of the Lord!" 19:38).[64] Jesus as benevolent ruler stands in contrast to the evil tyrant of the parable in Luke 19, a point reinforced by the fact that only in Luke (cf. Matt 25:14–30), does the absentee landlord assume the role of a king (βασιλεύς, *basileus*, Luke 19:12, 27). Further, Luke is the only writer who prefaces the parable with the note that Jesus told the parable of the pounds because the crowds "supposed that the kingdom of God was to appear immediately" (19:11). By employing the rhetorical device of the commonplace, Luke is able to contrast the tyranny of earthly kings with the humility and benefaction of king Jesus. Jesus' humility is seen in the so-called Triumphal Entry in the fact that he chooses to enter the city riding on a colt (19:34).[65] Jesus makes a similar point later in Luke at the Last Supper: "The kings of the Gentiles exercise lordship over them; and those in authority over them are called benefactors. But not so with you; rather let the greatest among you become as the youngest, and the leader as one who serves. For which is the greater, one who sits at table, or one who serves? Is it not the one who sits at table? But I am among you as one who serves" (Luke 22:24–27).

Chapter 5. Ekphrasis

We have already noted the relationship of *ekphrasis* ("descriptive speech, bringing what is portrayed clearly before sight"; see Theon 118.7; Patillon, 66) and Luke's penchant for describing events in very vivid and corporeal language, a habit which led to the identification of Luke in later traditions as the painting evangelist. At least part of that tradition owes its roots to Luke's use of vivid language, writing for the eye as much as the ear, and it would be profitable to examine some of those stories in this light (think of the accounts of the ascension, Acts 1:3–11, and Pentecost, 2:1–11).

Chapter 6. Speech-in-character

Prosopoiea demanded that the rhetor devise speeches that fit the character of the speaker. Plausibility and verisimilitude were essential for meeting the rhetorical needs of narrative, whatever its genre. J. C. Lentz's *Luke's Portrait of Paul* is a fine recent example of those studies that have attempted to show how the speeches of Paul in Acts confirmed the picture of Paul as a man of virtue and an educated Hellene.[66]

Chapter 7. Encomium and Invective

Theon treats encomium and invective together in the same chapter, noting that speeches can be given in praise or criticism. Todd Penner and Phil Shuler, among others, have explored various encomiastic aspects of Luke-Acts.[67]

Chapter 8. Synkrisis

Theon defines synkrisis as that "which shows what is better and what is worse" (Theon, 112.23–24; Patillon, 78). He makes it clear that such comparisons are only effective when the two persons or objects being compared are similar in their value and worthiness. Fearghus O'Fearghail has explored the opening chapters of Luke as an extended synkrisis of Jesus with John the Baptist, which extends all the way to Luke 4:44.[68]

On Inflection

Every beginning language student is aware that Greek is a highly inflected language, but, in light of the *progymnasmata*, the significance of that fact for NT interpretation has not been fully appreciated.[69] Inflecting the main subject or topic (κλίσις, *klisis*) was one of the first exercises taught to beginning students of elementary rhetoric and provided a transition from the study of grammar to the study of rhetoric since the exercise focused on the rhetorical function of inflection.[70] Theon gives a rather full description of how such inflection is to take place in his discussion of *chreia* and fable and refers back to it in his discussion of narrative (85.29–31; Patillon, 48). In his chapter on "Fables," Theon asserts:

> Fables should be inflected, like *chreia*, in different grammatical numbers and oblique cases. . . . The original grammatical construction must not always be maintained as though by some necessary law, but one should introduce some things and use a mixture (of constructions); for example, start with one case and change in what follows to another, for this variety is very pleasing (74.24–35, passim-75; Patillon, 33; see also 101.10–103.2).

Quintilian (9.1.34) also comments briefly on the use of inflection as a rhetorical device. Following a discussion of the effects of repetition, he suggests: "Other effects may be obtained by the graduation or contrast of clauses, by the elegant inversion of words, by arguments drawn from opposites, asyndeton, paraleipsis, correction, exclamation, meiosis, the employment of a *word in different cases* (in multis casibus), moods and tenses. . . ." And again at 9.3.37:

> At times the cases and genders of the words repeated may be varied, as in 'Great is the goal of speaking, and great the task, etc.'; a similar instance is found in Rutilius, but in a long period. I therefore merely cite the beginnings of the clauses. Pater hic tuus? Patrem nunc appellas? Patris tui filius es? [Is this your father? Do you still call him father? Are you your father's son?] This figure may also be effected solely by change of cases, a preceding which the Greeks call πολύπτωτον [*polyptōton*].

What Theon calls κλίσις (*klisis*), Quintilian refers to as πολυπτωτον (*polyptōton*); but the phenomenon is the same. Inflection was more than just an ornamental figure of style designed to please the esthetical tastes of the audience. In fact, Quintilian included inflection in his discussion of figures of thought, a "class of figure, which does not merely depend on the form of the language for its effect, but lends both charm and force to the thought as well" (9.3.28; LCL). And the function of inflection was for emphasis (see Quintilian, 9.3.67) and to attract the audience's attention to the subject under discussion (Quintilian, 9.3.27).

Any student of elementary rhetoric then would have been accustomed to inflecting the main topic or subject of a *chreia*, fable, or narrative, and presumably an ancient audience would have been naturally, almost instinctively, able to identify the main subject by hearing the topic inflected in the various cases of the Greek noun. If true and if Luke were the student of rhetoric that I think him to have been, then we might expect Luke to have used this inflection convention to provide rhetorical markers as to the topic or subject of various parts of the Lukan narrative. We may test this hypothesis by exploring whether a topic is ever so inflected in Luke and Acts.

Speeches in Acts and parables in Luke, in addition to the narrator's prose, are the major forms of communication in Luke-Acts. Thus, it would be reasonable to expect to find examples of inflected subjects in these three kinds of communication.[71]

Speeches in Acts

We might first examine the speeches of the Lukan Paul, since, as we already noted, previous studies have demonstrated that in Acts, Paul is fully aware of and deftly employs the various components of deliberative, epideitic, and especially juridical speech in various addresses in Acts. When we turn to Paul's Areopagus speech (Acts 17:22–31), we find in fact that the five occurrences of "God" or θεός (*theos*) are inflected in four cases (Nominative, Genitive, Dative, and Accusative) within a matter of a few verses: v. 23—dative; v. 24—nominative; v. 27—accusative; v. 29—genitive; v. 30—nominative. This inflection would suggest that the topic of Paul's Areopagus speech was God, a not so surprising fact since this speech is well known for its lack of explicit Christological formula.

We find a similar pattern in Paul's speech before Agrippa (Acts 26), where again, θεός (*theos*) is inflected in four cases: v. 6—genitive (θεοῦ); v. 8—nominative (θεός); v. 18—accusative (θεόν); v. 20—accusative (θεόν); v. 22—genitive (θεοῦ); v. 29—dative (θεῷ). Interestingly, it is only after Agrippa accuses Paul of being "mad with much learning," that Paul finishes his inflection by using θεός (*theos*) in the dative case, ironically confirming for the authorial audience at least the second half of Agrippa's claim that Paul has much learning, or at least enough to know how grammatically to inflect the subject of his speech. That God, not Christ, is the subject of the defense speech is somewhat more surprising than the Areopagus speech given the various claims of the "Christological climax" of Paul's defense.[72]

Parables in Luke

Among the parables in Luke, the last parable in Luke 15 proves a fascinating case. The parable in Luke 15:11–32 has long been known in

English as the Parable of the Prodigal Son, and this is probably still the most popular title of the parable. No less prominent a figure than Joachim Jeremias, however, in his classic study of the parables, suggested that this parable is more aptly described as a "parable of the Father's Love."[73] But even Jeremias's judgment could not derail the tide of subsequent interpreters, many of whom still see the parable as predominately about the prodigal younger brother. Joel Green's comments are characteristic: "as important as the father is to this parable, center stage belongs to the younger son."[74]

Does the grammar of inflection help us understand better how the authorial audience may have heard this parable? The term "son" occurs eight times in Luke 15:11–32, once in the accusative case (and plural, v. 11) and seven times in the nominative singular, in reference to the prodigal (15:13, 19, 21 twice, 24, 25, 30). We might reasonably expect that the subject of a parable or story would occur most frequently in the nominative case; however, if we take seriously the role of grammatical inflection in the educational system of late antiquity, then we might not be surprised to learn that not only does the word "father" occur twelve times in the parable, it appears in all five cases at least once, and in four cases, including the vocative (a rarity in Luke) at least twice: nominative—vv. 20, 22, 27, 28; genitive—v. 17; dative—vv. 12, 29; accusative—vv. 18, 20; vocative—vv. 12, 18, 21. The conclusion seems irresistible that an ancient audience hearing Luke 15, who were conditioned (even unconsciously) upon "hearing" a word inflected to identify that term as the subject of the story at hand, would have naturally understood that the subject of the parable was the Father and his love.

First-Level Narration

In Luke-Acts, we find that the narrator employs this same strategy of inflection in the telling of his stories.[75] I cite two examples.[76] The first four occurrences of "people" (λαός, laos) in Luke 1, appear in four different cases: v. 10—genitive; v. 17—accusative; v. 21—nominative; v. 68—dative. Since, with one notable exception (Acts 15:14, which proves the rule), all the occurrences of λάος (laos) in Luke and Acts refer to the Jewish people, this phenomenon perhaps gives grammatical and rhetorical underpinning to the importance Luke assigns to the Jewish setting of the birth of Jesus in the infancy narrative.

In Acts 9, which records the conversion/call of Saul, the term "disciple" (μαθητής, mathētēs) occurs six times in four cases and in both singular and plural: v. 1—accusative plural; v. 10—nominative singular; v. 19—genitive plural; v. 25—nominative plural; and v. 26—dative plu-

ral and nominative singular. Again the inflection functions rhetorically
to signal to the audience that whatever else the call/conversion of Paul
may be about, it is in the first instance a narrative about the role of the
disciples, the Christian community, in that call, an emphasis that all but
drops out in Paul's subsequent re-telling of the event in chs. 22 and 26.[77]

We should not be alarmed that Luke does not use inflection to
mark the subject of every story. Quintilian rightly warned that these figures are only effective "if the figures are not excessive in number nor all
of the same type or combined or closely packed, since economy in their
use, no less than variety, will prevent the hearer from being surfeited"
(9.3.27; LCL).

Nor should we view the use of inflection as a particularly elegant
rhetorical device. Remember it was one of the first exercises practiced by
the beginning student of rhetoric, who quickly passed on to more chal-
lenging exercises. In fact, Quintilian recognized that inflection and
other figures like it "derive something of their charm from their very re-
semblance to blemishes, just as a trace of bitterness in food will sometimes tickle the palate" (9.3.27; LCL). But its "ordinary" nature might
argue for its effectiveness as a rhetorical device in signaling the importance of the inflected term for the understanding of the narrative in
which it is couched. Certainly this seems to be that for which Theon
hoped. In one of the chapters in "Listening to What is Read," preserved
only in the Armenian versions, Theon comments: "In listening, the
most important thing is to give frank and friendly attention to the
speaker. Then the student should recall the subject of the writing, identify the main points and the arrangement, finally recall also the better
passages" (Patillon, 105–106).[78] At the least the practice of inflection deserves further reflection both as it was practiced in the ancient world,
and as it may have been employed in Luke and Acts.

Conclusion

One of the most exciting and productive advances in New Testament studies in the past twenty years has been the various explorations
of the literary features of the Gospels. These "holistic" readings of texts,
often dubbed "narrative criticism," represented a new approach to the
historical-critical methods of form and redaction criticism that had
dominated Gospel studies in the previous generation. The literary
model adapted by biblical critics was shaped and forged by secular theo-
rists reading nineteenth- and twentieth-century novels, and thus one of
the most common and forceful criticisms leveled at narrative criticism

was that it is inappropriate and certainly anachronistic to impose this model on first-century texts that do not share the literary conventions and social settings of the modern novel. For those of us still interested in understanding Luke's strategies as a storyteller, this criticism continues to have a nagging persistence. Based on this preliminary investigation into the preliminary exercises, however, I argue that the *progymnasmata* and the rhetorical traditions, conventions, and strategies that they represent help make sense of the rhetorical conventions and strategies employed by Luke the storyteller.

Notes

1. This chapter is based on a paper that I presented at the international meeting of the Society of Biblical Literature in Rome, Italy, in July 2001. I thank Todd Penner for the invitation to participate in a session on "New Directions in the Study of Luke/Acts" and for the helpful comments from its participants.

2. B. H. Streeter, *The Four Gospels* (London: Macmillan, 1924), 548.

3. See, e.g., Ernst Haenchen, *The Acts of the Apostles: A Commentary* (trans. Bernard Noble, et al; Philadelphia: Westminster, 1971), 90 n. 1.

4. Haenchen, *Acts*, 104.

5. Mark Allen Powell, *What Are They Saying About Luke?* (New York: Paulist, 1989), 5–15. Powell (10) has also briefly commented on the relationship between these references to Luke the "literary artist" and the traditions of Luke the painter: "At some point in church history, a legend arose that Luke was a skilled painter . . . . This is not, however, what scholars mean when they say that Luke is an artist. The reference, rather, is to his literary art, his skill in composing a narrative." Powell may have too quickly dismissed the possible links between Luke the consummate literary writer and Luke the "skilled painter."

6. Robert Tannehill, *The Narrative Unity of Luke-Acts* (2 vols; Philadelphia: Fortress, 1986), 1:1. See also Gerhard Krodel, *Acts* (ACNT; Minneapolis: Augsburg Press, 1986), 15, who calls Luke "a great storyteller" who "could sketch vivid scenes"; further, J. N. Aletti, *L'art de raconter Jésus Christ: L'écriture narrative de l'évangile de Luc* (Paris: Seuil, 1989); and Talbert, *Literary Patterns, Theological Themes, and the Genre of Luke-Acts*, 1–5, who chronicles efforts to understand the literary genius of Luke.

7. Jerome, *Commentary on Isaiah*, 3.6 (PL 24.98).

8. Jerome, *Epistual ad Damasum*, 20.4.

9. Jerome, *Vir. ill.*, 7.

10. John Chrysostom, *Hom. Act.* 1.

11. Jacobus de Voragine, *The Golden Legend* (trans. William Granger Ryan; Princeton: Princeton University Press), 2:251.

12. *Golden Legend*, 2:252.

13. Quintilian *Institutio Oratoria* (trans. H. E. Butler; LCL; New York: G. P. Putnam's Sons, 1922), 8.3.62.

14. Quintilian, 9.2.40.

15. [Pseudo-Cicero], *Ad Herennium* (trans. Harry Caplan; LCL; Cambridge: Harvard University Press, 1964), 4.39.51.

16. Quintilian, 12.10.2. In 12.10.3–6, Quintilian discusses a number of specific painters and sculptors and follows that by a discussion of oratory style.

17. Theon, *Progymnasmata*, 118.7; Patillon, 66; (Spengel, 118). The translation cited here is by George A. Kennedy, *Progymnasmata: Greek Textbooks of Prose Composition Introductory to the Study of Rhetoric* (Fort Collins, Colo.: Chez l'auteur, 1999), ii (Spengel, 70). I have used the critical edition of the Greek text found in Michel Patillon and Giancarlo Bolognesi, eds., *Aelius Théon. Progymnasmata* (Paris: Les Belles Lettres, 1997). See also James R. Butts, "The Progymnasmata of Theon: A New Text with Translation and Commentary" (Unpublished dissertation; Claremont Graduate School, 1987). For simplicity's sake I use the standard numbering system of Leonard Spengel, ed., *Rhetores Graeci*, 2 vols. (Leipzig: Teubner, 1854–1856). Unless otherwise noted, all translations of Theon are mine and based on the Patillon edition.

18. Theon, *Progymnasmata*, 7.53–55 (Spengel, 119).

19. Theon, *Progymnasmata*, 1.85–89.

20. For another such attempt, see Robert Morgenthaler, *Lukas und Quintilian. Rhetorik als Erzählkunst* (Zürich: Gotthelf, 1993).

21. George Kennedy, "The Speeches in Acts," in *New Testament Interpretation through Rhetorical Criticism* (Chapel Hill: University of North Carolina Press, 1984), 114–40. See also Clifton C. Black, II, "The Rhetorical Form of the Hellenistic Jewish and Early Christian Sermon: A Response to Lawrence Wills," *HTR* 81 (1988): 1–8; Jerome Neyrey, "The Forensic Defense Speech and Paul's Trial Speeches in Acts 22–26: Form and Function," in *Luke-Acts: New Perspectives from the Society of Biblical Literature Seminar* (ed. C. H. Talbert; New York: Crossroad, 1984), 210–24; Philip E. Satterthwaite, "Acts against the Background of Classical Rhetoric," in *The Book of Acts in Its Ancient Literary Setting* (ed. Bruce W. Winter and Andrew D. Clarke; vol. 1 of *The Book of Acts in Its First Century Setting*, ed. Bruce W. Winter; Grand Rapids: Eerdmans, 1993), 337–79; Marion L. Soards, "The Speeches in Acts in Relation to Other Pertinent Ancient Literature," *ETL* 70 (1994): 65–90; Soards, *The Speeches in Acts: Their Content, Context, and Concerns* (Louisville: Westminster John Knox, 1994); F. Veltman, "The Defense Speeches of Paul in Acts," in *Perspectives on Luke-Acts* (ed. C. H. Talbert; Perspectives in Religions Studies Special Studies Series 5; Macon, Ga.: Mercer University Press, 1978), 243–56; D. F. Watson, "Paul's Speech to the Ephesian Elders (Acts 20.17–38): Epideictic Rhetoric of Farewell," in *Persuasive Artistry: Studies in New Testament Rhetoric in Honor of George A. Kennedy* (ed. D. F. Watson; JSNTSup 50; Sheffield: Sheffield Academic Press, 1990), 184–208; Bruce Winter, "The Importance of the *Captatio Benevolentiae* in the Speeches of Tertullus and Paul in Acts 24:1–21," *JTS* 42 (1991): 505–31; Winter, "Official Proceedings and the Forensic Speeches in Acts 24–26," in *Acts* (ed. Winter and Clarke), 1:305–36; D. Zweck, "The *Exordium* of the Areopagus Speech, Acts 17.22, 23," *NTS* (1989): 94–103; and now also, Derek Hogan, "Paul's Defense: A Comparison of the Forensic Speeches in Acts, *Callirhoe*, and *Leucippe and Clitophon*," *PRSt* 29 (2002): 73–87.

22. Philip Satterthwaite, "Acts against the Background of Classical Rhetoric," 378, concludes: "At point after point Acts can be shown to operate according to conventions similar to those outlined in classical rhetorical treatises."

23. R. O. P. Taylor, *Groundwork for the Gospels, With Some Collected Papers* (Oxford: Blackwell, 1946). Taylor's rationale is persuasive to me, that as a Hellenic citizen, the "Christian was bound to pursue the art of pleading, both in his

own defense and in the work of persuading others. . . . It was only natural that he should use the methods in vogue. And in the work of the Rhetores, we have an exposition of their methods" (75).

24. Willi Braun, *Feasting and Social Rhetoric in Luke 14* (SNTSMS 85; Cambridge: Cambridge University Press, 1995), 146.

25. Quintilian, in fact, refers to the preliminary exercises as part of the educational curriculum of young boys (*Inst.*, 1.9). On the role of rhetoric in the educational curricula of antiquity, the standard works remain S. F. Bonner, *Education in Ancient Rome* (Berkeley: University of California Press, 1977); D. L. Clark, *Rhetoric in Graeco-Roman Education* (New York: Columbia University Press, 1957); H. Marrou, A *History of Education in Antiquity* (London: Sheed & Ward, 1956).

26. In addition to the text of Aelius Theon (cited above), other surviving *progymnasmata* include those by Hermogenes of Tarsus (second century; critical edition in H. Rabe, ed., *Hermogenes Opera* [Rhetores Graeci 10; Leipzig: Teubner, 1913], 1–27); English translation in C. S. Baldwin, *Medieval Rhetoric and Poetic (to 1400) Interpreted from Representative Works* (New York: Macmillan, 1928), 23–38; Aphthonius of Antioch (fourth century; critical edition in H. Rabe, ed., *Aphthonii Progymnasmata* [Rhetores Graeci 10; Leipzig: Teubner, 1926], 1–51); English translation in R. E. Nadeau, "The *Progymnasmata* of Aphthonius in translation," *Speech Monographs* 19 (1952): 264–85; an on-line translation of Aphthonius by Professor Malcolm Heath, Head of the Classics Department at the University of Leeds, may also be found at www.leeds.ac.uk/classics/resources/rhetoric/index.htm; Nicholaus of Myra (fifth century; critical edition in J. Felten, ed., *Nicolai Progymnasmata* [Rhetores Graeci 11; Leipzig: Teubner, 1913]; no English translation available). English translations of, introductions to, and notes about Theon, Hermogenes, Aphthonius, and Nicolaus (along with selections from some others) may be found in George Kennedy, *Progymnasmata.*. An English translation of them, along with the Greek text, may also be found in Butts, "The Progymnasmata of Theon." A fifth document, a commentary on Apthonius's *Progymnasmata* attributed to John of Sardis is available in the Teubner edition, *Ioannis Sardiani Commentarium in Aphthonii Progymnasmata* (ed. Hugo Rabe; Leipzig: Teubner, 1928).

27. Butts (181 n. 36) rightly observes: "This statement is clear evidence that T[heon] understood the *progymnasmata* as providing instruction for literary activity ranging far beyond the technical parameters of rhetoric."

28. Kennedy, *Progymnasmata*, v.

29. As recently as 1994, Duane Watson was able to write, "a thorough and balanced assessment of the rhetoric of the Gospels has yet to be written" ("Notes on History and Method," in *Rhetorical Criticism of the Bible: A Comprehensive Bibliography with Notes on History and Method* [Biblical Interpretation 4; Leiden: Brill, 1994], 115).

30. For the theoretical underpinnings of the notion of the "authorial audience," see Peter J. Rabinowitz, *Before Reading: Narrative Conventions and the Poetics of Interpretation* (Ithaca: Cornell University Press, 1987); idem., "Truth in Fiction: A Reexamination of Audience," *Critical Inquiry* 4 (1977), 126; M. A. Tolbert, *Sowing the Gospel: Mark's World in Literary-Historical Perspective* (Minneapolis: Fortress, 1989), 52–55; Warren Carter, *Matthew: Storyteller, Interpreter, Evangelist* (Peabody, Mass.: Hendrickson, 1996); Charles H. Talbert,

"Conversion in the Acts of the Apostles: Ancient Auditors' Perceptions," *Literary Studies in Luke-Acts: Essays in Honor of Joseph B. Tyson* (ed. Richard P. Thompson and Thomas E. Phillips; Macon, Ga.: Mercer University Press, 1998), 141–54.

31. See Richard Bauckham, "For Whom Were the Gospels Written?" in *The Gospel for All Christians: Rethinking the Gospel Audiences* (ed. Richard Bauckham; Grand Rapids: Eerdmans, 1998), 9–48; also Luke Timothy Johnson, "On Finding the Lukan Community: A Cautious Cautionary Essay," *SBLSP* (ed. Paul J. Achtemeier; Missoula, Mt.: Scholars Press, 1979), 87–100.

32. Butts, 7. Theon himself acknowledges that others had written on the subject of preliminary exercises (1.15–16) and can even refer (1.18) to "traditional exercises."

33. Modified from Kennedy, *Progymnasmata*, viii.

34. Treated as a form of the *Chreia*.

35. Theon discusses refutation and confirmation in connection with narrative.

36. Prominent among that literature are Burton L. Mack and Vernon K. Robbins, *Patterns of Persuasion in the Gospels* (Sonoma, Calif.: Polebridge, 1989); Burton L. Mack, *Rhetoric and the New Testament* (GBS; Minneapolis: Fortress, 1990); Vernon K. Robbins, *The Tapestry of Early Christian Discourse: Rhetoric, Society, and Ideology* (London: Routledge, 1996); and idem, *Exploring the Texture of the Texts: A Guide to Socio-Rhetorical Interpretation* (Philadelphia: Trinity, 1996). This interest in the *chreia* tradition has led also to the collection and publication of the *chreia* exercises of prominent *progymnasmata*; see R. F. Hock and E. N. O'Neil, eds., *The Chreia in Ancient Rhetoric:* Volume 1, *The Progymnasmata* (SBLTT 27; Atlanta: Scholars Press, 1986). On studies particular to the Gospel of Luke or with significant sections devoted to Luke, see K. Berger, "Hellenistische Gattungen im Neuen Testament," (*ANRW;* ed. H. Temporini and W. Haase; 2.25.2; Berlin: Walter de Gruyter), 1031–432; Willi Braun, *Feasting and Social Rhetoric in Luke 14;* William R. Farmer, "Notes on a Literary and Form-Critical Analysis of Some of the Synoptic Material Peculiar to Luke," *NTS* 8 (1961/62): 301–16; R. Meynet, *L'Évangile selon saint Luc: Analyse rhétorique* (2 vols.; Paris: Cerf, 1988).

37. Richard B. Vinson, "A Comparative Study of Enthymemes in the Synoptic Gospels," in *Persuasive Artistry: Studies in New Testament Rhetoric in Honor of George A. Kennedy* (ed. D. F. Watson; JSNTSup 50; Sheffield: Sheffield Academic Press, 1991), 119–41; W. Wuellner, "The Rhetorical Genre of Jesus' Sermon in Luke 12.1–13.9," in *Persuasive Artistry: Studies in New Testament Rhetoric in Honor of George A. Kennedy,* 93–118.

38. In addition to the works cited above, see Vernon K. Robbins, "The Woman Who Touched Jesus' Garments: Socio-Rhetorical Analysis of the Synoptic Accounts," *NTS* 33 (1987): 502–15; "Progymnastic Rhetorical Composition and Pre-Gospel Traditions: A New Approach," in *The Synoptic Gospels: Source Criticism and the New Literary Criticism* (ed. Camille Focant; BETL 110; Leuven: Leuven University Press, 1993), 111–47; "Using Rhetorical Discussions of the Chreia to Interpret the Pronouncement Stories," *Semeia* 64 (1994): xii–xvi.

39. Vernon K. Robbins, "From Enthymeme to Theology in Luke 11:1–13," *Literary Studies in Luke-Acts. Essays in Honor of Joseph B. Tyson* (ed. Richard P.

Thompson and Thomas E. Phillips; Macon, Ga.: Mercer University Press, 1998), 191–214.

40. Robbins, "From Enthymeme to Theology," 214.

41. See especially Mary Ann Beavis, "Parable and Fable: Synoptic Parables and Greco-Roman Fables Compared," *CBQ* 52 (1990): 473–98; also Beavis, "Ancient Slavery as an Interpretive Context for the New Testament Servant Parables with Special Reference to the Unjust Steward (Luke 16:1–8)," *JBL* 111 (1992): 37–54.

42. C. H. Dodd, *Parables of the Kingdom* (London: Nisbet, 1935; repr., New York: Scribner, 1961), 17.

43. Fitzmyer, *The Gospel according to Luke*, 1:1105. Talbert, *Literary Patterns, Theological Themes, and the Genre of Luke-Acts*, 153, comes closer to acknowledging the unity of the interpretations by noting that they are held together by a "complex web of interlocking devices."

44. In that sense, Craig Blomberg's attempt to see each of the interpretations as reflecting the point of view of one of the characters in the parables is closer to Theon's account than most modern interpreters (see *Interpreting the Parables* [Downer's Grove, Ill.: InterVarsity Press, 1990]).

45. Though beyond the parameters of this chapter, which are limited to the final form of the Lukan writings, one cannot help but wonder if the historical Jesus had been also a rhetorical Jesus, that is, whether such elaborate elaborations on a fable could not in fact have gone back to Jesus himself.

46. On Theon's chapter on narrative and its relevance for NT study, see also Vernon Robbins, "Narrative in Ancient Rhetoric and Rhetoric in Ancient Narrative," (*SBLSP* 35; Atlanta: Scholars Press, 1996), 368–84.

47. Theon appears to use the terms διήγησις (*diēgēsis*) and διήγημα (*diēgēma*) interchangeably (see 5.2–4), while other writers, such as Hermogenes (4.9–15), distinguish between the two arguing that διήγημα (*diēgēma*) refers to the elementary exercise and διήγησις (*diēgēsis*) is equivalent to the "statement of facts" portion of a speech (the *narratio*). To further complicate matters, when Theon does seem to distinguish between the two terms it is in direct opposition to Hermogenes's distinction, e.g., for Theon διήγησις (*diēgēsis*) refers to the elementary exercise of story-writing and διήγημα (*diēgēma*) is the "statement of facts" part of a speech (see 60.5; Patillon, 2).

48. We will save the discussion of clarity for the next chapter on Luke's prologue.

49. Brevity is also a topic of discussion in the handbook tradition (see *Rhetoric ad Alexandrum*, 84.17–181; Cicero, *Inv.* 1.28; Pseudo-Cicero, *Rhetorica ad Herennium*, 1.14).

50. While it is clear that Theon views ἱστορία (*historia*) as the combination of narratives (60.6; Patillon, 2), it is not clear whether Theon thinks of ἱστορία (*historia*) exclusively in terms of historiography. Certainly ἱστορία (*historia*) includes historiography, but it does not seem to be limited to it. After reviewing all the occurrences of ἱστορία (*historia*) (60.4, 6; 67.4; 70.3, 6, 12; 77.15; 80.17; 81.2, 7; 83.25, 31; 87.23; 91.15; 121.2; 122.30; 123.1; conveniently indexed by Patillon, 199), the general distinction rather seems to be between prose writing and poetry (see esp. 123.1).

51. While Theon here spends much space discussing the paraphrasing of one author by another, he does also mention, quite positively it seems,

Demosthenes, who not only transferred material from one speech to another, but even repeated material within a single speech (64.1; Patillon, 6–7).

52. Since there is no comparative material for Acts, we will limit our comments to the Gospel.

53. E. P. Sanders, *Tendencies of the Synoptic Tradition* (Cambridge: Cambridge University Press, 1969), 69–82. Sanders analyzed the texts in seven different categories: 1) Old Testament quotations in one Gospel but not the others; 2) speeches longer in one than in the others; 3) speeches present in one but not the others; 4) dialogues in one but not the others; 5) scenes and events in one but not the others; 6) actions in one but not the others; and 7) differences in length within the same pericope.

54. According to A. M. Honoré ("A Statistical Study of the Synoptic Problem," *NovT* 10 [1968]: 95–147), there are 84 pericopae in the triple tradition material. In those pericopae (see chart, 96), Mark uses 8,630 words compared to Luke's 7,884 words (see Matthew with 8,336). In addition, there are six pericopae in common between Mark and Luke not found in Matthew (139). In those passages, Mark uses 357 words compared to Luke's 274 words.

55. Henry Cadbury, "Four Features of Lucan Style," *Studies in Luke-Acts* (ed. Leander E. Keck and J. Louis Martyn; Nashville: Abingdon, 1966), 89.

56. Sanders, *Tendencies*, 87.

57. Theon evidently considered plausibility/persuasiveness (πιθανός, *pithanos*) and its cognates) as the key element to narrative: "For it is always necessary to keep what is plausible in a narrative; for this is its best quality" (79.28–29; Patillon, 40). On plausibility see also Quintilian, 4.2.32; *Rhetorica ad Alexandrum* 30.143b.1–4; Cicero, *Inv.* 1.21.29–30. See also Theon's comments on plausibility/persuasiveness in the fable at 76.35–77.9.

58. I am indebted to the work of my student, Derek Hogan, for much of what follows. He and the other students in my doctoral seminar on Luke and Rhetoric in the fall of 1999 provided the initial stimulus for this investigation.

59. Joseph Fitzmyer, *Luke*, 1:563; R. Alan Culpepper, *Luke* (*NIB* 9; Nashville: Abingdon, 1997), 116. Joel Marcus, *Mark 1–8* (AB 27A; Garden City: Doubleday, 1999), 178, suggests that Mark is "responsible for moving the call of the first four disciples (1:16–20) forward to the beginning of this section; originally, perhaps, it followed the healings and exorcisms in 1:21–34 (see Luke 5:1–11, where Peter begins to follow Jesus only after witnessing a miracle)."

60. Given their propositional nature, thesis and law seem less likely to bear fruit in any analysis of a larger narrative; thus their exploration will be delayed for another occasion.

61. For example, see *The* Preliminary Exercises *Attributed to Hermogenes* in *Progymnasmata: Greek Textbooks of Prose Composition and Rhetoric* (SBLWGRW 10; ed. and trans. George A. Kennedy; Atlanta: Society of Biblical Literature, 2003), 79; *The* Preliminary Exercises *of Aphthonius the Sophist* in *Progymnasmata*, 101–5; *The* Preliminary Exercises *of Nicolaus the Sophist* in *Progymnasmata*, 144–47; *Selections from the Commentary on the* Progymnasmata *of Aphthonius Attributed to John of Sardis* in *Progymnasmata*, 199–201.

62. Culpepper, *Luke*, 362–64. Culpepper is here extending Robert Alter's observation about literary type scenes (discussed in *The Art of Biblical Narrative* [San Francisco: HarperCollins, 1981], 47–62) to include social conventions as well. As Culpepper notes (362 n. 212), he and I had discussed this nomenclature while he was writing his commentary. We might also note in passing that Alter's

notion of a literary "type scene" (so effectively applied to Luke-Acts by Robert Tannehill), might rather have been heard by the authorial audience as an example of "paraphrase" (saying the same thing well a second or more times), which Theon discusses extensively in his introduction (62.10–64.25) and in chapter 15 in the Armenian version (Patillon, 107–8).

63. Though this does not this rule out this particular interpretation for the Matthean version of the story.

64. This point is highlighted by the fact that in the Matthean and Markan versions of the Triumphal Entry, reference to "the *King*" who "comes in the name of the Lord" is missing (see Matt 21:9/Mark 11:9; but see John 12:15).

65. This tradition is common to all four Gospels. Jesus' humility in this scene is a point widely recognized in the commentaries. His humility and pacifism (in contrast to the militaristic pomp and circumstance of the Roman *Adventus*, which celebrated the return home of the victorious warring Emperor) is reflected in some early Christian sarcophagus art where Jesus is shown riding the donkey side-saddled (for a discussion, see Thomas Mathews, *The Clash of the Gods: A Reinterpretation of Early Christian Art* [rev. ed.; Princeton: Princeton University Press, 1999]).

66. J. C. Lentz, *Luke's Portrait of Paul* (SNTSMS 77; Cambridge: Cambridge University Press, 1993). See also Derek Hogan, "The Forensic Speeches in Acts 22–26 in Their Literary Environment" (PhD diss., Baylor University, 2006).

67. Todd Penner, "Narrative as Persuasion: Epideitic Rhetoric and Scribal Amplification in the Stephen Episode in Acts," *SBLSP* 35 (1996), 352–67; Philip Shuler, "The Rhetorical Character of Luke 1–2," *Literary Studies in Luke-Acts* (ed. Thomas Phillips and Richard Thompson; Macon, Ga.: Mercer University Press, 1998), 173–89.

68. Fearghus O'Fearghail, *The Introduction to Luke-Acts: A Study of the Role of Luke 1,1–4,44 in the Composition of Luke's Two-Volume Work* (AnBib 126; Rome: Pontifical Biblical Institute, 1991). Abraham Smith also explores synkrisis in his analysis of Stephen; see Smith, " 'Full of Spirit and Wisdom': Luke's Portrait of Stephen (6:1–8:1a) as a Man of Self-Mastery," in *Asceticism and the New Testament* (ed. L. E. Vaage and Vincent L. Wimbush; New York: Routledge, 1999), 97–114. Best known in among the ancients perhaps is Plutarch's *Lives*, but numerous other examples of *syncrisis* in the literature of antiquity can be found in F. Focke, "Synkrisis," *Hermes* 58 (1923): 327–68.

69. On the occurrence of inflection in Latin poetry (with some reference to Greek literature as well), see Jeffrey Wills, *Repetition in Latin Poetry: Figures of Allusion* (Oxford: Clarendon Press, 1996), 188–268.

70. Nicolaus, 4.18–19, suggests that more advanced students could skip the exercise of grammatical inflection and move on to elaborating, condensing, refuting, or confirming.

71. I have limited my examples to instances where the term under consideration has been inflected in the four main cases (nominative, genitive, dative, and accusative) within a reasonably short and well-marked narrative unit, one that would presumably be recognizable to an attentive audience.

72. See, among others, Robert O'Toole, *The Christological Climax of Paul's Defense Speech in Acts 26* (AnBib 78; Rome: Pontifical Biblical Institute, 1971). The pattern is not limited to Paul's speeches. For example, a similar pattern emerges in Stephen's speech in Acts 7. Stephen uses the word θεός (*theos*) seventeen times in the chapter, twelve times in the nominative (vv. 2, 6, 7, 9, 17, 25,

32[twice], 35, 37, 42, 45), three times in the genitive (vv. 43, 46, 56), and once in the dative (v.20) and accusative (v. 40). Again, that God is the subject of Stephen's rehearsal of Israel's holy history is really not surprising, but the inflection of θεός (*theos*), along with the fact that θεός (*theos*) is the last word in the speech proper provides grammatical and textual moorings for this theological conclusion.

73. Joachim Jeremias, *The Parables of Jesus* (2d rev. ed.; trans. S. H. Hooke; New York: Charles Scribner's Sons, 1972), 128.

74. Joel B. Green, *The Gospel of Luke* (NICNT; Grand Rapids: Eerdmans, 1997), 578.

75. Robert Funk uses the term "first-level narration" to describe the narrator's telling of the story as opposed to second-level narration, e.g., a character's speech (second level narration, e.g., Jesus or Paul); or third-level narration, e.g., the report of a character's speech in a second-level narration (e.g., the Prodigal Son's speech before his father). See Funk, *Poetics of Biblical Narrative* (Sonoma, Calif.: Polebridge, 1988).

76. If we take Theon's comment at 74.24–25 to suggest inflecting the subject in only the oblique cases (genitive, dative, accusative), then another interesting pattern emerges. Only in Acts 12 and 28 do we find the narrator inflecting in the oblique cases. In Acts 12, we find 12:5—accusative; 12:22—genitive; 12:23—dative; and 12:24—genitive. In one instance, θεός (*theos*) is used to refer to 'a god,' and not Yahweh God (v.2). In chapter 28, we find θεός (*theos*) inflected again only in the oblique cases: 28:6—accusative; 28:15—dative; 28:23—genitive; and 28:31 genitive. Again, θεός (*theos*) is used once to refer to "a god" and not the God (v. 6). Furthermore, it is God in ch. 12 and not Herod or Peter, and God in ch. 28 and not Paul who is so inflected and thus presumably the subject of each respective passage. Additionally, θεός (*theos*) occurs in the last verse of each chapter. Not only is this observation significant for the interpretation of each passage, it may provide the textual and rhetorical markers for the overall structure of Acts. Many scholars take 13:1 with its shift to Paul and the Gentile mission to mark the beginning of a major new section in Acts. If our analysis of the inflection is correct, then the audience (familiar with the telling and re-telling of the story and upon retrospective patterning) would have been prepared for such a major shift by the rhetorical markers left by the oblique inflection of God.

77. Equally important may be the emphasis on "Lord" (κυριός, *kurios*) in Acts 9. The word occurs in the nominative—9:10, 11, 17; genitive—9:1, 28, 31; accusative—27, 35, 42; and vocative—9:5, 10, 13; (but not dative).

78. At this point, I am relying on Kennedy's English translation (*Progymnasmata*, 50) of Patillon's French translation of the Armenian version of a lost Greek text. As such, as Kennedy rightly observes, these sections "would be of dubious value for detailed interpretation." Nonetheless, my general conclusion seems warranted.

CHAPTER 3

Luke 1:1–4 and Ancient Rhetoric

Introduction

In the previous chapter we looked at Luke the storyteller as a practitioner of Greco-Roman rhetoric. That is, both the Gospel and Acts reflect a rhetorical tradition that helps to shape the ways in which the story is told. When the modern audience is attuned to these ancient rhetorical practices, they are better able to understand how Luke's first audience would have understood the story as Luke tells it. In the previous chapter we explored Luke the storyteller in light of the *progymnasmata* tradition in general; in this chapter, we seek to examine one specific text in much more detail. The movement is from the macro level to the micro level, or from the wide-angle lens to the telephoto, as it were. The combined effect shows that a fruitful way to hear the text of Luke and Acts is to hear it as an ancient audience attuned to rhetorical traditions might have heard it, and we seek to illustrate that both broadly (chapter two) and more narrowly (this chapter).

Luke's preface has received extensive analysis in the scholarly literature.[1] Still, there are many unresolved questions. Does the preface belong to the genre of historiography[2] or does it fit better within the category of scientific treatises?[3] Is the preface limited to the Gospel[4] or does it extend to Acts as well?[5] Does Luke intend to criticize his predecessors' attempts to write an account of Jesus or does he stand in basic continuity with them?[6] In this chapter we will demonstrate that, when read in light of ancient rhetoric, especially the *progymnasmata*, Luke does indeed intend to criticize his predecessors for their failure to write a rhetorically "complete and well-ordered" narrative of Jesus.[7]

As we noted in the last chapter, rhetorical analyses of the Lukan writings have tended to focus on enthymemes and *chreia* in the Gospel and on the speeches in Acts.[8] If Luke were familiar with writing exercises similar to those discussed by Theon (as argued in Chapter 2), it is important to tease out the implications of this fact for understanding the impact of Luke's preface upon his authorial audience, who presumably also knew how to respond appropriately (if unconsciously) to the effects of persuasive rhetoric.

Theon and the Art of Writing Narrative

Many have noted the use of the term, διήγησις (*diēgēsis*), in ancient historiography,[9] but the term was not confined to historical writing.[10] In fact, it was an important one in the rhetorical handbook tradition.[11] Theon has an entire chapter devoted to exercises in narrative writing, and it is in this connection that the term διήγησις (*diēgēsis*) occurs. As we noted in Chapter 2, Theon used the word διήγησις (*diēgēsis*) in the first chapter of his *Progymnasmata* to describe the elementary exercise of writing a "narrative" (1.26–29).[12] In his chapter, "On the Narrative," Theon defines a "narrative" as λόγος ἐκθετικὸς πραγμάτων γεγονότων ἢ ὡς γεγονότων (*logos ekthetikos pragmatōn gegonotōn ē hōs gegonotōn* "an explanatory account of matters, which have occurred or as if they have occurred"; 5.1). Cicero's definition of a narrative is remarkably similar to Theon's: "The narrative is an explanation of events that have occurred or supposedly occurred" (*Inv.* 1.29.27). Likewise with Quintillian: "The narrative is an exposition, useful for persuasion, of that which has been done or is supposed to have been done" (*Inst.* 4.2.31). The similarity between these statements is all the more striking since Theon was dealing with the elementary exercise of writing a story and Quintillian and Cicero were discussing a section of the rhetorical speech.[13]

This tradition may have been called to mind in Luke's use of the term διήγησις (*diēgēsis*) in his preface. The point here is not that Luke is writing a rhetorical handbook; obviously he is not. Nor is it the case that these connections to the rhetorical tradition prove that Luke is *not* writing in historiographical mode, since the historians (as well as the ancient biographers and novelists) also were sensitive to the effects of rhetoric in their writing.[14] These comments, in effect, are not relevant to questions about the genre of Luke's Gospel and Acts. But they do affect our understanding of Luke's relationship to previous attempts to tell the story of Jesus. For Luke, from a rhetorical perspective, these attempts failed *as narratives*. But why? As we shall see, Luke judged previous attempts to compile narratives about Jesus as inadequate because they either lacked sufficient coverage of the topic at hand or they did not arrange the story in a rhetorically compelling way.

The Rhetorically Complete Narrative

Theon begins his chapter on narrative by listing the six elements of a narrative: "1) the character can be either one or many; 2) the act done by the character; 3) the place in which the activity was done; 4) the time during which the activity was done; 5) the manner of the activity; and 6) the reason for these things" (5.3–11). Failure to address each of these elements in some fashion or another constitutes what Theon would call an "incomplete" (ἐλλιπής, *ellipēs*) narrative (5.10). Theon then amplifies each of these elements. About the first, "character," Theon says, "Inseparably connected with the 'character' are: race, physical nature, training, disposition, age, fortune, motive, action, speech, death, what is after death" (5.12–14). Cicero elaborates even further on what constitutes attributes of "character" (*Inv.*, 1.24–34). What Theon calls "physical nature" (φύσις, *physis*), Cicero calls *naturam* and includes whether or not the character is divine, human or animal, and the character's gender, place of birth, and family.

These observations are helpful when we turn to Luke's Gospel. We do not know the extent of the πολλοί (*polloi*, the "many," Luke 1:1), though it should be noted that the use of this term and its cognates was a known rhetorical device employed in the beginning of narratives and speeches (see Sir 1:1; Heb 1:1; Acts 24:2, 10) and should not therefore be pressed to mean a large number. Perhaps it is best to render the term in English as "several."[15] The interpreter's assessment of the extent of the "many" will, of course, be determined by his or her solution to the Synoptic Problem. While I obviously cannot solve this issue here, I will assume that Luke knew at least Mark and will draw on that Gospel to illustrate Luke's dissatisfaction with Mark as a rhetorical "narrative."

One of the problems that Luke would have had with Mark's Gospel was that in beginning with the public ministry of Jesus and omitting any reference to his birth, Mark presented an incomplete rhetorical narrative in terms of Jesus' φύσις (*physis*). Missing from Mark is an account of Jesus' family, his place of birth, and an explicit confirmation of his divinity. All of these elements are present in Luke 1–2. Luke refers to "those who were, from the beginning, eyewitnesses who were servants of the message."[16] For the authorial audience familiar with the opening line of Mark, the use of the word "beginning" (ἀρχῆς, *archēs*) in Luke 1:2 would have had strong echoes with Mark 1:1, "The beginning (ἀρχή, *archē*) of the good news of Jesus." While there is much scholarly discussion of the meaning of ἀρχή in Mark 1:1,[17] many early readers of Mark interpreted it to refer to the beginning of Jesus' story with his baptism by John the Baptist as seen in Augustine's observations: "Note that Mark mentions nothing of the nativity or infancy or youth of the Lord. He has made his Gospel *begin* directly with the preaching of John" (*Harm.*, 2.6.18).

Mark's Gospel began with John's preaching and Jesus' baptism. Mark's beginning, while perhaps the place to start the "good news," is for Luke inappropriate for a "narrative." Luke claims that he has received the message from those servants of the word who were eyewitnesses from the beginning. And for Luke that beginning properly included the story of Jesus' birth and his family. In fact, to be a complete narrative from a rhetorical perspective, Luke's story had to include these elements about Jesus' φύσις (*physis*).

So who were these "eyewitnesses from the beginning"? Many have taken this phrase to refer to the tradition passed on by the apostles, and certainly the apostles would be included among these eyewitnesses.[18] For Luke, these "servants/eyewitnesses from the beginning" also included those who witnessed the events surrounding the birth of Jesus. Mary the mother of Jesus and Simeon would surely count as eyewitnesses who were servants. In Luke 1:38, after Gabriel has revealed to Mary God's plan for her to bear the child, Jesus, Mary responds: " 'Here am I, the servant (δούλη, *doulē*) of the Lord; let it be with me according to your word.' " In the Magnificat, she exclaims that God "has looked with favor on the lowliness of his servant (δούλης, *doulēs*)" (1:48). Later in the infancy narrative, when Simeon, whom Luke describes as "righteous and devout, looking forward to the consolation of Israel" (2:25), receives the Christ child in his arms, he "praised God, saying, 'Master, now you are dismissing your servant (δοῦλον, *doulon*) in peace, according to your word; for my eyes have seen your salvation . . .' " (2:29–30).

The appeal to eyewitnesses/servants from the beginning does not serve to insure historical reliability (as some have claimed), but it does fit Luke's need to present a narrative, which is, rhetorically speaking, complete. If Luke's copy of Mark ended at 16:8, Luke might also have regarded this story as rhetorically incomplete in its ending also, since it did not have the requisite account of events that occurred after the character's death (see Theon, 5.14). His claim, then, to have investigated carefully everything from the start (1:3), when read in light of the rhetorical exercises for story-writing, informs the audience that what is to follow is a properly executed narrative, rhetorically complete in its coverage of the story of Jesus from start to finish.

The Rhetorically Well-Ordered Narrative

Presentation was an issue of concern to the rhetoricians. Remember Theon's words: "The virtues of a narrative are three in number: clarity, conciseness, and plausibility (or persuasiveness); above all, if it is possible, the narrative should have all the desirable qualities" (79.20–22; Patillon 40).

Clarity is an important (perhaps the most important) aspect of narrative, according to Theon, and one way clarity is achieved is through the "arrangement" (τάξις, *taxis*) of the subject matter: "Guard also against confusing the times and the order of the events . . . For nothing confuses the thought more than these things" (80.26–29; Patillon, 41). By order in the narrative, Theon does not imply any kind of strict historical or chronological order. Theon does seem to distinguish between unintentionally "mixing up . . . the order of events" (τὸ μὴ συγχεῖν . . . τὴν τάχιν τῶν πραγμάτων, *to mē synchein . . . tēn taxin tōn pragmatōn*), which he says "one must guard against" (φυλακτέον, *fylakteon*) and the elementary exercise of intentionally "changing the order of events" (5.229, Patillon, 50), of which he approves.

Theon comments further:

> We shall, however, rearrange the order in many [Armenian version: five] ways. For it is possible, beginning with the middle to run back to the beginning, then to come back to the final portions—as Homer has done in his *Odyssey*. . . . It is also permissible, beginning with the end, to go on to the middle, and thus to come back to the beginning—as Herodotus teaches us in his third book. . . . Furthermore, it is possible, beginning with the middle, to go on to the end, then to conclude with the beginning. And again, it is possible, beginning with the end, to return to the beginning and to conclude with the middle events. And it is also possible, beginning with the first things, to shift to the final parts and to stop with the middle. So much for the rearrangement of order. (86.9–87.13; Patillon, 48–50)

This transposition often occurs in shorter pericopae within narratives in Homer and Herodotus. Not all later rhetorical treatises agreed with this practice of transposing the order, especially those associated with judicial speeches that may have revolved around preserving the exact sequence of events (see *Rhetorica ad Alexandrum* 30.1438a.28–31; *Rhetorica ad Herennium* 1.9.15). Quintilian, however, in support of this procedure, writes: "Neither do I agree with those who assert that the order of our narrative should always follow the actual order of events, but I have a preference for adopting the order that I consider most suitable" (4.2.83).

Luke is likewise concerned with the presentation of events in the narrative. He claims that after he has thoroughly investigated everything, he will write "in order" (καθεξῆς, *kathexēs;* 1:3). What exactly does Luke mean by this term? The word has variously been understood to refer to 1) general chronological order;[19] 2) salvation history;[20] 3) a complete presentation without gaps;[21] 4) a continuous series;[22] 5) a literary systematic presentation;[23] 6) a persuasive order;[24] and 7) getting the story straight.[25]

The position taken in this chapter is similar to 6) and 7), though I am attempting to buttress the argument for a rhetorically persuasive order by appealing to the *progymnasmata* tradition. Our first clue comes in Luke's use of the word καθεξῆς (*kathexēs*) elsewhere in his writings (Luke 8:1; Acts 3:24; 11:4; 18:23). Of those occurrences, surely the most significant is the use of the term in Acts 11:4. When the Jerusalem church heard about Peter's associations with Gentiles, they sent an envoy to question him about these events. The narrator notes that Peter began to explain "in order" or "step by step" (καθεξῆς, *kathexēs*). The modern reader expecting the story to be told in chronological sequence will be surprised to hear that Peter begins by reversing the order of presentation of the visions: His own vision precedes that of Cornelius (see Acts 10 where Cornelius's vision is narrated first, followed by Peter). But the word "in order" has little to do with chronological or linear order. Rather, Peter (and in a larger sense the narrator) is seeking to present the events in a manner which his audience will find convincing. As Robert Tannehill has observed:

> Peter presents the narrative "in order" (11:4). The order is a narrative order, but it is not the same as the order of events in chapter 10. Peter begins not with Cornelius' vision but with his own vision. . . . A sequence of events led Peter to change his mind. Now his audience is being led through the same sequence so that they can appreciate and share Peter's new insight.[26]

For Luke, καθεξῆς (*kathexēs*) here has nothing to do with chronological order and everything to do with a rhetorically persuasive presentation. That was what Peter was attempting to do in Acts 11, and it is what Luke purports to do in preface to his Gospel.

By claiming that he will narrate his story "in order," in the preface to his Gospel, Luke strongly hints that his literary predecessors did not achieve the very important feature of "clarity" in their narratives. In Luke's opinion, the πολλοί (polloi, Matthew or Q and Mark, among others) have fallen short of the clarity that was rhetorically indispensable to the narrative.[27] In other words, the πολλοί (polloi) were acceptable, even authoritative, for Luke as *sources* to be drawn upon, but they were inadequate as well-constructed and persuasive *narratives*.

Luke purports to write a rhetorically persuasive presentation and thus reworked his sources with rhetorical deftness and in ways that his audience did in fact appreciate. Examples of these rhetorical strategies were discussed in the last chapter. What was Luke's goal in presenting a rhetorically compelling, well-ordered narrative? That, too, is stated clearly in the preface: "so that you may know the truth concerning the things about which you have been instructed" (1:4). The language here suggests that the audience in mind is primarily Christian and that the purpose of Luke's Gospel is one of instruction and assurance of "the events that have been fulfilled among us" (1:1). Here for theological reasons, Luke departs from the rhetorical tradition that views narrative as "an explanatory account of matters which have occurred or as if they have occurred" (Theon, 5.1). Luke's narrative, rather, is about matters that have been prophesied, whether by the Jewish Scriptures, living prophets, or heavenly messengers, and have now been fulfilled through the words and deeds of Jesus.[28] Luke's motive in writing includes an attempt to present these events that have been fulfilled and about which the audience has already been instructed in such a rhetorically compelling order that the authorial audience finds the narrative's truthfulness confirmed.

Comparison with the *progymnasmata* may shed further light on certain exegetical difficulties associated with the preface to Luke's Gospel. The term, for example, "attempt" (ἐπιχειρέω, epicheireō, literally, "take into hand") is a major interpretive difficulty for understanding Luke's attitude. The term is sometimes used in a neutral sense of "undertaken" (Polybius, *His.* 2.37.4), even in literary prefaces (Josephus, *Ag. Ap.* 1.2). Elsewhere, however, the term is used in a negative sense: "they have attempted but did not succeed" (Josephus, *Life* 9.40.65; *Herm. Sim.* 92.6). The term occurs only twice elsewhere in the Lukan writings, and in both instances, it is used in this negative sense. "He [Saul] spoke and argued with the Hellenists; but they were attempting (unsuccessfully) [ἐπεχείρουν, epecheiroun] to kill him" (Acts 9:29). "Then some itinerant Jewish exorcists attempted (unsuccessfully) [ἐπεχείρησαν, epecheirēsan] to use the name of the Lord over those who had evil spirits . . ." (19:13).

Luke's own use of the term, while in and of itself not decisive, must be read in light of our conclusions about Luke's rhetoric in the preface. Luke claims, unlike his predecessors, to write a rhetorically complete ("having investigated everything thoroughly from the beginning") and rhetorically well-ordered (καθεξῆς) narrative. Thus, the authorial audience, familiar with Luke's use of the word ἐπιχειρέω (*epicheireō*) in Acts and also cognizant of the rhetorical claims Luke is making in the preface, upon rehearing Luke 1:1 would, in all likelihood, have understood the term ἐπεχείρησαν (*epecheirēsan*) in its pejorative sense: "many have attempted unsuccessfully to write a rhetorical narrative." So, on the one hand, Luke shows his continuity with those previous attempts to narrate the Jesus story by beginning with a term, ἐπειδήπερ (*epeidēper*), "since" or "inasmuch" that rightly suggests a causal relation between these earlier narratives and Luke's own narrative, and he identifies with his predecessors in the phrase ἔδοξε κἀμοὶ . . . γράψαι (*edoxe kamoi . . . grapsai,* "it also seemed to me . . . to write"). Luke writes because others have written. Here Luke intends to stand in the tradition of those who had earlier narrated the matters that had been fulfilled. On the other hand, of course, Luke does write, and the very act of writing seems to imply some criticism of previous attempts.[29] Further, Luke distinguishes between his complete and well-ordered narrative and his predecessors' failure to produce such a rhetorically competent narrative.

Conclusion

Some commentators have denied altogether that Luke is in any way critical of his predecessors.[30] Others have allowed that Luke may have intended some veiled criticism of his predecessors; often words like "guarded," "discrete," "subtle," "muted," or "subdued," are used.[31] Occasionally, interpreters think Luke is less ambivalent in his criticism.[32] From our study, we concur with this latter view. Luke identified with his predecessors ("it seemed good also to me") and was willing to use their material as sources for his own presentation. But in light of what constituted a rhetorically complete and well-ordered narrative in the ancient *progymnasmata* tradition at work in the Hellenistic period, the authorial audience would have heard loud and clear Luke's criticisms of his predecessors' attempts to write in terms of their inadequate content and/or lack of a rhetorically compelling order. If that criticism seems overly subtle or muted to the modern interpreter, perhaps it is because our ears have become dull to the persuasive rhetoric that filled the air of the ancient Mediterranean world.

Notes

1. Preeminent among the more recent literature on the Lukan prefaces is Loveday Alexander, *The Preface to Luke's Gospel: Literary Convention and Social Context in Luke 1.1–4 and Acts 1.1* (SNTSMS 78; Cambridge: Cambridge University, 1993). See also I. Howard Marshall, "Acts and the 'Former Treatise,'" in *The Book of Acts in Its Ancient Literary Setting* (ed. Bruce W. Winter and Andrew D. Clarke; vol. 1 of *The Book of Acts in Its First Century Setting*, ed. Bruce W. Winter; Grand Rapids: Eerdmans, 1993), 163–82; Darryl W. Palmer, "Acts and the Ancient Historical Monograph," in *The Book of Acts in Its Ancient Literary Setting*, 1–29, esp. 21–26.

2. So, among others, Terrence Callan, "The Preface of Luke-Acts and Historiography," *NTS* 31 (1985): 576–81; Gregory E. Sterling, *Historiography and Self-Definition: Josephus, Luke-Acts, and Apologetic Historiography* (NovTSup 64; Leiden: E. J. Brill, 1992): 339–50; W. C. van Unnik, "Once More, St. Luke's Prologue," *Neot* 7 (1963): 7–26.

3. So especially, Alexander, *Preface*.

4. So E. Haenchen, "Das 'Wir' in der Apostelgeschichte und das Itinerar," *ZTK* 58 (1961): 363; H. Schürmann, *Das Lukasevangelium* (2 vols.; HTKNT; Freiburg: Herder, 1969), I:4; John Nolland, *Luke 1–9:20* (WBC 35a; Dallas: Word, 1989), 12.

5. So I. Howard Marshall, *Commentary on Luke* (NIGTC; Grand Rapids: Eerdmans, 1978), 39; Robert Maddox, *The Purpose of Luke-Acts* (Studies of the New Testament and its World; Edinburgh: T&T Clark, 1982), 4–6; Green, *The Gospel of Luke*, 10; G. Klein, "Lukas 1,1–4 als theologisches Programm," in *Zeit und Geschichte: Dankesgabe an Rudolf Bultmann zum 80. Geburtstag* (ed. Erich Dinkler; Tübingen: J. C. B. Mohr, 1964), 200; Fitzmyer, *The Gospel according to Luke I–IX*, 200.

6. Charles Talbert, *Reading Luke: A Literary and Theological Commentary on the Third Gospel* (New York: Crossroad, 1982), 7, has suggested that the strategy of criticizing one's predecessors, even though apparently missing or muted in Luke, was a typical feature of ancient prefaces.

7. I am in full agreement with Alexander's caveat that "the rules devised for prefaces in rhetoric were devised for a very specific situation [an oral speech] and are of limited usefulness outside that situation" (*Preface*, 17). However, an attempt to compare Luke's preface with the *progymnasmata*, with their interest in writing as well as speaking, does not seem subject to this criticism. Further, a perusal of Alexander's indexes of subjects and ancient authors shows no reference to the *progymnasmata* tradition.

8. The pioneering work on *chreia* tradition in the Gospels was Taylor's *Groundwork for the Gospels, With Some Collected Papers*, though he had few immediate followers. More recently, Taylor's insights have been refined, sharpened, and surpassed in a flurry of writings about *chreia* and enthymemes. For the references to that literature, see Chapter Two, nn. 33–36, xxx–xxxi under the heading *On Chreia*. On rhetorical analyses of the speeches in Acts, see n. 21 in chapter two under the heading "Luke and the Rhetorical Tradition."

9. See Sterling, *Historiography and Self-Definition*, 342; Darrell L. Bock, *Luke 1:1–9:50* (Baker Exegetical Commentary on the New Testament 3; Grand Rapids: Baker, 1994), 56.

10. A point noted by Fitzmyer, *Luke*, 292. And even when διήγησις (*diēgēsis*) is used in reference to historical writings, the rhetorical dimension may not be entirely out of view. Dionysius of Halicarnassus, one of the ancient historians most self-conscious about his rhetorical style, uses the term in *Ant. rom.*, 1.8.2. Even Lucian, who criticizes those historians who succumbed to rhetorical excess, understood that the "power of expression" (*dynamis hermēneutikēs* [δύναμις ἑρμηνευτικης]) was an indispensable element of effective historiography (see *How to Write History*, 34). It is certainly possible then to read the reference to διήγησις (*diēgēsis*) in history writing as including the element of persuasiveness (see *How to Write History*, 55). Van Unnik (12–13) is right to conclude that, for Lucian, "narrative . . . is a technical term for the well-ordered, polished product," but wrong to imply that it is used exclusively of the "historian's work."

11. Alexander, *Preface*, 111, notes the technical sense of the word in the rhetorical handbooks, but she does not comment on its use in the *progymnasmata*; on this point, see below.

12. For more on Theon's notion of "narrative," see that section in chapter 2.

13. The term πραγμάτα ("matters" or "events") was also employed in the handbook tradition (see Theon's definition, and the Latin equivalents in Cicero and Quintillian) and was not particularly well-suited to the historian's craft; contra Nolland, 1:7.

14. See Stanley E. Porter, ed., *Handbook of Classical Rhetoric in the Hellenistic Period 330 B.C.–A.D. 400* (Leiden: Brill, 1997), esp. the chapters on "Historical Prose," by Stefan Rebenich, 265–338; "Biography," by Richard A. Burridge, 371–92; and "The Rhetoric of Romance," by Ronald F. Hock, 445–66.

15. Cadbury's caveat ("Commentary on the Preface of Luke," Appendix C in *The Beginnings of Christianity*, Part I [ed. F. S. Foakes-Jackson and Kirsopp Lake; London: Macmillan, 1933], 493) that "one must not press πολλοί here to mean *very many* predecessors in Gospel authorship," has been widely followed in subsequent scholarship, e.g., among others, J. Bauer, "POLLOI," *NovT* 4 (1960): 263–66; Nolland, *Luke*, 1:6. But see now Alexander's defense, in light of the scientific treatises (*Preface*, 114–15), that "Luke meant what he said" (115).

16. This translation presumes, along with the majority of commentators (see among others, Bock, *Luke*, 58; Fitzmyer, *The Gospel according to Luke*, 294), that the eyewitnesses and servants mentioned in Luke 1:2 refer to the same group (governed by the single article οἱ) and not two separate groups (contrary to Krister Stendahl, *The School of St. Matthew* [ASNU 20; Lund: Gleerup, 1954], 32–34).

17. On the various interpretations of ἀρχή (*archē*), see M. Eugene Boring, "Mark 1:1–15 and the Beginning of the Gospel," *Semeia* 52 (1990): 52–53.

18. Fitzmyer, *The Gospel according to Luke*, 294, argues that the apostles are in view here, but Green, *The Gospel of Luke*, 42, rightly notes that the list quickly expands to include others.

19. Bock, *Luke*, 63; Marshall, *Commentary on Luke*, 43; Alfred Plummer, *A Critical and Exegetical Commentary on the Gospel according to S. Luke* (5th ed.; ICC; Edinburgh: T&T Clark, 1901), 5.

20. G. Schneider, *Das Evangelium nach Lukas* (2 vols; ÖTK 3; Gütersloh: Mohn, 1977), 1:128–31; Bock, *Luke*, 63; R. J. Dillon, "Previewing Luke's Project from His Prologue (Luke 1:1–4)," *CBQ* 43 (1981): 218–23.

21. Klein, "Lukas 1,1–4 als theologisches Programm," 194–96; Mussner, "καθεξῆς im Lukasprolog," 253–55.

22. M. Völkel, "Exegetische Erwägungen zum Verständnis des Begriffs καθεξῆς im lukanischen Prolog," *NTS* 20 (1973–74): 289–99.

23. Fitzmyer, *The Gospel according to Luke*, 298–99.

24. Green, *The Gospel of Luke*, 43–44; Luke Timothy Johnson, *The Gospel of Luke* (SP 3; Collegeville, Minn.: Liturgical, 1991), 4.

25. D. P. Moessner, "The Meaning of καθεξῆς in the Lukan Prologue as the Key to the Distinctive Contribution of Luke's Narration among the 'Many,'" in *The Four Gospels 1992. Festschrift Frans Neirynck* (ed. F. Van Segbroeck, et al.; Leuven: Leuven University Press, 1992), 1527–28. Schneider, *Das Evangelium nach Lukas*, 1:128–31, offers critique of #3 and #4.

26. Robert Tannehill, *The Narrative Unity of Luke-Acts: A Literary Interpretation*, 144.

27. This, of course, would also be one way to understand Papias' famous criticism of Mark, recorded by Eusebius (*Hist. eccl.* 3.39.15): "Mark, having become the interpreter of Peter, wrote down accurately whatever he remembered of the things said and done by the Lord, but *not however in order*" (my emphasis).

28. On the Lukan theme of prophecy and fulfillment, see "Excursus A: The Fulfillment of Prophecy in Luke-Acts," in Talbert, *Reading Luke*, 234–40; also Darrell L. Bock, *Proclamation from Prophecy and Pattern: Lucan Old Testament Christology* (JSNTSup 12; Sheffield: JSOT Press, 1987); Paul Schubert, "The Structure and Significance of Luke 24," in *Neutestamentliche Studien für Rudolf Bultmann zu seinem siebzigsten Geburtstag* (ed. W. Eltester; BZNW 21; Berlin: Walter de Gruyter, 1957), 165–86.

29. See Johnson, *Luke*, 29–30.

30. So Bock, *Luke*, 56; Green, *The Gospel of Luke*, 37; Marshall, *Commentary on Luke*, 40; Nolland, *Luke*, 1:6.

31. F. Bovon, *Das Evangelium nach Lukas*, vol. 1: *Lk 1,1–9,50* (EKKNT 3/1; Neukirchen-Vluyn: Neukirchener Verlag), 34; Culpepper, "Luke," 40; Fitzmyer, *The Gospel according to Luke*, 291–92; M. Goulder, *Luke: A New Paradigm* (JSNTSup 20; 2 vols.; Sheffield: Sheffield Academic Press, 1989), I.199; Sterling, *Historiography and Self-Definition*, 345, Talbert, *Reading Luke*, 7.

32. See Frederick W. Danker, *Jesus and the New Age: A Commentary on St. Luke's Gospel* (rev. and exp. ed.; Philadelphia: Fortress, 1988), 24; Johnson, *Luke*, 30.

PART TWO

LUKE THE INTERPRETER

CHAPTER 4

Interpreting Pagan Traditions: Friendship and Physiognomy

Introduction

We have seen from the last two chapters that Luke was familiar with the rhetorical conventions and strategies of the larger Mediterranean milieu of late antiquity.[1] Luke's knowledge also extended to social customs and cultural values common among the larger first-century culture in which early Christianity was situated. At times, Luke employed those social values in order to focus his argument about the social and moral obligations early Christians had among themselves and to the larger society. This seems to be the case with the *topos* of "friendship." At other times, Luke uses the language of a particular social value only in order to challenge and undermine it; such seems to be the case with the conventions of ancient physiognomy—the association of outer physical characteristics with inner qualities. We shall take up these two examples, friendship and physiognomy, in order to explore Luke's use and interpretation (and in some cases, rejection) of social customs and values held in common in the ancient world.

Friendship in Its Greco-Roman Context

Friendship was an important cultural value in the ancient world.[2] In classical times, Aristotle (*Eth. nic.* 8.4.2–6) claimed that there were three levels of friendship based on 1) *virtue* (which was very rare and enduring); 2) *pleasure* (where each friend derives the same benefit; e.g. friendship between two witty people); or *utility* (such friendship dissolves as soon as its profit ceases). For Aristotle, ideal friendship was based on equality; "Friendship is equality" (*Eth. nic.* 9.4.5); but by Hellenistic times, friendship (φιλία, *philia/amicitia*) covered a wide array of social relationships. The terms φιλία (*philia*)/*amicitia* and φίλος (*philos*)/*amicus* were elastic terms as they were used not only in reference to relationships shared among equals, but also those between non-equals.[3]

Patron-Client Friendships

One such relationship between non-equals was that between a patron and client.[4] A major characteristic of a patron-client relationship revolved around the client's dependency upon the patron to offer gifts and sustenance to the client in exchange for praise and special favors.[5] This type of relationship is akin to the political "friendship" that often existed between the Roman Empire and the various satellite states the empire had as its clientele.[6] Using the language of friendship to describe a patron-client relationship, however, is not appropriate between every patron-client relationship. As Martin Culy states, "while some 'friends' were clients, not all clients were 'friends.'"[7]

Friendships with Deities

Although Aristotle had claimed that friendship with the gods was impossible (*Eth. nic.* 8.1159a5), many subsequent writers did not hold this position. A third to second-century B.C.E. fragment from Hippodamus, for instance, mentions three types of friendships: "Some friendships, based on knowledge, are with the gods; others, based on mutual support, are with humans; still others, based on pleasure, are with animals" (*Strom.* 2.19.101.1).[8] The LXX identifies Moses as a "friend of God" (Exod 33.11), which influenced the thinking and terminology of Philo (*Moses* 1.156).[9] Similarly, the Stoic philosopher Epictetus considered himself as "a friend of the god" (*Disc.* 2.17.29; 4.3.9),[10] while the later Pythagoreans viewed friendship with God as the ultimate goal of a pious life (Sextus, *Sent.* 86b).[11]

Friendship in Luke and Acts

According to Alan Mitchell, "Luke uses friendship more than any other NT author, adding it in some places in the Gospel where it is lacking in synoptic parallels (Luke 7:6; 12:4 15:6; 21:16)."[12] Luke's flexible use of the language of friendship reflects the varying Hellenistic perceptions of friendship. First, we see Luke using the term friend in relationship to presumed social equals: "When he [the shepherd] comes home [after finding the lost sheep], he calls together his *friends* and neighbors, saying to them, 'Rejoice with me, for I have found my sheep that was lost!'" (Luke 15:6; see 15:9, 29). Second, we find the Lukan use of friendship language in relationship to subordinates: "When he [Jesus] was not far from the house, the centurion sent *friends* to him . . ." (Luke 7:6; see John 4:51 where "servants" is used). In other places, "friend" functions as a *patron:* "The Son of man has come eating and drinking; and you say 'Behold a glutton and a drunkard, a *friend* of tax collectors and sinners!'" (Luke 7:34). Oftentimes, the references to friendship are in relationship to reciprocity and obligation (see Luke 14:12–14; 21:16; Acts 10:24), a point we shall pursue more fully in our consideration of the parable of the friend at midnight (Luke 11:5–8).[13]

Furthermore, the concept, discussed earlier, of having a friendship with the divine in the context of the Greco-Roman world sheds significant light on the prologue of Luke's Gospel, in which the Gospel is addressed to a certain Θεόφιλος (*Theophilos*), literally "friend of God" (1:3). Although Θεόφιλος (*Theophilos*) was a common name during and after the third century B.C.E. and probably a specific individual to whom Luke was writing,[14] the readership of the Gospel would certainly not have been limited to a single individual. Ancient prefaces generally addressed an audience beyond that of a single individual, even when a single individual is specifically named in the preface (e.g. Josephus, *Ag. Ap.* 1.1–18). Thus, when subsequent readers (e.g. Origen) claimed that every reader of Luke's Gospel is a "friend of God," although they did not necessarily acknowledge Θεόφιλος (*Theophilos*) as an original recipient, they did, however, recognize a readership beyond that of a single individual.[15] Although it is easy to discredit readers such as Origen for failing to recognize that Θεόφιλος (*Theophilos*) may have been an actual person to whom Luke was writing, one should not completely dismiss such an observation since such a reading does take into account an audience that extends beyond Θεόφιλος (*Theophilos*). It is unknown exactly how early readers of Luke would have actually considered themselves as the "friends of God" to whom Luke was writing. While such a practice could have been original to Origen in the second to third century C.E., it is also possible that this practice reflects an earlier tradition.[16] Although it is not entirely clear how a first-century Greco-Roman audience would have heard Θεόφιλος (*Theophilos*) in Luke's prologue (as simply the name of the person who originally received the gospel, or, more symbolically, themselves as the "friends of God"), from a literary standpoint at least, Θεόφιλος (*Theophilos*) does nicely accentuate Luke's friendship motif.

Friendship in Luke 11:5–8

Although interpreters and scholars of the past have long read the parable of the friend at midnight in Luke 11:5–8 within its immediate (11:1–13) and overall Lukan context (often in connection with the parable of the unjust judge in 18:1–8[17]), most of the attention has tended to focus on persistence in prayer[18] and/or the matter of God's faithfulness in answering such prayer.[19] Only recently have scholars began to take note of the *topos* of friendship in the parable,[20] albeit few have commented on what such a *topos* contributes to the whole of Luke's narrative and how a first-century audience would have responded to it. Consequently, several questions concerning the parable remain unanswered. For instance, is it significant that the Lukan Jesus uses the word φίλος (*philos*) a total of four times within this brief parable that consists of only two sentences? If so, then how would Luke's audience, presumably within a Greco-Roman context, have heard the parable within the immediate and overall context of Luke's Gospel?

Friendship as a Primary Topos of the Parable in Luke 11:5–8

We begin with a look at the rhetorical conventions Luke employed in this parable in service of the friendship *topos*. As we have already discussed, one of most elementary exercises for beginning students was that of inflecting the main subject of a given story or narrative in a variety of constructions for the purpose of drawing the audience's attention to that subject (see Chapter 2).

Of particular concern here is the hypothesis that Luke utilized inflection in order to signal a key *topos* of the parable in Luke 11:5–8. In the parable, Luke's multiple use of the word φίλος (*philos*) appears inflected twice in the accusative, once in the vocative, and once in the nominative. This variety of case construction not only suggests an intentional emphasis on the word φίλος (*philos*); the arrangement of the words in their respective cases also gives further clues regarding its emphasis. In order to give special attention to the accusative cases, as was expected when dealing with "fables," Luke places the first and last occurrences of φίλος (*philos*) in the accusative case, thus forming a grammatical frame around the parable. Not only does this place special emphasis on the word by its double occurrence in the accusative; the fact that it "begins in the accusative," a practice highly commended by Theon, is a further signal of the importance of φίλος (*philos*).

Because, as we noted, friendship language was often used to describe the relationship between two individuals of unequal status, such as a patron and client, using φίλος (*philos*) to describe the relationship between the petitioner and the sleeper of the parable does not assume that these two characters are of equal status. The question then arises, if the petitioner does not have bread in his house, should one expect a person of equal status to have bread available? On the contrary, given that the petitioner automatically knows who will have bread available and thus goes to him making a request depicts the situation of a client going to his patron for the needed sustenance. The duty of a patron demanded that bread be given to a petitioning client. According to Seneca the Younger, only rude patrons would ignore such a request from their clients:

> How many patrons are there who drive away their clients by staying in bed when they call, or ignoring their presence, or being rude? . . . How many, still hung-over and half-asleep from last night's drinking, will yawn disdainfully at men who have interrupted their own sleep in order to wait upon his awaking, and will mumble a greeting through half-open lips, and will need to be reminded a thousand times of the client's name? (*Brev. Vit.* 14.4)[21]

If the audience of the parable does indeed understand the sleeper as a patron and the petitioner as a client, then the comparison between the sleeper who answers (11:8) and the God who will answer (11:9–13) is much more explicit. This connection between the sleeping patron and God would have been especially clear to Luke's audience if its members conceived of God as a patron figure. Indeed, Bruce Malina has shown that the conceptual and linguistic references to God in the synoptic tradition construct an analogy that portrays God as a patron and humans as God's clients.[22] P. Spilsbury has also demonstrated that God as patron is similarly attested in Josephus, who depicts the relationship between God and Israel as one that is largely based upon the patron-client relationship.[23] In commenting upon the use of patron-client terminology in reference to God-human relations in the context of Roman religion, Spilsbury notes that

> the contractual nature of Roman religion is reflected in the use of words such as *officium, beneficium* and *gratia*. For example, prosperity and good luck are referred to as *beneficia* of the gods (see

Pliny, *Hist. Nat.* 12.1; Quintilian, *Declamationes* 268; Seneca, *Ep. ad Luc.* 8.3), and the gods deserved *gratia* in return (see Seneca, *Ep. ad Luc.* 119.16; Tacitus, *Ann.* 11.15).[24]

Accordingly, the analogy of God as patron is highly attested in the milieu of the Greco-Roman world, thus showing the connection between the sleeper who acts as a patron to the petitioner and God who acts as a patron to God's petitioners. Therefore, if Luke's audience would have conceivably identified with a patron described as a friend, and God portrayed as a patron, it is only natural to suppose that his audience would resonate with the idea of God depicted as a friend.

Noting the ideals of God as friend, God as patron, and patron as friend, creates what V. K. Robbins has called an "enthymemic network," e.g., a network that presumes the social, cultural, and ideological context in which the text was written that ultimately spurs—in the mind of the audience—contexts outside of the text itself.[25] Of primary importance to this section is the proposal that Luke and his audience would have simply assumed the various social ideals discussed above, and that the enthymemic network in the mind of Luke's audience would have served as a filter in how his audience heard the friendship *topos* in Luke and Acts.

The Parable's Friendship Topos in Its Lukan Context

The reverberations of the parable's friendship *topos* form an interlinking network with both its immediate Lukan context (11:1–13), as well as the overall plot of Luke's narrative. As the following paragraphs will demonstrate, Luke has signaled the parable's friendship *topos* in order to address an issue of God's character by showing how God is a reliable friend who will remain loyal to the obligations of friendship reciprocity.

Friendship with God and the Motif of 'Sleeping'

The initial rhetorical question in the parable expects a negative answer (11:5–7).[26] As shown earlier, only a rude patron would ignore the presence of his client by staying in bed. Such a scenario, however, warrants further consideration of the analogy between the sleeping friend who will answer (11:8) and God who will answer (11:9–13). How is the sleeping friend similar and/or dissimilar from the God whose character Luke is describing through the parable?

The predicament of the friend who sleeps when his petitioning friend has a need (11:5–7) is an image that is similar to the problem of a god who seemingly sleeps in spite of human injustice and suffering. References to a sleeping god appear in both Greek and Jewish literature. Homer's *Iliad*, for example, narrates an account in which Zeus "went to his couch, where of old he was wont to take his rest, when sweet sleep came upon him" (1:1611, LCL). The analogy of a sleeping god in reference to a god who is inactive in spite of human suffering, however, is much more explicit in Psalm 44.23: "Rouse yourself! Why do you sleep, O Lord? Awake, do not cast us off forever! Why do you hide your face? Why do you forget our affliction and oppression? . . . Rise up, come to our help" (see Ps 78.65). A similar reference appears in post-biblical Judaism in reference to the Levites who, before the reign of Hyrcanus, would cry daily, "Awake, why sleepest thou, O Lord?" (*b. Sota* 48a).

Friendship with God and the Issue of Reciprocity

An accusation of the inactivity of God, especially within the context of the parable's friendship *topos*, would have serious consequences on the friendship between God and Luke's audience. A grave violation to friendship, and one of the only reasons[27] for dissolving a friendship in the ancient world, was due to the activity or *inactivity* of an unreliable and disloyal friend who violated the obligations of friendship reciprocity. For instance, Xenophon's portrayal of the trial of Theramenes accounts for the dissolution of the friendship between Critias and Theramenes as due to charges of betrayal (*Hell.* 2.3.43).[28] Similar concerns of friendship loyalty are emphatically interwoven throughout Aesop's fables.[29] The fable of "the wayfarers and the bear" appropriately illustrates how the violation of friendship reciprocity[30] is a legitimate reason to terminate the friendship:

> Two friends were walking on the same street. When a bear appeared before them, the first one had time to climb a tree and hide there, while the other, being close to being caught by the bear, fell to the ground and pretended to be dead. As the bear moved her snout close to him and smelt him, he held his breath; for it is said that this animal does not touch the dead. When the bear left, the one who was on the tree asked him what the bear told him in his ear. And he answered 'not to travel from now on together with the kind of friend who does not assist in time of danger' (P65).[31]

As the conclusion of this fable implies, only a disloyal friend will refuse to help his or her friend when placed in a situation of immediate danger or hardship.[32] The fable also highlights the element of betrayal[33] that comes to surface when a friend is disloyal. The ethical implications of the fable of "the wayfarers and the bear" illustrate the demands placed upon the sleeper when his petitioning friend asks for assistance in a time of need, which also reveals why the petitioner is so concerned to provide bread for his traveling friend. In both of these relationships (i.e., the friendship between the sleeper and the petitioner, and that between the petitioner and the traveler) the continuation of the friendship between each character is at stake. This raises a few questions: Does Luke's presentation of the parable address an audience that considered God a disloyal friend who had violated the obligations of friendship reciprocity and therefore betrayed them? If so, is Luke's audience considering terminating their friendship with God? Furthermore, what does Luke's presentation of the parable communicate about the friendship between God and Luke's audience? While attempts to answer the former two questions are beyond the scope of this section, the latter question warrants attention from the immediate context of the parable.

The Parable's Immediate Context

In its immediate context, the parable serves an illustrative[34] purpose by providing an example that complements a larger section (11:1–13) addressing the issue of prayer. Such a usage of the parable is analogous to a practice given in the preliminary rhetorical exercises of Hermogenes, which notes that one of the uses of the Greek fable was that of using the fable to give an example of the issue at hand (4; = Kennedy, *Protogymnasmata* 75). This rhetorical practice called for students to place "the statement explaining the moral" of the fable either at the beginning or end of the fable (4; = Kennedy, *Protogymnasmata* 75). Similarly, Luke provides commentary for understanding the moral of the parable in the subsequent verses (11:9–13). The image of the sleeping friend in the parable stands in parallel to the image of the father who knows how to give good gifts to his children (11:11–13). In both of these images, Luke uses an argument from the lesser to the greater (Aristotle, *Rhet.* 2.23.4)[35] to show how if one can expect a friend and a father to answer his or her requests, how much more should one expect God, the divine friend and father, to answer his or her requests.

The object of God's giving, however, only becomes clear when one considers the brief section (11:2–4) immediately preceding the parable. Responding to a certain disciple who asked how one should pray, the Lukan Jesus gives a prayer that begins with the request "let your kingdom come" and ends with the petition "do not lead us into trial (πειρασμός, *peirasmos*)." The first request points forward to 11:13, where the Lukan Jesus assures his disciples that God will give the "Holy

Spirit to those who ask." The presence of the Holy Spirit in Luke-Acts is the evidence that the kingdom of God has come (Luke 1:34–35; Acts 1:4–8).[36] Moreover, the presence of the kingdom carries an eschatological connotation implying a deliverance from trials (πειρασμός, *peirasmos*, Luke 22:28).[37] In Luke, πειρασμός (*peirasmos*) is characterized by opposition that often results in suffering (8:13; 22:28; Acts 20:19).[38] Therefore, as a unit, 11:1–13 assures Luke's audience that God will not violate the ideals of friendship reciprocity, but will remain a loyal friend by granting deliverance from trials and the sufferings that accompany them.

The Parable within the Context of Luke's Narrative

By showing how God is the reliable friend who answers the requests of God's petitioners, the parable in its immediate context accentuates a Lukan concern regarding the realization of God's justice (7:29) in spite of the marginalization (4:18–19; 6:20–23) and/or sufferings (13:2; see Acts 9:16) of the innocent. While the parable displays the character of God by showing how God will answer the requests of those who pray with shamelessness[39] during times of trial, it also points forward to the parable of the unjust judge, which will portray the character of God in a similar way by showing how God will answer the requests of those who pray with persistence (18:1–8). After the parable of the unjust judge, the theme of God's justice is realized more clearly. Now, not only will God answer the requests of those who pray for deliverance from trials (11:1–13), God will grant justice to those who do not lose heart and pray with persistence (18:1–8). Later in the narrative, although the Lukan Jesus has difficulty in urging the disciples to pray lest they "enter into trial (πειρασμός, *peirasmos*)" (22:40, 46), he himself ultimately becomes the model of his own teachings when he prays for deliverance (22:41–42)[40] prior to becoming an "innocent" (δίκαιος, *dikaios*) sufferer (23:4, 13–15, 22, 47).[41] In the end, one sees the results of such prayer when he receives his vindication in the form of resurrection (24:1–12), which gives a fitting closure to the issue of the justice of God in Luke's narrative.

Noting the significance of Luke's rhetorical emphasis of the friendship *topos* in Luke 11:5–8, this section of the chapter has sought to create a framework for understanding how the friendship *topos* functioned within the context of Luke's narrative and especially in the parable of the friend at midnight. By considering the general usage of the term φίλος (*philos*) in the ancient world, we see that the Third Evangelist has constructed a cultural, sociological, and ideological network in which the parable functions to show that God is a reliable friend, who will remain loyal to the obligations of friendship reciprocity by answering the requests of God's petitioners despite situations of trial and suffering. The parable, therefore, plays a vital role in the Lukan concern to communicate the reality of God's justice despite human suffering by showing how God will answer the requests of those who pray "lead us not into trial" (11:4).[42]

Luke and the Physiognomic Consciousness

Physiognomy in the Ancient World

We turn now to another cultural convention popular in the ancient world, the study and practice of physiognomy. Luke and his audience lived in a world in which it was commonplace to associate outer physical characteristics with inner qualities, a world in which it was assumed that you can, as it were, judge a book by its cover.[43] The study of the relationship between the physical and the moral was known as "physiognomy." In one of a handful of extant technical treatises on this topic, the author of the pseudo-Aristotelian tractate claims: "The physiognomist takes his information from movements, shapes, colors, and traits as they appear in the face, from the hair, from the smoothness of the skin, from the voice, from the appearance of the flesh, from the limbs, and from the entire stature of the body" (806a.28–34).[44] This method is based on the assumption that "soul and body react on each other; when the character of the soul changes, it changes also the form of the body, and conversely, when the form of the body changes, it changes the character of the soul" (808b.12–15).

Interest in physiognomy was not limited to those who wrote such technical treatises. Elizabeth Evans has convincingly demonstrated that from Homer through at least the third century C.E., physical descriptions of characters in epic, histories, drama, and fiction, as well as in medical writings, were used by writers "as an aspect of characterization in classical writers."[45] Thus there developed a widespread "physiognomic consciousness" that permeated the Greco-Roman thought world.[46] What follows is a small sample of a large data base of texts from Greek and Latin sources.[47]

> [Suetonius' description of Augustus]: His teeth were wide apart, small, and ill kept; his hair was slightly curly and inclined to golden; his eyebrows met. His ears were of moderate size, and his nose pro-

jected a little at the top and then bent slightly forward. His complexion was between dark and fair. He was short of stature, but this was concealed by the fine proportion and symmetry of his figure, and was noticeable only by comparison with some taller person standing beside him. (Suet. *Aug.* 79)

No other part of the body supplies greater indications of the mind—this is so with all animals alike, but especially with man—that is, indications of self-restraint, mercy, pity, hatred, love, sorrow, joy. (Pliny *Nat. Hist.* 11.141–145)

This "physiognomic consciousness" is also clearly inscribed in Jewish and Christian sources. One sees, for example, an interest in the inner qualities reflected in the outer characteristics in the Jewish Scriptures themselves. In 1 Sam 9:2 Saul is described as "a handsome young man. There was not a man among the people of Israel more handsome than he; he stood head and shoulders above everyone else." One thinks also of David, who "was ruddy and had beautiful eyes, and was handsome" (1 Sam 16:12). However these texts would have been understood by *their* authorial audience, by the first and second centuries, C.E., they fit nicely into the pattern of a "physiognomic consciousness."

There is also in Israel's Scriptures critique of placing too much emphasis on physical appearances. In that same text that gives a physical description of David, Samuel, who is looking for Saul's replacement among Jesse's sons, David's older siblings, is told by God: "Do not look on his appearance or on the height of his stature, because I have rejected him; for the Lord does not see as mortals see; they look on outward appearance, but the Lord looks on the heart" (1 Sam 16:7). Nonetheless, the physiognomic consciousness is detectable in post-biblical Judaism in the Dead Sea Scrolls.

[The righteous person is one] whose eyes are neither dark nor light, whose beard is sparse and medium curly, whose voice resonates, whose teeth are fine and regular, who is neither tall nor short but is well built, whose fingers are thin and long, whose thighs are hairless, the soles of whose feet and whose toes are as they should be: he possesses a spirit eight parts from the House of Light and one in the House of Darkness. This is the birth sign under which such a person shall be born. (4Q186, frag. 2 col. 1.1–8; see also 4QCryptic 3:4; 4QMess ar. 1:2)

The appearance of his face is as of a wild man. His right eye is like a star rising at dawn and the other is unmoving. His mouth is one cubit, his teeth are a span long, his fingers like scythes, the soles of his feet two span, and on his forehead an inscription "Antichrist." (*Apoc. Ezra*, 4:29–32)

Likewise some early Christian texts reflect this physiognomic consciousness.

> [Paul] a man small of stature, with a bald head and crooked legs, in a good state of body; with eyebrows meeting and nose somewhat hooked, full of friendliness; for now he appeared like a man, and now he had the face of an angel. (*Acts Paul* 3)

> "A fool raises his voice in laughter," says the Scripture (Eccl 21:23); but a clever man smiles almost imperceptibly. (Clement of Alexandria, *Paed.* 2.5; see also *Paed.* 2.7, 46; 3.3, 5, 11)

> Modesty must be guarded in our very movements and gestures and gaits. For the condition of the mind is often to be seen in the attitude of the body . . . Thus, the movement of the body is a sort of voice of the soul. (Amb. *Off.* 1.18.67, 70–71; see also Tertullian, *Cult. fem.* 2.1, 8, 13, *An.* 5, 20, 25, 32; St. Gregory of Nyssa, *Fun. Orat.* 7.5, 8.10, 18.5; Basil, *Lit.* 1.2, 20–21, 132–135)

Physiognomy and the Healing of the Lame Man

In this section we will examine the character of the lame man in Acts 3–4 in connection with this "physiognomic consciousness" in order to see if this exercise might shed any additional light on this text. [48] In doing so, I am not denigrating the considerable insight that scholars have already provided into this very important story, but I am seeking to explore features of the text that traditional exegesis has tended to neglect.[49] I am attempting to understand how this story, whatever its historical base, would have been heard by Luke's authorial audience.[50] My thesis is that Luke used physiognomic language to lure the audience into the story. He argues that membership in the eschatological community of the Way requires rejecting the assumption that physical appearance is directly connected to moral character. As such, the story of the lame man joins with others in introducing physiognomic categories only to subvert them, e.g., the bent woman of Luke 13, Zacchaeus in Luke 19, blind Saul in Acts 9, and the Ethiopian Eunuch in Acts 8, among others.[51]

I begin by noting briefly the structure of Acts 3:1–4:31 and its placement in the narrative of Acts. This story is a well-defined narrative segment. Narrative summaries on either side of our text in 2:41–47 and

4:32–35 make it a text "readily isolated from what precedes and what follows."[52] Furthermore this narrative segment is comprised of four scenes, 3:1–10, 3:11–4:4, 4:5–22; 4:23–31, demarcated by temporal and spatial shifts.[53] The temporal shift from Day 1 to Day 2, effected by a "nocturnal pause" between 4:4 and 4:5, causes Scenes 1–2 and 3–4 to be more closely related to each other.[54]

The Healing of the Lame Man
Acts 3:1–4:31

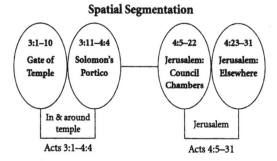

The theme of healing is found in every scene, either with specific reference to the lame man (3:7, 16; 4:9–10, 22) or to healing in general (4:30).[55] The healing of a lame man also has parallels in the ministry of Jesus (Luke 5:17–26) and Paul (Acts14:8–18).

With this brief description of the literary contours of our narrative, let us begin with our physiognomic analysis. In many ways, the key text is Acts 3:7b, where the narrator, in recounting the healing, notes that "immediately his feet and ankles were made strong." This verse was a favorite among those who advanced the thesis that Luke's so-called medical vocabulary proved that the author was a physician.[56] Of course, Henry Cadbury dismantled this thesis, and the legacy of Cadbury has been that subsequent commentators often omit any reference to these terms (e.g., Fitzmyer) or when they do comment, usually do so only to point out that "feet" and "ankles" are *not* medical terms (e.g., Haenchen).[57]

When we turn to the physiognomic handbooks, we see that feet and ankles are indeed the object of physiognomic consideration. About ankles, the author writes:

> Those who have strong and well-jointed ankles are brave in character; witness the male sex. Those that have fleshy and ill-jointed ankles are weak in character; witness the female sex. (Pseudo-Aristotle, *Physiogn.* 810a.25–29; see also Adamantius 7; Pseudo-Polemo, 18 [Förster, 357])[58]

In a culture where the "physiognomic consciousness" pervaded, the lame man's weak ankles would have been viewed as an outward physical sign of his inner weak moral character, his μαλακός (*malakos*), his "soft," "timid," "cowardly," or "effeminate" nature.[59] This weakness is confirmed by his presentation in the narrative as a passive participant. The lame man "is carried"; he is "laid daily at the gate"; "Peter took him by the right hand"; and "raised him up."[60]

The man's moral weakness is confirmed also by Peter's reference in 4:9 to the lame man as an ἀνθρώπου ἀσθενοῦς (*anthrōpou asthenous*), though not the same word as ps-Aristotle, certainly in the same semantic range (see Louw & Nida). The phrase ἀνθρώπου ἀσθενοῦς (*anthrōpou asthenous*) is translated "cripple" or "sick" in most modern translations, but literally means "weak man."[61] The various forms of the *ἀσθεν-* (*asthen-*) stem do often refer to a physical infirmity (see Luke 4:40; 5:15; 9:2; 10:9; Acts 5:15, 16; 9:37; 19:12; 28:9), but the term can carry a moral or metaphorical sense (see BDAG and Louw & Nida), which Luke also knows (see Acts 20:35; Luke 13:11).[62] Thus Peter's description of the man here as "weak" refers both to his former physical *and* moral state.

That the audience would have viewed the lame man negatively is further confirmed by the attitude in antiquity toward the disabled generally and the lame specifically. Classicist Robert Garland in his study, *The Eye of the Beholder: Disability in the Graeco-Roman World,* observes that the lame

> who probably constituted the largest number of disabled persons in the ancient world, probably fared better than the blind in economic terms since there were many more skilled and semi-skilled occupations of a sedentary nature that were available to them. These in-

cluded pottery-making, vase-painting, leather-working, and metal-working, as well as banking, retailing and teaching.[63]

If this statement is true, then the authorial audience of Acts might be even more perturbed by the passivity of the lame man, given that some occupations were presumably open to him that would not have been available to other disabled persons.[64] In this view, the man of Acts 3–4 is not only lame but lazy, since, from the perspective of the ancient audience, he did not seek any level of self-sufficiency, but rather relied entirely upon the generosity of unnamed family and friends to carry him to the temple in order to beg alms.[65]

The disabled, and the lame in particular, in the ancient world were also objects of ridicule and derision.[66] Garland comments at length on the cheap and often lewd humor associated with the Greek symposium.

> *Crippled dancers* feature prominently on Corinthian pots, as, for instance, on an alabastron which depicts a padded dancer with clubbed feet who is about to have his leg pulled away by another dancer—to the side-splitting laughter no doubt of the drinkers witnessing this prank. Whether scenes like these were acted out by genuine cripples or by actors taking their parts makes no difference. Evidently the joke was deemed sufficiently amusing to bear frequent repetition in the artistic repertoire, which presumably reflects its popularity at symposia.[67]

As an example of this kind of ribald and denigrating humor, consider Plutarch who "informs us that the typical kinds of commands which an insensitive symposiarch or master of drinking might give to test the guests' ability to hold their liquor included ordering a stammerer to sing, a bald man to comb his hair, or *a lame man to dance on a greased wineskin*" (emphasis mine, *Mor.* 621e).[68] We might note in passing that such derisive ridicule was not limited to the pagan world. This point is underscored in the late first-century Jewish document *4 Ezra,* which, in an exhortation to good works, commands: "Do not ridicule a lame man" (*4 Ezra* 2:21).[69] Or consider the *Apocryphon of Ezekiel* (first century B.C.E.–first century C.E.), whose point about the need to reunite body and soul in the resurrection depends on the assumption that alone, a lame man and a blind man, are each only "half a man."[70]

Whether or not lame worshippers were formally and ritually excluded from the first-century temple is a hotly debated and probably irresolvable issue. Nonetheless, the location of the lame man at "the threshold of the temple enclosure" raises question as to whether or not the authorial audience would have inferred from this reference that the man was socially ostracized, lying, as it were, "outside" the boundaries of institutional religion.[71] The healing that ensues then would have been dramatic: a healing of the body and a transformation of the soul, underscored in part by the movement from outside to inside the Temple precinct.[72]

Luke's interest in feet is no simple fetish! The physiognomic understanding of "weak ankles" (and feet) combined with the reality of the derision of the disabled in Greco-Roman society and the possible social exclusion hinted at by his location "outside" the gate, would have caused the audience of Acts 3–4 to view the lame man as a thoroughly negative character, a morally weak and passive man who is unable to stand on his own two feet.[73]

Furthermore, the strengthening of the lower extremities would be an outward sign of his newly found inner moral strength of character, what ps-Aristotle calls εὔρωστος (eurōstos, "stout," "strong," or "robust"—LSJ, 731). A few examples from ancient pagan, Jewish, and Christian sources will help delineate the meaning of the term. In his novel, Achilles Tatius uses term to describe a "robust" or "muscular" sailor (Leuc. Clit. 2.17.3; 3.4.1). Josephus uses this term to describe one Jewish archer named Mosollamus who was intelligent and "robust" (εὔρωστος, eurōstos; Ag. Ap. 1.201.4). The Sibylline Oracles uses the word to refer to a "bracing" (εὔρωστος, eurōstos) storm (3.369). Eusebius, in a quotation attributed to Clement, describes the moral corruption of a young man, whose rush away from God was like an "unbroken and powerful (εὔρωστος, eurōstos) horse" (Hist. eccl. 3.23.10). In an interesting passage, Plutarch claims (in relation to the character of Aemilius) that the spirit (ψύχη, psychē) that is "vigorous and strong" (εὐρωστία καὶ ἰσχύς, eupōstia kai ischys) "is neither spoiled nor elated by the insolence which prosperity brings, nor humbled by adversity" (Plutarch, Tim. 2.5). Though Luke does not use the term εὔρωστος (eupōstos), he "shows" the restored "vigor" and "robustness" of the lame man's character through the physical manifestations of leaping up, standing, and walking (Acts 3:9). The outer physical healing thus provides empirical proof for the inner moral and spiritual transformation, a point underscored by the double sense of σώζω (sōzō) in 4:9 as both "heal" in a physical sense and "save" in a moral/spiritual sense, a double entendre that conforms nicely to physiognomic expectations.

We see this point borne out in the narrative as well. The lame man moves from inactivity to walking, from paralysis to praise. He also moves from sitting to clinging (Acts 3:11) to standing unassisted, alongside Peter and John. As such he shares in the "boldness" (παρρησία, parrēsia) of the apostles (4:13),[74] a point noted long ago by John

Chrysostom: "So great was the boldness of the [lame] man; that even in the judgment-hall he has not left them. For had they said that the fact was not so, there was he to refute them."[75] Chrysostom, building on the use of the word θεωρέω (*theōreō*) in Acts 4:13, where the religious authorities "saw" the apostles' boldness, also claims that this boldness was not confined to words, but rather was "seen" in the apostles' "body language": " . . . [Not only by their words,] but by their gesture also, and their look and voice . . . they manifested the boldness with which they confronted the people."[76] Even though he does not speak, the lame man's boldness is seen also in his "body language," as he boldly takes his stand in solidarity with the persecuted apostles, and his transformation is complete.

If this were the whole story, then it would appear that Luke had previously followed the physiognomic conventions. The lame, morally weak man becomes a whole, morally bold man. As such, physiognomic prejudices and conventional cultural expectations are confirmed. But this is not all there is to Luke's story. If the lame man's body language in standing with the bold apostles fulfills physiognomic conventions, his leaping and praising God in the temple defies them.

Maud Gleason claims that deportment, the way one carries oneself, was also a tell-tale sign of a person's character. Furthermore, it was the walk of the lion, which "in the zoological shorthand of physiognomy," represented the ideal.[77] Ps-Aristotle echoes this sentiment in his description of the lion as "the most perfect share of the male type" (809a.15–16). After describing the fine features of the lion's head and back, the author proceeds to speak of the lion's lower body:

His legs are strong and muscular, his walk is vigorous, and his whole body is well-jointed and muscular. . . . He moves slowly with a long stride and swings his shoulders as he moves. These then are his bodily characteristics; in character he is generous and liberal, magnanimous and with a will to win; he is gentle, just, and affectionate towards his associates. (809b.30–36)

By contrast, Polemo describes the effeminate or cowardly: "You may recognize him by his provocatively melting glance and by the rapid movement of his intensely staring eyes . . . his loins do not hold still, and his slack limbs never stay in one position. He minces along with little jumping steps" (*Adam.* 2.52.1.415–416F).[78]

This interest in the physiognomic implications of one's gait was not limited to the physiognomic handbooks. Aristotle speaks of the "great-souled man" *whose step is slow,* whose voice is low, and whose speech is measured and deliberate (see Arist. *Eth.Nic.* 1125a34). Dio Chrysostom observes: "Walking is a universal and uncomplicated activity, but while one man's gait reveals his composure and the attention he gives to his conduct, another's reveals his inner disorder and lack of self-restraint" (*Or.* 35.24).[79]

This concern about the "hasty gait" is also seen in later Christian texts as well. Clement said, "A noble man should bear no sign of effeminacy upon his face or any other portion of his body. Nor should the disgrace of unmanliness ever be found in his movements or his posture" (*Paed.* 3.11.73–74). "Modesty must be guarded in our very movements and gestures and gaits. For the condition of the mind is often to be seen in the attitude of the body . . . Thus, the movement of the body is a sort of voice of the soul" (Ambrose, *Off.* 1.18.67, 70–71).[80]

What then are we to make of the lame man's actions recorded in Acts 3:8: "And leaping up, he stood and walked and entered the temple with them, walking and leaping and praising God"?[81] Form-critically this action is typically labeled the "demonstration of healing," but it certainly goes beyond the typical demonstration (see Luke 5:25; Acts 14:10). The lame man has moved from total inactivity to excessive activity; he does not "walk like a man."

More than one commentator has focused on the intertextual echoes with Isa 35:6. In that eschatological vision we hear that "the eyes of the blind shall be opened, and the ears of the deaf unstopped; the *lame shall leap like a deer*" (in which the same verb for "leap" is used in Greek Isa 35:6 as in Acts 3:9). The image is of the restoration of Israel as part of the vision of God as cosmic king.[82] How would an authorial audience, familiar with physiognomic conventions regarding deportment, hear this intertextual allusion to Isaiah's eschatological vision? With not a little ambivalence, I suspect. Just as lions are consistently depicted as the most courageous and noble of animals, so deer (ἔλαφος, *elaphos*) are depicted in a consistently negative fashion in physiognomy for cowardice: "For the *deer*, the hare and sheep are the most timid of all animals" (806b.8; see 807a.20; 811a.16; 811b.3; 811b.7).[83]

The Lukan authorial audience, shaped by a physiognomic consciousness, would expect the lame man to "prowl like a lion," not "leap like a deer"! But this seems to be exactly Luke's point. There is continuity with the physiognomic categories up to a point, but there is also discontinuity, as Luke breaks the physiognomic stranglehold that says how you look determines your moral character.[84]

As in other places, Luke invokes the categories of physiognomy only to overturn them (the bent woman [Luke 13:10–17], the Ethiopian eunuch [Acts 8:26–39], etc.). I cite briefly one other example to make this point. Zacchaeus was short in stature, a fact that, like the lame man's disability, would have earned him the scorn of the audience (e.g., he is called a "sinner" by the folk of Jericho). The physically small were, according to physiognomy, "small or mean in spirit." Nonetheless, his encounter with Jesus causes him to resolve to restore the money he had stolen four-fold and to give half his money to the poor. Jesus, in turn, pronounces him a "son of Abraham" (Luke 19:9), this despite the fact that not one cubit is added to his stature by worry or wonder-working. Though still short, salvation/healing comes to Zacchaeus' house that day. Each of these characters would have been viewed by Luke's auditors as morally weak, corrupt, or even evil, yet Luke claims that the eschatological community is comprised of such as these, a community in which "God shows no partiality" (Acts 10:34).

Nor does the lame man, cowardly, lazy, effeminate though he may have been, simply conform to the physiognomic standards of the day and immediately comport himself with a slow, dignified gait, showing by his outward deportment that he is a man of courage, or vigorous character, in other words, a "manly man." Rather, Luke shows that the formerly lame man, by leaping like a deer and praising God, is a member of the eschatological community of God![85] It is more important, in Luke's opinion, for one to respond appropriately to the benefaction of God than to worry about whether or not one's deportment is appropriately "masculine" according to cultural convention. [86]

The authorial audience experiences both continuity with and discontinuity from physiognomic conventions, as Luke subverts them in the name of Jewish eschatological expectation.[87] As in Isaiah, the lame man in Acts symbolizes the potential restoration of Israel (see Acts 1:6) as part of the establishment of God's cosmic reign, inaugurated by Jesus and continued through the ministry of the apostles and Paul. In this light, it is difficult to resist giving symbolic value to the more than forty years of the lame man's illness in terms of the exiled and restored Israel.[88] In Acts, where the Christian enterprise is called the "Way," we should not be surprised to find that the healing of the man born lame functions in a paradigmatic and symbolic way (much as the man born blind in John 9 functions in the Fourth Gospel, in which believing is symbolized as a kind of seeing). [89]

Conclusion

Luke was thoroughly familiar with the pagan social customs and values of his days. At times, he employed those values in order to call the Christian community to reciprocal obligation (as with friendship); at other times, he introduces the pagan value in order to correct it (as with physiognomy). We should not be surprised to see that Luke expects his audience to hear in what Fred Danker has called a "twofold tonality" in terms of hearing the text in light of both the Jewish and Greco-Roman milieu:

> At all times it must be kept in mind that Jewishness does not mean ignorance of Greco-Roman cultural tradition, and being Greco-Roman (i.e., of non-Jewish ancestry) does not imply ignorance of Jewish tradition. Thus, on the one hand, the evangelist's Greco-Roman auditors would grasp meaning in terms of continuity of Luke's text with their own cultural context. Conversely, they would find themselves encouraged, because of Luke's specific story line, to transpose their encounter with his text into a Christian key.[90]

This is exactly what Luke does in the case of friendship and physiognomy. Luke has used the friendship *topos* to highlight the reciprocal obligation of Christian to Christian, and in the case of the parable of the friend at midnight to reassure his audience that, despite the apparent inactivity of God, God is a reliable friend who will, graciously and willingly, come to the aid of his followers, his friends.

Likewise, Luke has used (and ultimately subverted) Greco-Roman physiognomic conventions to lure his audience into his story and then, employing allusions to the Old Testament (especially Isa 35), he encourages them to accept his conclusion that the lame man's healing is paradigmatic for the potential restoration of Israel within the establishment of the cosmic reign of God. The lame man's character is transformed through the presentation of the character of the lame man. In other words, the literary character(ization) of the lame man is unfolded in the story of the transformation of the lame man's (moral) character. And this without uttering an audible word in the story! Ambrose was right, "the movement of the body is a sort of voice of the soul"!

Hopefully, this chapter has demonstrated the exegetical payoff of examining the pagan social customs and values of the larger Greco-Roman world in which Luke lived and wrote. We turn now to consider how Luke interpreted the traditions of another sub-culture of that ancient world, first-century Judaism.

Notes

1. An earlier version of this section on friendship was originally cowritten with Justin R. Howell, a PhD student at the University of Chicago.

2. For a thorough assessment of friendship in late antiquity, see Martin M. Culy, "Jesus—Friend of God, Friend of His Followers: Echoes of Friendship in the Fourth Gospel," (PhD diss., Baylor University, 2002), 55–108. See also J.-C. Fraisse, *Philia: La Notion d'Amitié dans la Philosphie Antique* (Bibliothèque d'Histoire de la Philosophie; Paris: Librairie Philosophique J. Vrin, 1974); S. N. Eisenstadt and L. Roniger, *Patrons, Clients and Friends: Interpersonal Relations and the Structure of Trust in Society* (Themes in the Social Sciences; Cambridge: Cambridge University, 1984); J. T. Fitzgerald, ed., *Greco-Roman Perspectives on Friendship* (SBLRBS 34; Atlanta: Scholars Press, 1997); D. Konstan, *Friendship in the Classical World* (Key Themes in Ancient History; Cambridge: Cambridge University Press, 1997); and R. Metzner, "In aller Freundschaft. ein frühchristlicher Fall freundschaftlicher Gemeinschaft (Phil 2.25–30)," *NTS* 48 (2002): 111–31.

3. See Eisenstadt and Roniger, *Patrons, Clients and Friends*, 52–64; Benjamin Fiore, "The Theory and Practice of Friendship in Cicero," in *Greco-Roman Perspectives on Friendship*, 73; Konstan, *Friendship in the Classical World*, 7; and Culy, "Jesus—Friend of God," 57.

4. See Richard Saller, *Personal Patronage Under the Early Empire* (Cambridge: Cambridge University Press, 1982), 11–15; idem, "Patronage and Friendship in Early Imperial Rome: Drawing the Distinction," in *Patronage in Ancient Society* (ed. Andrew Wallace-Hadrill; London and New York: Routledge, 1989), 49–62.

5. See Saller, *Personal Patronage*, 13–15; See Konstan, *Friendship in the Classical World*, 136.

6. Eisenstadt and Roniger, *Patrons, Clients and Friends*, 53; Edward N. O'Neil, "Plutarch on Friendship," in *Greco-Roman Perspectives on Friendship* (ed. John T. Fitzgerald; Atlanta: Scholars Press, 1997), 109.

7. Culy, "Jesus—Friend of God," 68.

8. J. C. Thom, "'Harmonious Equality': The *Topos* of Friendship in Neopythagorean Writings," in *Greco-Roman Perspectives on Friendship*, 83.

9. Konstan, *Friendship in the Classical World*, 167, 170; see Josephus (*Ant.* 5.115–16); as noted by P. Spilsbury, "God and Israel in Josephus: A Patron-Client Relationship," in *Understanding Josephus: Seven Perspectives* (JSPSup 32; ed. Steve Mason; Sheffield: Sheffield Academic Press, 1998), 189–90.

10. Konstan, *Friendship in the Classical World*, 169; Thom, "Harmonious Equality," 86–87; and Culy, 'Jesus—Friend of God', 82.

11. Thom, "Harmonious Equality," 87; and Culy, "Jesus—Friend of God," 82.

12. Alan C. Mitchell, "'Greet the Friends by Name': New Testament Evidence for the Greco-Roman *Topos* on Friendship," in *Greco-Roman Perspectives on Friendship*, 237.

13. On this, see also Alan C. Mitchell, "The Social Function of Friendship in Acts 2:44–47," *JBL* 111 (1992): 255–72.

14. See Fitzmyer, *The Gospel according to Luke*, 1:299–300; and Nolland, *Luke*, 1:10.

15. Culpepper, "Luke," 9:40.

16. See Vernon. K. Robbins, "The Social Location of the Implied Author of Luke-Acts," in *The Social World of Luke-Acts: Models for Interpretation* (ed. J. H. Neyrey; Peabody, Mass.: Hendrickson, 1991), 320–23.

17. See for example: A. Plummer, *The Gospel according to Luke* (ICC; 5th ed.; Edinburgh: T&T Clark, 1989), 298; W. F. Arndt, *The Gospel according to St.*

Luke (Bible Commentary; Saint Louis, Mo.: Concordia, 1956), 297; K. Berger, "Materialen zu Form und Überlieferungsgeschichte neutestamentlicher Gleichnisse," 33–36; Talbert, *Reading Luke*, 132; J. Nolland, *Luke*, 2:622; and Luke Timothy Johnson, *The Gospel of Luke*, 179. Conversely, K. Haacker discredits this connection in "Mut zum Bitten. Eine Auslegung von Lukas 11,5–8," *TBei* 17 (1986): 5 n. 11.

18. See Calvin, *Commentary on a Harmony of the Evangelists, Matthew, Mark, and Luke* (Grand Rapids: Eerdmans, 1949), 1:354; Arndt, *Luke*, 297; and Fitzmyer, *Luke*, 2:910.

19. Rightfully so, this is contended by Fitzmyer, *Luke*, 2:910; Talbert, *Reading Luke*, 132; Nolland, *Luke*, 2:621–27; and Culpepper, "The Gospel of Luke," 9:237.

20. J. D. M. Derrett gives the most thorough treatment of friendship in the parable in "The Friend at Midnight: Asian Ideas in the Gospel of St. Luke," in *Donum Gentilicium: New Testament Studies in Honour of David Daube* (ed. E. Bammel, et al.; Oxford: Clarendon, 1978), 78–87. Also commenting on the issue of friendship in the parable are Fitzmyer, *Luke*, 2:911; Nolland, *Luke*, 2:623–24; Johnson, *Luke*, 178; Culpepper, "The Gospel of Luke," 9:236; Bernard Brandon Scott, *Hear Then the Parable: A Commentary on the Parables of Jesus* (Minneapolis: Fortress, 1989), 90–91; and Green, *The Gospel of Luke*, 446–49.

21. This translation follows that of J.-A. Shelton in *As the Romans Did: A Sourcebook in Roman Social History* (2d ed.; New York: Oxford University Press, 1998), 14–15.

22. Bruce Malina, "Patron and Client: The Analogy Behind Synoptic Theology," *Forum* 4 (1988): 2–32. See also J. J. Pilch and Bruce Malina, ed., *Biblical Social Values and Their Meaning: A Handbook* (Peabody, Mass.: Hendrickson, 1993), 133–37; and Bruce Malina, *The New Testament World: Insights from Cultural Anthropology* (rev. ed.; Louisville: Westminster John Knox, 1993), 102.

23. Spilsbury, "God and Israel in Josephus," 172–91.

24. Ibid., 178–79.

25. Robbins, "From Enthymeme to Theology in Luke 11:1–13," 191–92. Here Robbins defines an enthymeme as "an assertion this is expressible as a syllogism. A special characteristic of an enthymeme is to leave a premise or conclusion unexpressed, with a presumption that the premise or conclusion is obvious from the overall context. Enthymemic discourse, then, is discourse that presumes a context to fill out its meanings."

26. "Who of you," τίς ἐξ ὑμῶν (*tis ex humōn*) is a common way to introduce a rhetorical question that always expects a negative answer (e.g., Luke. 11:11; 12:25; 14:28; 15:4; 17:7).

27. According the Neopythagorean writings, "the only acceptable grounds for ending a friendship is a serious and irreparable moral defect in the other" (*Vit. Pyth.* 232 = *Vit. Pyth.* 102); as quoted in Thom, "Harmonious Equality," 100.

28. See J. T. Fitzgerald, "Introduction," in *Greco-Roman Perspectives on Friendship*, 7 n. 10.

29. M. A. Beavis has demonstrated the close relationship between parable and fable and the legitimacy of reading the Greek fables in parable research. She has shown how parable and fable have similarities in narrative structure, content, religious and ethical themes, the elements of surprise or irony, and the secondary morals or applications ("Parable and Fable," *CBQ* 52 [1990]: 473–98).

30. C. A. Zafiropoulos gives extensive treatment to the violations and obligations of friendship reciprocity as reflected in the *Augustana* Collection of Aesop's Fables in *Ethics in Aesop's Fables: The Augusta Collection* (Mnemosyne Supplements 216; Leiden: Brill, 2001), 81–145, esp. 81–98.

31. As quoted in Zafiropoulos, *Ethics in Aesop's Fables*, 90.

32. See Sir 6.7, where a true friend is gained only through testing. Only during times of crisis will a friend prove his or her true worth. Conversely, a friend who is not entirely committed is likely to abandon their friends in pressing situations (6:14–17). A true friend, however, will maintain his or her faithfulness throughout (6:14–17). See also W. H. Irwin, "Fear of God, the Analogy of Friendship and Ben Sira's Theodicy," *Bib* 76 (1995): 551–59; and Metzner, "In aller Freundschaft," 112–13.

33. See Zafiropoulos, *Ethics in Aesop's Fables*, 86–98.

34. See E. Cuvillier, "*Parabole* dans la Tradition Synoptique," *ETR* 66 (1991): 25–44, esp. 40–43. Here Cuvillier describes the Lukan parables as illustrations or word-images that are used in the rhetorical process of urging its audience toward making a decision—a usage of parable that comes close to the Aristotelian conception of parable.

35. See Nolland, *Luke*, 2:629.

36. See Talbert, *Reading Luke*, 131; see Luke 3:22; 4:18.

37. See Jesus' instructions to the disciples to pray lest they come into time of trial (Luke 22:40, 46). See also Jas 1:12; 1 Pet 1:6; 4:12; 2 Pet 2:9; and Rev 3:10.

38. See Tannehill, *The Narrative Unity of Luke-Acts*, 1:239–40.

39. As K. Snodgrass has demonstrated, all pre-Lukan usages of ἀναίδεια (*anaideia*) imply a sense of "shamelessness" ("*Anaideia* and the Friend at Midnight [Luke 11:8]," *JBL* 116 [1997]: 505–13), rather than the commonly rendered idea of "persistence" (e.g., NIV, NJB, and NRSV). See also A. F. Johnson, "Assurance for Man: The Fallacy of Translating *Anaideia* by 'Persistence' in Luke 11:5–8," *JETS* 22 (1979), 123–31; and Haacker, "Mut zum Bitten," 1–6.

40. Note that Jesus addresses God as "father" in both Luke 11:1–4 and in the prayers of the passion narrative (22:42; 23:[34], 46); as noted by Robert Tannehill in *Luke* (ANTC; Nashville: Abingdon, 1996), 187.

41. See other characters deemed as δίκαιος (*dikaios*) in 1:6; 2:25; 14:12–14; 23:50.

42. We might also compare and contrast the notion of "friendship" in Luke-Acts with that of the closely related, and sometimes overlapping cultural custom of "hospitality" (ξενία, *xenia*); see especially Andrew Arterbury, *Entertaining Angels: Early Christian Hospitality in its Mediterranean Setting* (New Testament Monographs 8; Sheffield: Sheffield Phoenix Press, 2005).

43. Of course, not all "moderns" would have been ignorant of physiognomic theories. The writings of Johann Caspar at the beginning of the nineteenth century revived the practice of physiognomy; see Lucy Hartley, *Physiognomy and the Meaning of Expression in Nineteenth-Century Culture* (Cambridge: Cambridge University Press, 2001).

44. Several systematic studies were devoted to the topic. Among the best known are a third-century B.C.E. document, *Physiognomica,* attributed (inaccurately) to Aristotle; *On Physiognomy,* a work by the second-century C.E. rhetorician, Polemo of Laodicea; and two later documents from the fourth century, C.E., *Physiognomonica* by Adamantius the sophist; and an anonymous Latin handbook, *de Physiognomonia*. These texts were collected, edited, and published

by Richard Förster, ed., *Scriptores Physiognomonic Graeci et Latini* (2 vols.; Lipsius: Teubner, 1893). See A. M. Armstrong, "The Methods of the Greek Physiognomists," *Greece & Rome* 5 (1958): 53, and J. Mesk, "Die Beispiele in Polemos Physiognomonk," *Wiener Studien* 50 (1932): 51–67.

45. Elizabeth C. Evans, "Physiognomics in the Ancient World," *TAPA* 59 (1969): 5.

46. Evans, "Physiognomics in the Ancient World," 6.

47. For others, see Evans, "Physiognomics in the Ancient World."

48. Among scholars who have explored physiognomy in relationship to the NT, see Abraham Malherbe, "A Physical Description of Paul," first published in *HTR* (1986): 170–75 (repr., *Paul and the Popular Philosophers* [Minneapolis: Fortress, 1989], 165–70); Dale B. Martin, *The Corinthian Body* (New Haven: Yale University Press, 1995); Bruce J. Malina and Jerome H. Neyrey, *Portraits of Paul: An Archaeology of Ancient Personality* (Louisville: Westminster John Knox, 1996); J. Massyngbaerde Ford, "The Physical Features of the Antichrist," *JSP* 14 (1996): 23–41; Karl Olav Sandnes, *Belly and Body in the Pauline Epistles* (SNTSMS 120; Cambridge: Cambridge University Press, 2002).

49. Dennis Hamm, though he does not explore physiognomy in any way, argues for the symbolic and paradigmatic value of the lame man's story for Luke's theology, and in that sense, his work stands closest to what I am attempting to do. See M. Dennis Hamm, S. J., "This Sign of Healing. Acts 3:1–10: A Study in Lucan Theology," (PhD diss., St. Louis University, 1975); idem, "Acts 3:12–26: Peter's Speech and the Healing of the Man Born Lame," *PRSt* 11 (1984): 199–217; idem, "Acts 3:1–10: The Healing of the Temple Beggar as Lucan Theology," *Bib* 67 (1986): 305–19.

50. On the notion of the "authorial audience," see Chapter 2, p. 19. On questions of historicity of this story, see Gerd Luedemann, whose representative skepticism toward miracle is still the dominant view in modern NT scholarship: "There is no historical nucleus to the tradition of the miracle story in vv. 1–10. Those who are lame from their childhood are (unfortunately) not made whole again" (*Early Christianity according to the Tradition in Acts: A Commentary* [Minneapolis: Fortress, 1989], 54). For a defense of the historicity of miracles in Acts, generally, see Colin Hemer, *The Book of Acts in the Setting of Hellenistic History* (WUNT 49; Tübingen, J. C. B. Mohr, 1989), 439–43. On the question of miracles in Acts, see the balanced presentation by Charles Talbert in *Reading Acts: A Literary and Theological Commentary on the Acts of the Apostles* (New York: Crossroad, 1997), 251–53.

51. This section is part of a larger project, *Body and Character in Luke and Acts* (Grand Rapids: Baker, 2006).

52. Funk, *The Poetics of Biblical Narrative*, 83. See also Mikeal Parsons, "Acts," in *Acts and Pauline Writings* (Mercer Commentary on the Bible, vol. 7; ed. Watson Mills, et al.; Macon, Ga.: Mercer University Press, 1997), 9.

53. For a slightly different proposal of the structure of Acts 3–4, see Talbert, *Reading Acts*, 51–52. It is unusual to have such a long, connected segment, since NT narratives are noted for the episodic nature; see Stephen Moore, "Are the Gospels Unified Narratives?" *SBLSP* 26 (1987): 443–58.

54. The figure below is taken from Funk, *The Poetics of Biblical Narrative*, 86, 87. Used by permission.

55. Parsons, "Acts," 9.

56. W. K. Hobart (*The Medical Language of St. Luke* [Dublin: Hodges, Figgis, 1882; repr., Grand Rapids: Baker, 1954]) was probably not the first to comment on this verse, but he surely made more of it than most have.

57. In one of the few recent works to treat the "medical" dimensions of the text, John Wilkinson, himself a medical missionary, has suggested (*Health and Healing: Studies in New Testament Principles and* Practice [Edinburgh: Handsel, 1980], 88) that the most probable diagnosis for the lame man in Acts 3–4 "is a severe degree of clubfoot or what is known medically as congenital talipes equino-varus."

58. The comments about feet (here the more familiar ποῦς, *pous*) are similar: "Those who have well-made, large feet, well-jointed and sinewy, are strong in character; witness the male sex. Those who have small, narrow, poorly-jointed feet, are rather attractive to look at than strong, being weak in character; witness the female sex. Those whose toes of the feet are curved are shameless, just like creatures which have curved talons; witness birds with curved talons." (810a.15–22).

59. See BDAG, 613 for definitions of and references to μαλακός (*malakos*).

60. As Funk notes (*Poetics of Biblical Narrative*, 64): "The lame man is the 'subject' of the mini-narrative. This does not mean that he is the agent of the principal action, but that the narrative is 'about' him."

61. RSV, NIV = "cripple"; NAS = "sick man"; NRSV = "someone who was sick."

62. In Paul's Ephesian farewell address, he claims, "In all things I have shown you that by so toiling one must help the weak (ἀσθενούντων, *asthenountōn*), remembering the words of the Lord Jesus, how he said, 'It is more blessed to give than to receive'" (Acts 20:35). Here the weak do not necessarily seem to be limited to those with physical ailments. Elsewhere (see Parsons, *Body and Character*, chapter 4) I have argued that the phrase "spirit of weakness" in the story of the bent woman likewise carries a moral and metaphorical meaning. Forms of the ἀσθεν- (*asthen-*) stem occur in ps-Arist. 807b.8, 10 in a description of the signs of a coward (δειλοῦ σημεῖα, *deilou sēmeia*), "weak eyes" and a "weak thigh" (see also 810.b11, 27), but these references appear to refer to physical, not moral, weakness (though of course they are signs of the morally weak or cowardly).

63. Robert Garland, *The Eye of the Beholder: Deformity and Disability in the Greco-Roman World* (Ithaca, N.Y.: Cornell University Press, 1995), 34.

64. The role as blacksmith of club-footed, fire-god Hephaistos, a "solitary misfit among an unageing population of divinely perfect deities" in the Greek Olympiad thus "conforms to an authentic social reality, metal-working being one of the few professions available to the lame" (Garland, *The Eye of the Beholder*, 61–62). This negative presumption on the auditors' part could be true whether or not, historically speaking, metal-working was an actual occupation that the lame man could have held in Jerusalem.

65. Efforts to avoid such "burdens to society" probably explain why, according to Garland, such a small percentage of the congenitally disabled survived infancy. Quoting Garland (*The Eye of the Beholder*, 12): " . . . the Greeks and the Romans would have had little compunction about withholding the necessities of life from any infant whom they deemed incapable of growing up to lead a full, active and *independent* existence" (emphasis mine). That this man "lame from birth" had survived infancy only to be a burden on those around

him was no doubt for some proof positive of the wisdom of infanticide of
the congenitally disabled (Jewish resistance to such practices notwithstanding).
In his treatise on *Gynaecology,* the second-century writer Soranos has a section
entitled "How to recognize a newborn child that is worth raising," in which he
writes that the child "should be perfect in all its parts, limbs and senses, and
have passages that are not obstructed, including the ears, nose, throat, urethra
and anus. Its natural movements should be neither slow nor feeble, its limbs
should bend and stretch, its size and shape should be appropriate, and it should
respond to external stimuli" (2.6.5).

66. Two cripples feature prominently in this derision of the disabled in
Homer's writings. See Hephaistos (*Il.* 1.600 discussed in the text and *Od.* 8) and
Thersites (*Il.,* II.217–19)).

67. Garland, *The Eye of the Beholder,* 84.

68. Cited by Garland, *The Eye of the Beholder,* 85.

69. Another popular and degrading "gag" was to have the crippled serve as
wine-pourers at the symposium. In fact, in one of the more familiar scenes on
Greek pottery, the divine ironsmith, crippled Hephaistos, pours the wine for the
Olympiad symposium, which causes "unquenchable laughter" to break out (*Il.*
1.600; see Figure 2). As Garland notes, "The incident involving Hephaistos as
wine-pourer is made all the more comical by the fact that in real life, just as in
myth, the role of wine-pourer was usually reserved for a young man of out-
standing beauty . . . by prompting comparison with that graceful and perfect-
limbed youth, the ungainly Hephaistos becomes a natural vehicle for parody"
(*The Eye of the Beholder,* 84).

70. For a translation of the surviving fragments of the text, see J. R. Mueller
and S. E. Robinson, "Apocryphon of Ezekiel," in *OTP,* 492–95.

71. F. Scott Spencer, *Journeying through Acts* (Peabody, Mass.: Hendrickson, 2004), 55, suggests that this text laid the foundation "for stereotyping crippled persons throughout Israelite society, not just in priestly circles, as 'dead
dogs'; that is pathetic, impotent, despicable creatures (2 Sam. 9.8)." Joachim
Jeremias, *Jerusalem in the Time of Jesus* (Philadelphia: Fortress, 1969), 117, cites
m. Shab. 6.8 in order to argue that those who were ambulatory (with assistance)
were allowed into the Temple, while "for those who were altogether lame or leg-
less and had to be carried around on a padded seat, this was forbidden. The impotent man in Acts 3:2 is probably an example of this." Beverly Gaventa, *Acts*
(ANTC; Nashville: Abingdon, 2003), 84, is right to point out that the restrictions found in Lev 21:16–18 "apply only to priests who are offering sacrifices."
More relevant, however, may be the rather difficult passage in 2 Sam 5:8, "The
blind and the lame shall not come into the house," to which the LXX translators
add "of the Lord." Some take this text to reflect, at least on the part of
Hellenized Jews in the second century, B.C.E., the assumption that the blind and
the lame are excluded from entering the Temple precincts; see especially, Saul
M. Olyan, "'Anyone Blind or Lame Shall Not Enter the House': On the Interpretation of Second Samuel 5:8b," *CBQ* 60 (1998): 218–27.

72. A similar symbolic use of space may be seen in Luke 16:20 in which Lazarus lies at the gate (πυλών, *pulōn*) of the rich man. The term Luke uses here, θύρα
(*thyra*), literally "door," is also used metaphorically in Acts 21:30 to speak of a
"door of faith." In this light, perhaps we should spend less time trying to locate
the historical "Beautiful" Gate and more time contemplating its potential symbolism. The term ὡραία (*ōraia*) can refer to time ("timely") or space ("beautiful").

If Luke knows the same textual tradition as Paul (see BDAG, which cites cod. Q), he may have had in mind here an allusion to the "beautiful feet" of Isa 52:7, which proclaim the good news of "peace" and "salvation/healing" (σωτηρίαν, *sōtērian;* see also Sir 26:18 where the phrase "beautiful, well-formed" feet, πόδες ὡραῖοι, *podes ōraioi,* also occurs). Hence, the irony of the situation heightens, as a man with crippled feet sits at the "Timely/Beautiful" Gate awaiting the timely arrival of the "beautiful feet" of the apostles who will proclaim to him the "good news" and make for him salvation/healing in the name of Jesus. On this, see Mikeal C. Parsons, "Christian Origins and Narrative Openings: The Sense of a Beginning in Acts 1–5," *RevExp* 87 (1990): 412.

73. Furthermore, the note that the man was "lame from birth" might have been understood to suggest some kind of divine retribution for transgression. Congenital birth defects and even infant mortality were associated with sinfulness in the writings of Jews (2 Sam 12:15b–23; *Ruth Rabbah* 6.4), Christians (John 9:2), and Greeks (Hesiod, *Op.* 1.235; Herodotus, *Hist.* 1.105; 4.67). Some illuminating imprecations have been found inscribed on Greek tomb monuments from the Roman Imperial period, which threaten potential tomb-robbers with the punishment that their wives will give birth "not in accordance with Nature" (SEG 18.561.7). Non-congenital transgressions were also viewed as the cause of disabilities: "After they [the Israelites] sinned [in making the golden calf] not #? days passed before there were among them persons with issue and lepers, lame and blind, dumb and deaf, mentally disabled and retarded" (*Songs of Songs Rabbah* 4:7; see Luke 5:20–24).

74. The term παρρησία (*parrēsia*) was particularly associated with the "frank speech" of the Cynic philosophers (see Dio Chrysostom, *Or.* 32:11; 77.1–78.37, 45; esp. Lucian of Samosata, *The Dead Come Back to Life;* cited by Luke Timothy Johnson, *The Acts of the Apostles,* 78). See also S. B. Marrow, "*Parrhesia* and the New Testament," *CBQ* 44 (1982): 431–46.

75. John Chrysostom, *The Homilies on the Acts of the Apostles* (Oxford: John Henry Parker, 1851), 143.

76. Chrysostom, *Homilies on Acts,* 147. For other occurrences of θεωρέω (*theōreō*) in Luke-Acts, see Luke 10:18; 14:29; 21:6; 23:35, 48; 24:37, 39; Acts 3:16; 4:13; 8:13; 9:7; 10:11; 17:16, 22; 19:26; 20:38; 21:20; 25:24; 27:10. All of these usages have the sense of physical seeing or beholding, thus supporting Chrysostom's interpretation of this verse.

77. Maud W. Gleason, *Making Men: Sophists and Self-presentation in Ancient Rome* (Princeton: Princeton University Press, 1995), 61–62.

78. See also *Phys.* 61.1.276F; *Anon. Lat.* 98.2.123–124F; on gait specifically, see *Anon. Lat.* 76.2.100F; see Suetonius, *On Insults,* 66. Gleason (*Making Men,* 80) concludes:

> The physiognomists, astrologers, and popular moralists of antiquity thought in terms of degrees of gender-conformity and gender-deviance. They shared a notion of gender identity built upon polarized distinctions . . . that purported to characterize the gulf between men and women but actually divided the male sex into legitimate and illegitimate members . . .

79. See also Demosthenes who "concedes the unattractiveness of a hasty gait" (*Or.* 37.52; 45.77). Likewise, Cicero condemns a hasty gait as an impediment to masculine *dignitas* (*Off.* 1.131).

80. See also Tertullian, *Cult. fem.* 2.1, 8, 13, *De Anim.* 5, 20, 25, 32; St. Gregory of Nyssa, *Fun. Or.* 7.5, 8.10, 18.5; Basil, *The Letters*, 1.2, 20–21, 132–35.

81. I see the emphases in this text as part of Luke's intentional rhetoric, contrary to C. K. Barrett (*A Critical and Exegetical Commentary on the Acts of the Apostles* [ICC; Edinburgh: T&T Clark, 1994], 1:184) who claims: "How Luke came to write such a clumsy sentence is another question to which no answer seems satisfactory; it is perhaps best to leave the sentence as one of a number of indications that Acts did not receive a final stylistic revision."

82. On the messianic role of the Israelite community in God's cosmic kingship, see Edgar W. Conrad, *Reading Isaiah* (OBT; Minneapolis: Fortress, 1991). Regarding Israel's destiny in Isaiah, Conrad (145) writes, "The vocation of the Davidic kingship, once the function of individuals such as Ahaz and Hezekiah, has become the vocation of the community." I am indebted to my colleague, Jim Kennedy, for this reference.

83. In fact, when the writer wants to highlight the necessity of using peculiar characteristics of animals, rather than common ones, he contrasts lions and deer: "So that, when a man resembles an animal not in a peculiar but in a common characteristic, why should he be more like a lion than a deer?" (805b.18). This interest in deportment could explain Luke's unusual choice of the word βάσις (*basis*) in Acts 3:7 (a NT hapax). BDAG, 171, claims that "in our lit[erature] that with which one steps, usually of the area below the ankle, foot." Sometimes the emphasis appears to be on "that with which" and at other times on "steps" or movement (e.g., the term βάσις, *basis*, can in pagan literature refer to "measured steps or movement"; see LSJ). We find in Aristophanes this reference: "what we should be doing . . . is first of all to halt the graceful step of our circular dance" (πρωτον εὐκύκλου ξορείας εὐφυᾶ στῆσαι βάσιν , *proton eukuklou xoreias euphua stēsai basin, Thesm.* 968). Louw and Nida, 100, claim, "βάσις is a more technical term for the foot than is πούς." Or consider the words of one of Aeschylus's characters who claims: "I have no strength left in me nor can I go upright (ἀκταίνειν βάσιν, *aktainein basin*). I run with the aid of my hands, not with any nimbleness of limb" (*Eum.* 36). And, interestingly, it is the term used to describe the lion's gate in the passage cited from Pseudo-Aristotle above. To think Luke means to say that the lame man's ankles and "step/gait" were strengthened is tantalizing, but ultimately unprovable.

84. By this point, I do not intend to diminish the emotional dimension of this text. It is difficult, if not impossible, for an able-bodied person to comprehend the excessive joy and display for its own sake in this kind of analysis. I am grateful to Dr. Rebecca Raphael for this insight.

85. On "praising God" as a "Lukan equivalent to faith" (so Talbert, *Reading Acts*, 53), see Luke 17:11–19; esp. vv. 18–19.

86. There are still other issues in this text to pursue along physiognomic lines. Among the various issues to pursue, there is the prominence of the healing as a sign, a σημεῖον (*sēmeion*, 4:16, 22). While surely the primary referent of this word are the "signs and wonders" performed by the apostles (and others) in Acts, it might be worthwhile exploring possible connections to the physiognomic tradition since the same term is a refrain throughout the handbooks with regard to the physical characteristics, e.g., the "marks" or "signs" (σημεία, *sēmeia*) of the "shameless man"; the "orderly man"; "low-spirited man"; etc. In fact, the term occurs no less than 53 times in the fifty pages of Greek text of Pseudo-Aristotle. Several commentators have noted the frequency of ἀτενίζω

(*atenizō*) "stare, gaze intently" in this and other healing stories. What light does physiognomy potentially shed on this phenomenon? We know that the "eyes" were among the most important feature to physiognomists: "The most favorable part for examination is the region round the eyes . . ." (814b.4–5). One wonders how an audience shaped by this physiognomic consciousness would hear the reference to Peter "staring" at the lame man and then his command to the lame man to "Look at us!" before healing him. Furthermore, there is the predictive aspect of physiognomy. For example, Ammanianus Marcellinus writes about physiognomists: "Gazing long and earnestly on his (Julian's) eyes . . . they divine what manner of man he would be, as if they had perused those ancient books, the reading of which discloses from bodily signs the inward qualities of the soul" (*Res Gestae* 25.8). This predictive element, while not missing in the Acts 3–4 account, is much clearer in the parallel in Acts 14, the healing of the lame man at Lystra: "Paul stared at him and saw that he had faith to be made well" (14:9).

87. Think here also of the father running to his son in the parable of the Prodigal Son (Luke 15:20). Hamm, "Acts 3,1–10," also suggests a possible LXX allusion in Luke's use of ἐξαλλόμενος (*exallomenos*) in Acts 3:9 and the reference to the remnant of Israel in Mic 2:13–14. "I will surely receive the remnant of Israel; I will cause them to return together as sheep in trouble (ὡς πρόβατα ἐν θλίψει, *ōs probate en thlipsei*), as a flock in the midst of their fold. They shall rush forth (ἐξαλοῦνται, *exalountai*) among men through the breach made before them; they have broken through and passed the gate and gone out of it, and their king has gone out before them and the Lord shall lead them." Remember that the sheep are numbered along with the deer as among the most timid. The boldness of belonging to the eschatological community requires the timidity of deer and sheep!

88. Indeed, such symbolic reading is tempting, despite Johnson's warning: "There is an obvious temptation to see a symbolic resonance here except that Luke uses the specific number forty (well-hallowed by the biblical tradition) so frequently" (*Acts*, 79; note that the references Johnson cites against giving forty a symbolic value could just as easily be used in its favor!) Consider Spencer's remarks (*Journeying through Acts*, 52):

> Apart from providing a symbol of hope for the poor and disadvantaged in Israelite society, the healed lame man also represents an image of restoration for the entire nation. We have already noted the connection to Isa. 35.6 where the leaping lame typify Israel's glorious deliverance from exile through the desert (see 35.1–10). . . . The lame man's restoration after forty years of paralysis establishes a key temporal link to this same national tradition. As God's saving purpose for ancient Israel was finally realized after forty years of stumbling and meandering through the wilderness, so the moment of fresh renewal—signalled by the dance of a forty-year cripple—has dawned upon the present Israel. To join this joyous dance, however, Israel must now follow the lead not only of Moses, but also of the promised 'prophet like Moses', the crucified and risen Jesus of Nazareth, in whose name alone God brings full salvation to his people.

Spencer's comments remarkably echo comments made well over a millennium earlier by the Venerable Bede (*Commentary on the Acts of the Apostles* [trans. Lawrence T. Martin; Kalamazoo: Cistercian, 1989], 51):

According to the historical sense, this [age] shows that the man's mature age [made him] invincible to detractors. Allegorically, however, [the passage signifies that] the people of Israel . . . in the land of promise continued always to limp along with the rites of idols together with those of the Lord.

89. Hamm, "The Healing of the Temple Beggar as Lucan Theology," 305. On this I disagree with S. John Roth, *The Blind, the Lame, and the Poor: Character Types in Luke-Acts* (JSNTSup 144; Sheffield: Sheffield Academic Press), 220–21, who denies any paradigmatic use of these healing stories in Acts.

90. Danker, *Jesus and the New Age*, 20–21.

Chapter 5

Interpreting Jewish Traditions: Jerusalem and the Suffering Servant

Introduction

First-century Judaism, out of which early Christianity emerged, was part of the larger Greco-Roman world in which early Christianity existed. Thus, Judaism, in both its "Palestinian" and "Hellenistic" varieties (to use the traditional nomenclature), had been shaped by and responded to some of the same pagan traditions which we examined in our last chapter.[1] To claim that Luke was an interpreter of Jewish tradition, then, is not mutually exclusive from the claim that he was an interpreter of pagan traditions. Both traditions moved in the larger Hellenistic currents of the day, although admittedly first-century Judaism(s) functioned as a discrete, if variegated, sub-culture of the larger Greco-Roman milieu in a way that some of the pagan traditions did not.[2]

So in this chapter we will consider two examples of Luke's interpretation and re-appropriation of Jewish tradition. Our strategy here is to explore the question of Luke's interpretation of Jewish tradition on both a macro- and micro-level. In the first instance we will look at Luke's view of the place of Jerusalem in the narrative world he has created and in the second at Luke's interpretation of a specific text of Jewish Scripture, Isa 53.

In neither case is it necessary to argue that Luke was a Jew in order to comprehend his interpretation of things Jewish. Nor does our argument presume that Luke, in his interpretation of Judaica, always "got it

right." On the other hand, we might rightly discard the widely held notion that Luke was a Gentile writing for a Gentile audience,[3] if by that we
mean that Luke was either woefully unfamiliar with things Jewish or totally disinterested in placing the story of Jesus and his followers within
its Jewish context.

Theological Cartography and the Place of Jerusalem on the Lukan Landscape

The cover of *The New Yorker* magazine on March 29, 1976, bears a
well-known image by Saul Steinberg. The most striking feature, of
course, is that it locates visually and spatially the city of New York at
the very center of the world. The map is, as such, an example of cosmological cartography, that is, the making of a map of one's symbolic universe. *The New Yorker* cover was immensely popular and spawned the
production of hundreds, perhaps thousands, of "copycats" through
which various towns, cities, states, and countries produced their own
versions of the map, propagandistically locating their own political
unit at the center.

Galileo's struggle to establish a heliocentric cosmology by disabus-
ing his fellow humans of the notion that the earth was at the center of
the universe is evidence of the stubborn tenacity with which people
cling to various forms of geocentricity and ethnocentricity, and images
like the *New Yorker* cover remind us that these notions are remarkably
resilient. So, while we may all carry maps of the world in our heads
shaped by our elementary school geography lessons, the globe in our
studies, and the breath-taking satellite photos of the earth on the TV or
the computer screen, at some level, we have these other symbolic maps
which locate various places and persons in spatial relationship to each
other in terms of their relative importance to the orbits of our daily
lives. We are all, then, cartographers of symbolic maps which order
our worlds.

Such cosmological cartography is not a recent phenomenon.[4] As
early as 600 B.C.E., the Babylonians had produced a cosmological map on
a clay tablet. Notable among its features are the placement of Babylon at
the center of the map and the placement of various topographical features (Euphrates River, mountains, oceans) in relationship to Babylon.[5]
In the text accompanying the map are described various beasts and re-
gions which lie beyond the ocean encircling the Babylonian world,
what will be called in later maps, the *terrae incognito*.[6] And there is evi-

dence that many other early cultures—Egyptians, Chinese, Mayans—so located their holy places at the center of the world.

But surely no group produced more such cosmological maps than Christian geographers of the medieval period.[7] In the section labeled, "The Geography of the Imagination," of his encyclopedic work, *The Discoverers,* Daniel Boorstin laments:

> Christian geographers in the Middle Ages spent their energies embroidering a neat, theologically appealing picture of what was already known, or was supposed to be known.

> Geography had no place in the medieval catalogue of the "seven liberal arts." . . . Lacking the dignity of a proper discipline, geography was an orphan in the world of learning. The subject became a ragbag filled with odds and ends of knowledge and pseudo-knowledge, of Biblical dogma, travelers' tales, philosophers' speculations, and mythical imaginings.[8]

Over six hundred of these so-called *Mappae Mundi* have survived from the medieval period. Their makers were responsible for what Boorstin calls "the Great Interruption." Most famous of these medieval maps are the *T-O maps* credited to Isidore of Seville (560–636), a renowned encyclopedist and historian who succeeded his brother as bishop of Seville in c. 600 C.E.[9] The Isidorian T-O map is thus named because the whole inhabited earth was depicted as a circular dish (an "O"), divided by a T-shaped flow of water. East was put at the top, which was what was then meant by 'orienting' a map.[10] Above the 'T' was the continent of Asia, which was associated with Noah's son Shem; Africa in the South is linked with Ham; Europe is associated with Japheth. Jerusalem was either presumed or shown to be at the center of the world, the *umbilicus terrae,* as the Latin Vulgate put it.[11]

The *Madaba map* is a sixth-century C.E. mosaic of Palestine and Lower Egypt with legends in Greek.[12] This map is the earliest extant Christian map. Here Jerusalem is given a prominent position and an exaggerated size. The "Holy City" is "portrayed in great detail as an oval walled city with its principal gateway in the north."[13] We see here with the Madaba map a tradition of Christian scholars visualizing the *Terra Sancta,* the Holy Land with its accompanying Holy City, at the center of the inhabited world. I propose in this part of the chapter to trace the authorial audience's understanding of one particular place, Jerusalem, within the plot of Luke-Acts by comparing it with other depictions of Jerusalem in other Jewish writings of late antiquity.

Obviously, with Luke-Acts, I am dealing with literary texts, verbal maps, as it were, and not drawn or visual maps. Few drawn maps from antiquity are extant today, even from the Greeks who made such rich contributions to scientific cartography, though the ancients did occasionally draw their mental maps and models. The fact that none of these survived is not an irreparable loss. If we have sufficiently detailed verbal descriptions which convey clear visual images, we can translate these onto paper.[14]

The question is whether or not the Lukan writings are open to such cartographic interpretation. I am not arguing that Luke stands in the scientific geographical tradition of Eratosthenes, Strabo, and Ptolemy. It is interesting in this regard that Strabo and others credit Homer with being the founder of the study of geography,[15] even though Homer was a poet, not a philosopher (using Strabo's terminology), and even though Homer evidently never intended to draw a map. Strabo is forced to admit, in the course of defending Homer against his critics, that Homer at times "was wont to add a mythical element to actual occurrences, thus giving flavor (ἡδύνων, *hēdynōn*) and adornment (κοσμῶν, *kosmōn*) to his style."[16]

Luke, too, "added flavor and adornment to his style" with his abiding interest in and use of geographical references in his theological agenda. Luke's interest in spatial features and spatial metaphors can be quantified to an extent. With the help of semantic domain lexicons, a close examination of the New Testament writings shows that only the book of Revelation comes anywhere close to the consistent quantity and variety of geographical terms found in Luke and Acts.[17] Thus, while Luke was not a geographer per se, he was interested in geography, and it has been instructive to create a map of Luke's symbolic world based on his literary texts. We now turn our attention to the place of Jerusalem on the Lukan landscape.

Mapping the Lukan Landscape: The Place of Jerusalem in Luke-Acts

In his watershed redactional study, *The Theology of St. Luke*, Hans Conzelmann argues that with the Gospel of Luke "the process by which the scene [of Jerusalem and its surrounding setting] becomes stylized into the 'Holy Land' has begun."[18] The legacy of Conzelmann in modern scholarship is not hard to find. Luke Johnson claims: "The geographical structure of Luke-Acts makes Jerusalem the center of Luke's narrative."[19] And Joseph Fitzmyer concludes: "Though Luke never uses the expression, Jerusalem functions for him as 'the navel of the earth.'"[20] In this view, Luke's understanding of Jerusalem as the "Holy Land" or the umbilicus terrae may logically be viewed to have culminated in the Mappaemundi of medieval Christian scribes which visually and literally located Jerusalem at the center of the world.

On the other hand, W. D. Davies claimed that Luke recognized that "what we might call a demotion of Jerusalem" was "a necessity for the Church of his day."[21] He continued: "In Jewish expectation Jerusalem was the city of the End: an eschatological mystique surrounded it. Early Christians could easily succumb to this mystique, and some, as we shall see in Acts, were tempted to do so. Luke was aware of that mystique and of its accompanying seduction. He saw that it was necessary, quite deliberately, to transcend it."[22]

I argue that Jerusalem was neither intentionally marginalized or "demoted" by Luke as Davies suggests, nor was it the stylized as the "Holy Land" as Conzelmann argued, but rather was presented in ambivalent terms. My contribution to this discussion will be to place Luke's view of Jerusalem within the context of first-century Jewish views of Jerusalem with which one may presume Luke's authorial audience would have been familiar.[23] In order to accomplish this task, I am interested, then, in a literary analysis which lays bare the spatial relations of Luke's narrative world, what I am calling an exercise in symbolic cartography, thereby gaining theological insight into the symbolic world of Luke and Acts and Jerusalem's place within it.

I begin by noting two cartographic categories necessary for our analysis. We may from the Lukan writings construct either a topographical map or a geopolitical map.[24] A topographical map depicts spatial relationships that would be observed from an aerial photograph or a relief map. Geopolitical space refers to spatial areas which are defined by human-made boundaries of civic or governmental units. The implied reader of Luke-Acts will know that God is creator of both topographical and the geopolitical space. In Acts 4:24, the Christian community at prayer draws on an Old Testament topos: "Lord God, who made the heaven and earth and sea and everything in them." This phrase occurs verbatim in the Greek version of Exod 20:11, Neh 9:6, Isa 37:16, Ps 145:6. In his speech to the Lycaonians of Lystra, Paul also refers to the "living God who made the heaven and the earth and the sea and all that is in them" (14:15). According to Paul's Areopagus speech, the God who is Lord of topographical space is also the same God who "made from one person every nation to live on all the face of the earth, having determined allotted periods and the boundaries of their habitation" (17:26). The word "boundaries" (ὁροθεσίας, *horothesias*) occurs only here in the

NT, though elsewhere in the larger Greco-Roman world it carries (as here) the geopolitical sense of borders or boundaries between nations.

On a topographical map one would see rivers, lakes, seas, wilderness areas, mountains, cities and villages (although not their names), and roads, that is, the physical features of the earth, both natural (for example, mountains) and human-made (for example, roads). We must include on this topographical map Luke's view of a three-tiered universe, one we have come to expect in the writings of biblical and post-biblical Judaism. There is the earth, with heaven above, and hell or Hades below. What is interesting to me is how relatively little interest Luke shows in providing detailed descriptions of either the tier above, heaven, or the tier below, Hades.

It is, instead, the middle tier, the earth's surface, on which the attention of Luke's audience is fixed. And as the readers adjust their vision from the more global picture of the three-tiered universe to the specific features of the Lukan landscape, they encounter a variety of topographical features: natural places like the countryside, the desert, fields, rivers, valleys, mountains, hills, lakes, grain fields, seacoasts, rocks, holes, nests, and human-made spaces like cities and villages, roads, streets, wells, courtyards, temples, houses, and synagogues. A number of these, such as the desert, mountains, and countryside, have special significance along the Lukan landscape.

One topographical feature is worthy of comment, in light of our quest to locate Jerusalem in Luke's symbolic world. The "road" or "way" (ὁδός, *hodos*) in Luke and Acts also plays an important role for the understanding of the authorial audience. The term, however, functions less as a static, physical setting in which certain action takes place (though this element is not entirely missing; see 9:57, 18:35, 19:36, 24:32). Rather the word is used to depict Jesus' career as a course or way. It is well-known that the central section of Luke's Gospel is set within the framework of a journey narrative. But the way of Jesus not only expresses his physical arrival in Jerusalem and his progress toward his passion. It also, at the outset, describes the journey as Jesus' ἀναλήμψις (*analēmpsis*), literally his "taking up." This "taking up" refers to the entire complex of events that forms Jesus' transit to the Father: his passion, death, burial, resurrection, and ascension/exaltation. Jesus' journeying along the way is also depicted in Luke as an "exodus." In the transfiguration scene in Luke 9:28–36, only Luke of the Synoptic Gospels reports that Jesus, Moses, and Elijah were speaking of Jesus' "departure" or exodus, which he was to accomplish at Jerusalem (9:31). The way of Jesus becomes paradigmatic for Jesus' followers: The journey motif fits "Luke's conception of the life of faith as a pilgrimage, always on the move."[25] It is not surprising, then, that the favorite term for the Christian movement in Acts is simply the "Way" (see 9:2; 19:9, 23; 22:4; 24:14, 22).

The goal of this journey of Jesus is Jerusalem, the city under discussion. This brings us to a discussion of geopolitical space in Luke's narratives. While there are some interesting comments to be made on a number of geopolitical sites in Acts, especially cities like Caesarea, Antioch, Ephesus, Athens, and Rome, as well as provinces like Judea and Samaria, our focus remains on Jerusalem. The evidence for the importance of Jerusalem for Luke is easy for the reader to find and is well-documented in the commentaries. Luke Johnson's comments are typical:

> The infancy account leads to the presentation of Jesus in the Temple (2:22) and his discovery there as a young boy (2:41–51). In the Lukan temptation account, the order of the last two temptations in Matthew is reversed, so that the climax is reached in Jerusalem (4:9). At the end of the Galilean ministry, the transfiguration account explicitly prepares for the journey to Jerusalem and Jesus' death there (9:31). The journey itself begins with a solemn announcement (9:51), and continues with multiple references to Jesus' destination (13:22, 33–44; 17:11; 18:31; 19:11, 28). Luke has all of Jesus' resurrection appearances take place in the environs of the city, and in the last of them, Jesus instructs the disciples, "stay in the city." (24:49)

> In Acts the geographical movement is *away* from Jerusalem. The ministry in Jerusalem (Acts 1–7) is followed by the evangelization of Judea and Samaria (8–12), then Asia Minor and Europe, ending in Rome. Each outward movement, however, also circles back to Jerusalem (see Acts 12:25; 15:2; 18:22; 19:21; 20:16; 21:13; 25:1). Luke is concerned to show that the expansion of Christianity into the wider world and among the Gentiles took place in continuity and communication with the original community in Jerusalem.[26]

On the other hand, there are ominous and negative images associated with Jerusalem. Along the way to Jerusalem, Jesus laments:

> Yet today, tomorrow, and the next day I must be on my way, because it is impossible for a prophet to be killed outside of Jerusalem. Jerusalem, Jerusalem, the city that kills the prophets and stones those who are sent to it! How often have I desired to gather your children together as a hen gathers her brood under her wings, and you were not willing! (Luke 13:33–34)

Later, Jesus foretells the destruction of Jerusalem with details unparalleled in the other Gospels:

When you see Jerusalem surrounded by armies, then know that its desolation has come near. Then those in Judea must flee to the mountains, and those inside the city must leave it, and those outside in the country must not enter it; for these are days of vengeance, as a fulfillment of all that is written. . . . and Jerusalem will be trampled on by the Gentiles until the times of the Gentiles are fulfilled. (21:20–24; see 19:11)

If one includes the image of the Temple depicted in Luke and Acts, the picture is even more ambivalent. On a positive note, the Gospel does begin and end in the Temple, but by the time we reach Stephen's speech in Acts 7, the Temple or at least the prevailing attitudes toward it is the object of Stephen's harsh critique: "Yet the Most High does not dwell in houses made with human hands" (7:48).

Acknowledging the theological centrality of Jerusalem for Luke, it still remains to be seen if Jerusalem occupies the central *place* in Luke's world. We find some clues in the Pentecost narrative. In Acts 2:5, we read that "there were devout Jews from every nation under heaven living in Jerusalem." The reference to "devout Jews from every nation under heaven living in Jerusalem" implies that Jerusalem is the mother-city of the world, because Jews are living in every nation with vv. 9–11 listing representative nations. The list of nations in Acts 2:9–11 may be an "update" of the Table-of-Nations tradition found in Gen 10, a point rarely examined by interpreters.[27]

The implied reader has already been introduced to the Table-of-Nations tradition in Luke 10:1 in the so-called mission of the seventy. The mission of the seventy foreshadows the Gentile mission. The textual problem of whether the number is seventy or seventy-two only serves to strengthen the connection with the Table of Nations tradition of Genesis, since the variant may go back to the differences between the Hebrew text of Genesis which lists 70 nations and the Greek, which lists 72.[28] From a very early point, then, early readers (the scribes) connected the mission of the seventy(-two) with the Table of Nations in Gen 10 to symbolize that their mission is a universal one.

The context in Acts 2 is an eschatological one, and it foreshadows the Gentile mission. In his Pentecost sermon, Peter interprets the gift of the Holy Spirit by reference to Joel 3. But he adds a significant phrase missing in the Greek text of Joel: "And it shall be, *in the last days, says God,* I will pour out my spirit on all flesh" (2:16). At the end of his speech, he will allude to inclusion of the Gentiles as recipients of the promise of salvation and spirit: "For the promise is for you, for your

children, and *for all who are far away, everyone whom the Lord our God
calls to him*" (2:39).

Mapping the Larger Context: Jerusalem in Post-Biblical Jewish Thought

How would Luke's implied reader have understood these references
to Jerusalem? Here we need to turn to extratexual information, by noting how Jewish interpreters variously viewed the cosmological place of
Jerusalem, roughly contemporary with the Lukan writings. The authorial audience of Luke-Acts may have been aware of at least four attempts to locate Jerusalem in relationship to the rest of the world.[29]

1. *The Table of Nations in Genesis 10 established Jerusalem at the center of the world and that position continues to be a present reality.* Some
texts draw on the Table-of-Nations tradition in Gen 10 to argue that the
establishment of Jerusalem at the center of the world, an act of God in
conjunction with the division of lands among the sons of Noah, is envi-
able and static. Jerusalem at the center of the world reflects present reality despite whatever outward appearances may have existed (including
the subjugation of the Jews by a foreign power). Most prominent among
these texts is *Jub.* 8–10. *Jubilees*, a document from the second century
B.C.E., evidently draws on the old Ionian world map.[30]

Though the Ionian maps of Anaximander and others are no longer
extant, it is traditionally accepted that these ancient maps were circular,
with Greece in the middle and Delphi at the very center. At the oracle in
Delphi there was purportedly an *omphalos* (navel), a stone that symbolized the center not only of east and west, but the connection between
higher and lower tiers of the three-tiered universe. It is not clear how seriously later Greeks took these maps. Herodotus offered a scathing critique of those maps (*Hist.* 4.36), and there was also the mythological
tradition which said that Zeus, in an attempt to find the center of the
world, released two birds flying east and west in opposite directions;
the birds collided with one another and fell to the earth at Delphi. The
omphalos was thus erected on the spot where the fowl fell!

The author of *Jubilees* evidently took this tradition very seriously
and envisaged the inhabited world as a roughly circular land mass surrounded by ocean. The center of the world—its 'navel' (*omphalos*) is
Zion, not Delphi, as on the Ionian map. *Jubilees* 8:12 reads: "And the lot
of Shem was assigned in the document as the middle of the earth." Later
Jubilees reports that "Mount Zion (was) in the midst of the navel of
the earth." For the writer of *Jubilees*, the Table of Nations, and Israel's

position in it, is seen to have timeless value and eternal validity, even for the second century B.C.E. when *Jubilees* was written.[31]

2. *Jerusalem is the center of the world as evidenced by the fact of the Diaspora.* A more modest claim regarding Jerusalem's central place in the present world argues that Jerusalem is rightly called the "mother city" because Jews live in every part of the inhabited world. This is the view of Philo of Alexandria, who, in his *Embassy to Gaius*, includes a letter allegedly by King Agrippa I to the Emperor Gaius. The relevant passage reads:

> While she (the Holy City), as I have said, is my native city, she is also the mother city not of one country, Judea, but of most of the others in virtue of the colonies sent out at different times to the neighboring lands ... So that if my own home-city is granted a share of your goodwill the benefit extends not to one city but to myriads of the others situated in every region of the inhabited world whether in Europe or in Asia or in Libya, whether in the mainlands or in the islands, whether it be seabord or inland. (281–283)

3. *Jerusalem is the center of the land of Israel, not of the world.* On the other end of the spectrum are those texts which, in light of historical realities, modified the view of Jerusalem at the center of the world. Most important of these writers is Josephus. In *Ant.* 1.122–147, Josephus presents his own updating of the Table-of-Nations tradition, which is very different from that of *Jubilees*. He does not follow *Jubilees'* schema of correlating the three sons of Noah with the three Ionian continents. More importantly, in light of the destruction of the Temple and fall of Jerusalem, he relinquishes the notion that Jerusalem is the center of the earth. When he does refer to Jerusalem as the "navel" (in *J.W.* 3.52) he restricts the concept to mean the "navel of the country [i.e., Judaea]," not the world.

4. *At the end times, Jerusalem will be (re-)established or once again recognized as the center of the world.* Other texts declare that Jerusalem will be (re)constituted or at least finally recognized again as being at the center of the world in an eschatological act of God. This view goes back at least to the time of Ezekiel where we read that in the eschatological battle between God and his enemy, the prince, Gog, will say, "I will go up against the land of unwalled villages ... to seize spoil and carry off plunder; to assail the waste place that are now inhabited, and the people ... who live at the navel of the world" (Ezek 38:10–12; see also Isa 66:17–20). This view was also seen in several Second Temple Jewish texts, roughly contemporary with Luke and Acts. In the *Psalms of Solomon* (a document likely from the first century C.E.), we read this eschatological vision:

Sound in Zion the signal trumpet of the sanctuary;
announce in Jerusalem the voice of one bringing good news,
for God has been merciful to Israel in watching over them.
Stand on a high place, Jerusalem, and look at your children,
from the east and the west assembled together by the Lord.
From the north they come in the joy of their God;
from far distant islands God has assembled them. . . .
Jerusalem, put on the clothes of your glory,
prepare the robe of your holiness,
for God has spoken well of Israel forevermore. (11:1–7)

First Enoch's eschatological vision of Jerusalem "at the center of the earth" (*1 En* 26:1) and the reference in *Sib. Or.* 5 to the "heavenly race of the blessed Jews, who live around the city of God in the middle of the earth, are raised up even to the dark clouds" (5:249–50) also bear witness to Jerusalem as the center of the world at the end-times.

For the authorial audience, the text of Luke-Acts does not explicitly refer to Jerusalem as the "center" of the world, as *Jubilees* does, neither does it limit its role to the land of Israel only, as Josephus does. Already in Isa 66:18–20, the Table-of-Nations tradition was updated by a partial list of "the nations," and a *pars pro toto* list also found in the *Sibylline Oracles* (3:512–519). Remember that both *Jubilees* and Josephus "update" the Table of Nations, though as we have seen, in ways very different from Luke.

It is difficult to escape the conclusion that the authorial audience would have understood Luke, like *Jubilees* and Josephus, to be drawing on the Table of Nations to locate Jerusalem on his symbolic map. But the authorial audience would have also presumably concluded that Luke is not willing either to state baldly that Jerusalem is in fact at the center of the world (as *Jubilees* does), or to demote Jerusalem to the center only of the land of Israel (as Josephus does); after all, Jews from every nation under heaven have come there. Rather, like Philo, Luke uses the fact of the Diaspora to imply that Jerusalem is still important, though he avoids Philo's language that Jerusalem is the "mother city." Luke asserts the importance of Jerusalem in an eschatological context foreshadowing the Gentile mission.

Luke, His Authorial Audience, and Jerusalem

To sum up: For the authorial audience presumably conversant with these various options for "locating" Jerusalem, Luke locates Jerusalem by drawing on a familiar "thesaurus"; the implied reader recognizes:

(1) Luke's use of Table-of-Nations tradition (with *Jubilees*, Isaiah, and Josephus); (2) the appeal (with Philo) to the Diaspora to establish Jerusalem's place; and (3) the eschatological setting of many references to Jerusalem (with Ezekiel, *Psalms of Solomon, 1 Enoch*, and the *Sybilline Oracles*). But Luke's view presents the implied reader with a fifth alternative, which at this point may be stated negatively: Jerusalem does not stand in the center of Luke's symbolic world.

This last statement contradicts Conzelmann's conclusion and flies into the face of much contemporary Lukan scholarship. If not at the center, then where? Luke conveniently answers that question for us twice. Jerusalem stands at the *end* of the story of Jesus as the goal of his journey and at the *beginning* of the story of the church as the starting point for Christian witness in the world. I will deal with this second point in more detail. At the end of Luke's Gospel, Jesus commands his disciples: "Thus it is written, that the Messiah is to suffer and to rise from the dead on the third day, and that repentance of sins is to be proclaimed in his name to all nations, *beginning from Jerusalem*. And you are witnesses of these things" (24:47–48). And in Acts 1:8: "you will be my witnesses in Jerusalem, in all Judea and Samaria, and to the end of the earth."

For Luke, Jerusalem is not the city of the end-time. His symbolic world does not picture the nations swarming to Jerusalem to receive the Gospel. Instead Jerusalem is associated with the end only in the sense that it stands at the beginning of the end, the beach-head for the Gentile mission. There is a spatial dimension to Luke's eschatology that is often overlooked. When the disciples ask Jesus "is this the time when you will restore the kingdom to Israel?" Jesus brushes aside their temporal question and replaces it with a spatial response: "It is not for you to know the times or periods . . . but you will be my witnesses in Jerusalem . . . to the end of the earth." There is a real sense in which for Luke the Parousia cannot occur until the Christian witness reaches the end of the earth. That is to say, the temporal dimension of eschatology is interrelated to its spatial dimension.

Many have identified the commission of Acts 1:8 exclusively with the Gentile mission and then argued that Luke has a "theology of glory," a triumphalist attitude that depicts the gospel steamrolling through the Mediterranean basin, converting anything that moves.[32] But while to be a "witness" in the Lukan world includes the Gentile mission, more generally it means to bear testimony to the redemptive work achieved by God through Christ, and often involves a dimension of suffering. Jesus' followers were not only witnesses *to* the suffering of the Messiah (24:47–48), they were to participate *in* the suffering of the Messiah.[33] In the first account of Paul's conversion (Acts 9), Ananias, functioning as representative of the church, receives the content of Paul's call: "Go, for he [Paul] is an instrument I have chosen to bring my name before Gentiles and kings and before the people of Israel; I myself will show him how much he must suffer for the sake of my name" (9:15–16; see 21:13). Certainly much of Paul's suffering in Acts is the direct result of his missionary activities, but his suffering is not limited to the Gentile mission. The last few chapters of Acts describe the journey of Paul, faithful witness to the gospel, to Rome, a place where there are already believers (see 28:14), yet he suffers and bears witness nonetheless.

Therefore, the commission in Acts 1:8 is for the disciples (and others!) to extend their Christian witness from Jerusalem and beyond. At times, that witness would involve evangelizing the unconverted Gentiles; at other times, as with Stephen, James, and Paul, it would involve bearing witness to a suffering Messiah by participating in the messianic suffering of the church. For Luke, the commission in Acts 1:8 is fulfilled just as much by Stephen in his martyrdom as by Paul in the Gentile mission, just as much by Paul in his suffering journey to Rome as by Peter's conversion of Cornelius.

At the conclusion of a well-known essay, Jonathan Z. Smith remarked, "'Map is not territory'—but maps are all we possess."[34] All too often in the history of Lukan scholarship, debate has turned to the relationship between the territory, that is, the historical events of early Christianity, and the map, the ways in which Luke represented, construed, and/or invented those events. As important as those issues often are, preoccupation with them can distract us from interpreting the texts in their final form as we have them. By focusing on map itself, the narrative construct Luke has provided as a vehicle for his theology, we see that Jerusalem is not the center of Luke's symbolic world. Furthermore, Luke is no Christian Zionist as Conzelmann implies, nor is Jerusalem simply demoted as Davies insists. Luke's view stated positively: Jerusalem was, on the one hand, an ending to the story of Jesus and, on the other, the beginning of the church's end-time witness, which included but was not exclusive to the Gentile mission.

The Use of Isaiah 53 in Acts 8

In our second example of Luke as interpreter of Jewish tradition we will examine a specific scene, the story of the Ethiopian Eunuch in Acts 8, as an example of how Luke interpreted Jewish Scripture, here Isaiah

53, in light of the expansion of the Christian movement into the non-Jewish world.

In her influential book, *Jesus and the Servant*, Professor Morna Hooker argues that "Jesus himself was not profoundly influenced by the Servant passages in particular."[35] To reach this conclusion, Professor Hooker engages in a detailed exegesis of the relevant NT passages, as well as exploring the general background and meaning of the Servant Songs of Deutero-Isaiah. I would like to take up her interpretation of Isa 53 in Acts 8 and offer an alternative way of reading that text. I am not attempting at this point to topple Professor Hooker's overall thesis, but rather to clarify and refine her interpretation of one of those passages that led to her conclusion. Re-assessing her exegesis of this one passage, however, does raise the question regarding her interpretation of other passages, which could ultimately lead to a reassessment of her total argument.[36]

Hooker's Interpretation of Acts 8

About the use of the Servant motif in Acts, Hooker concludes: "The account of the beliefs of the early Christians which is given in the Acts of the Apostles does not suggest that the primitive community ever thought of Jesus as 'the Servant' of Deutero-Isaiah."[37] She reaches this particular conclusion on the basis of her reading of the titles "servant" (παῖς, *pais;* 3:13, 26; 4:27, 30) and "Righteous One" (ὁ δίκαιος, *ho dikaios;* Acts 3:14; 7:52; 22:14) and especially the use of Isa 53 in Acts 8:

> in Acts 8 we find a quotation from Isaiah 53 actually applied to the sufferings and death of Christ. While it is evident from the context, however, that Philip interpreted the passage as a description of the Passion of his Lord, this by all means implies that he must have in mind an equation of the nature: Jesus=the Servant. For it must be stressed once again that the words which are quoted speak only of the *fact* of the sufferings and death of the Servant, and do not mention their *significance*. These facts, however, are precisely those features which were already present in the primitive kerygma, and which needed no passage from the Old Testament to suggest them. The significance of the quotation, therefore, must lie, not in any interpretation of the meaning of Christ's death, but in the fact that it is a foreshadowing of the events of the Passion. . . . [38]

Hooker refers to the use of Isaiah here in Acts 8 as a "'proof-text' from the Old Testament that these things could—and did—happen to the Messiah."[39]

Hooker arrives at her "proof-text" conclusion from a careful exegesis of Acts 8. She notes that Acts 8 provides "clear evidence for the use of Isa 53 in connection with Jesus' sufferings by at least one of the earliest members of the Church."[40] She continues, however, with these words: "thus, while it is clear that Philip was ready to interpret this chapter of Jesus, there is no proof that it was a passage of particular importance. . . ."[41] She quite rightly notes that the quotation of Isa 53 in Acts 8:32–35 consists of the last three lines of Isa 53:7 and the first three lines of 53:8. Curiously missing are the references to vicarious suffering in Isa 53 just prior to ("and the Lord laid on him the iniquity of us all"—Isa 53:6) and just after ("because of the iniquities of my people he was led to death"—Isa 53:8) the material quoted. Hooker concludes:

> The exact verbal agreement with the LXX suggests that he was quoting from a written source, and not from memory, so that the choice is not a haphazard one. It seems that the significance of Isa 53 lay, for the author of Acts at least, not in the connection between suffering and the sin of others, but in the picture of humiliation; thus yet again the chapter is used as a proof-text of the necessity for Christ's Passion, and not as a theological exposition of its meaning.[42]

Two conclusions Hooker draws here deserve further analysis: (1) Luke begins and ends the quotation of Isa 53 where he does to avoid making explicit reference to the vicarious suffering of the servant; (2) Acts 8 is to be taken as a "proof-text" and not as a "theological exposition" of the necessity of Christ's suffering. I return to both of these points in the analysis of Acts 8 which follows.

Reevaluating the Role of Isaiah 53 in Acts 8 and Beyond

I begin the analysis of Acts 8:25–40 by probing its literary structure. Most scholars are agreed that a chiastic structure

    A
        B
            C
            C'
        B'
    A'

shapes the unit, though they disagree about its details. The most significant aspects of any chiasm usually lie in the outer frame, on the one hand, and the center of the chiasm on the other. This passage is no different. On the outer ring, vv. 25 and 40, the chiastic structure is clear (following the Greek word order, but translated into English):

> v. 25   A they returned to Jerusalem
>   B to many villages of the Samaritans
>   C they [Peter and John] preached
> v. 40   C' he [Philip] preached
>   B' to all the cities
>   A' until he came to Caesarea

Likewise, most formal analyses locate at the center of the chiasm the citation from the Old Testament and the eunuch's questions. The quotation of Isa 53:7–8 is the only time in Acts when the narrator quotes the Old Testament directly, apart from the lips of an individual character. Hooker is misleading on this point when she attributes the citation of Isa 53 to the eunuch and not to the narrator of Acts: "It is strange that this first quotation should be found in the mouth of an unconverted Gentile, and not a Christian preacher, or even a Jew."[43] Her conclusion is even more off-base: "It cannot, therefore, be taken as evidence that this passage of Scripture was central in the Christian preaching of the time."[44] In fact, as the only Old Testament passage explicitly cited by the narrator, and as the middle citation of three important lengthy Old Testament quotations in the entire book of Acts (see the quotation of Joel 3 in Acts 2 and Isa 6 in Acts 28), this passage does have great significance for Acts as a whole. But what exactly is its significance?

The Eunuch in Late Antiquity

To answer this question, we return to the beginning of Acts 8:25–40. The rest of the opening unit is given over to a description of the man whom Philip meets: "an Ethiopian, a eunuch, a minister of the Candace, queen of the Ethiopians, in charge of all her treasure" (8:27). Each of those words conveys very important cultural information about this character.[45] Of these descriptors, the most import is that the man is a eunuch.

But what did the term "eunuch" mean in late antiquity? Some evidence for the view that "eunuch" is simply a royal title does exist. Genesis 39:1 reports that "Joseph was brought down to Egypt; and Potiphar an officer (εὐνοῦχος, *eunouchos*) of Pharoah. . . ." Potiphar was, of course, married so "eunuch" here probably refers to his standing in Pharoah's court. Some early Christian writings developed the notion of eunuch as a reference to those who remain celibate. Athenagoras wrote in *A Plea for the Christians:* "If to remain a virgin and *abstain from sexual intercourse* (εὐνουχία, *eunouchia*) brings us closer to God. . . ." (33.3; see Clement of Alexandria, *Stromata*, 3.1; Matt 19:12c[?]). Nonetheless the overwhelming number of instances of "eunuch" from the classical period to late antiquity refer to eunuch in the *physical* sense as one who was sexually mutilated (see Philostratus, *Life of Apollonius*, 6.42; Lucian, *Saturnalia*, 12) or, much more rarely, born with a congenital defect (see Aristotle, *Generation of Animals*, 2.7.25).

How is the reader to understand the word here in Acts 8? Clearly the nuance of celibacy is not at work here, and no interpreter has ever argued such. There is some debate about whether the word eunuch here should be taken literally to refer to castrated or mutilated persons (*castrati*) or whether it simply refers to the title of a court official. The advantage to this latter view is that the Ethiopian may be viewed as a Jewish proselyte returning home from temple worship and dutifully reading Isaiah. Even more important for some is the fact that if the Ethiopian eunuch is a Jewish proselyte, then Cornelius is still the first Gentile admitted for baptism.

Several factors mitigate against this view and in favor of understanding "eunuch" in its physical sense. First, the status of the Ethiopian as a high ranking official is established in 8:27 quite apart from the use of the term "eunuch." He was a "minister of the Candace, queen of the Ethiopians, in charge of all her treasure." The use of the term "minister" (δυνάστης, *dynastēs*) is interesting here. The only other occurrence in Luke and Acts is in the Magnificat where Mary pronounces that God has "brought down the mighty ones (δυνάστης, *dynastēs*) from their thrones and exalted those of low degree" (Luke 1:52). Furthermore, he has the wealth at his disposal to be driven in a chariot (see 8:27, 38) and to possess an expensive Greek scroll of Isaiah. To reduce the term "eunuch" to mean nothing more in this context than a "high-ranking official" is to render it redundant.

More likely then is the view that the Ethiopian eunuch here is a physically mutilated man. His service as a close advisor to a queen, the Candace, makes it likely he was castrated since male attendants for female royalty were often castrated (see Herodotus, 8.105; Esth 2:3, 14; 4:4–5). Further, for the remainder of the story the official is referred to, not as an Ethiopian (an exotic dark-skinned fellow) or as a "minister" or "official" (signifying power and wealth), but simply as the "eunuch" (8:34, 36, 38, 39). If this is his dominant, defining characteristic, then two questions emerge. What was the status of eunuchs in the Mediterranean world of late antiquity? How would Luke's readers have understood this text in light of the larger cultural script for eunuchs?

Eunuchs in antiquity "belonged to the most despised and derided group of men."[46] One of Herodotus's characters, Hermotimus, a eunuch, took revenge on the man who had castrated him and sold him as a slave into the court of Xerxes, calling the activity "the wickedest trade on earth" (8.104–106). Elsewhere, Lucian of Samosata tells of a supposed eunuch vying for a chair of philosophy in Athens. His assumed status as a eunuch (he claimed to be a eunuch to avoid charges of adultery) led to one of his opponent's invective that it was "an ill-omened, ill-met sight if on first leaving home in the morning, one should set eyes on any such person [a eunuch]." Eunuchs, he claimed, "ought to be excluded . . . not simply from all that but even from temples and holy-water bowls and all the places of public assembly" (*The Eunuch,* 6–11).

This attitude was prevalent among Greek-speaking Jews of the first century as well. Josephus wrote:

> Shun eunuchs and flee all dealings with those who have deprived themselves of their virility and of those fruits of generation, which God has given to men for the increase of our race; expel them even as infanticides who withal have destroyed the means of procreation. (*Ant.* 4.290–291)

Why were eunuchs thus demonized and ostracized in antiquity? In part, the answer lies in their ambiguous sexual identity. To quote Lucian again, a eunuch "was an ambiguous sort of creature like a crow, which cannot be reckoned either with doves or with ravens"; he was "neither man nor woman but something composite, hybrid and monstrous, alien to human nature" (*The Eunuch,* 6–11). Josephus comments along similar lines: "For plainly it is by reason of the effeminacy of their soul that they changed the sex of their body also. And so with all that would be deemed a monstrosity by the beholders" (*Ant.* 4.291). Likewise Philo of Alexandria claims that eunuchs were "men who belie their sex and are affected with effemination, who debase the currency of nature and violate it by assuming the passions and the outward form of licentious women" (*Spec. Laws* 1.324–25). In a culture where honor was gender-based, to be sexually ambiguous was to blur clear-cut gender roles and expectations and thus to bring shame upon oneself and one's community.[47]

Further, in Jewish thought, eunuchs, by belonging neither to the cultural expectations of male nor female, had violated purity codes.[48] Like amphibians who lived in two worlds but belonged to neither, eunuchs were considered unclean (see Lev 11). In addition, the physical body was thought to mirror the corporate social body, so a physical body that was damaged or mutilated had the potential of defiling the social body.[49]

This was especially true in Judaism where the physically defective, like eunuchs, were forbidden entry into the temple and interaction with the larger social body: "No one whose testicles are crushed or whose penis is cut off shall be admitted to the assembly of the Lord" (see Deut. 23:1). The Ethiopian eunuch, as Scott Spencer has noted, "embodied impurity as much as he exhibited shame. His ambiguous sexual identity ('neither male nor female') denied him a distinctive place on the purity map of the social body, even as his defective genital anatomy depicted his polluted map of the physical body."[50] It is this kind of person to whom Philip is directed by the Spirit to approach (8:29)—a man excluded, because of his physical condition, from participation in Jewish worship at the temple in Jerusalem, a man understood by Luke's readers to be a social outcast, living on the liminal in terms of his sexual identity, his religious identification, and his socio-economic status.

The Eunuch's Bible

Why, then, was the eunuch reading from Isa 53?[51] The social location of the eunuch discussed above is a crucial key for interpreting the citation of Isaiah within the social and literary world of Acts. The passage of Scripture which the eunuch was reading was, as Hooker notes, a verbatim quotation of a Greek version of Isa 53:7-8: "As a sheep led to the slaughter or a lamb before its shearer is dumb, so he opens not his mouth. In his humiliation, justice was denied him. Who can describe his descendants? For his life is taken up from the earth" (Acts 8:32-33). As Hooker points out, the passage quoted here takes up just after the reference to the servant's vicarious suffering and ends just before a similar note in Isa 53:8. The passage as it stands in Acts tends rather to emphasize the "humiliation" of the unnamed sufferer and perhaps also his vindication.

The key word here is "humiliation" (ταπείνωσις, *tapeinōsis*), found in the middle of the citation. In later Christian literature (see *1 Clement* and *Hermas*), this word is taken more in terms of Christian "humility," that is, as an example of a Christian virtue, enacted through rituals of penitence and fasting. Only rarely, however, does the word apply in antiquity to personal immorality (see, e.g., Sextus Propertius 1.10.27-28), and should not be so understood here. Rather, the reference to ταπείνωσις (*tapeinōsis*) here is to a "social position within Mediterranean society" which "was severely reprobative."[52] A passage from Lucian's *Somnium* is illustrative of the social ostracism conveyed by ταπείνωσις (*tapeinōsis*, see also Pollux *Onomasticon* 5.162–164). In this dream, Lucian is warned that should he choose a career in sculpture (rather than education) he will

> be nothing but a laborer, toiling with your body and putting in it your entire hope of a livelihood, personally inconspicuous, getting meager and illiberal returns, lowly in disposition (ταπεινὸς τὴν γνώμην, *tapeinos tēn gnōmēn*), an insignificant figure in public, neither sought by your friends nor feared by your enemies nor envied by your fellow-citizens, nothing but just a laborer, one of the swarming rabble, ever cringing. (*Sleep* 9)

Should, however, Lucian choose the life of education (*paideia*), his social fortunes will be reversed. If not, then his lot is surely one of an outcast:

> On the other hand, if you turn your back upon these men so great and noble, upon glorious deeds and sublime words, upon a dignified appearance, upon honor, esteem, praise, precedence, power and offices, upon fame for eloquence and felicitations for wit, then you will put on a filthy tunic, assume a servile appearance . . . with your back bent over your work; you will be a groundling, with groundling ambitions, lowly in every manner (πάντα τρόπον ταπεινός, *panta tropon tapeinos*) . . . you will make yourself a thing of less value than a block of stone. (*Sleep* 13)

It is not surprising, then, that the eunuch, whose access to wealth is tenuous at best and ironically dependant upon his socially debased position, should be drawn to this figure in Isaiah who, like the eunuch, is described as being in a state of "humiliation" and to whom, like the eunuch, "justice was denied" (Acts 8:33).

Furthermore, this figure in Isaiah is not only socially marginalized, but also depicted as unclean or polluted. The Isianic figure is identified as a slaughtered lamb and a shorn sheep (Acts 8:32). Both similes from the Jewish map of purity evoke images of pollution. Dead bodies, whether animal carcasses or human corpses, were unclean and taboo to the touch (see Lev 11:24–40; 21:1–4). Likewise, priests were required to follow certain regulations regarding shaving their bodies: "They shall not make bald spots upon their heads, or shave off the edges of their beards . . ." (Lev 21:5; see also Num 6:1–21; see Acts 21:21–26). Again, the eunuch in Luke's narrative would have closely identified with the Isianic figure since both are depicted as ritually unclean. He, too, is like a lamb before its "cutter," reduced to silence in humiliation (Acts 8:32–33).

To be sure, within Judaism there existed the eschatological vision of Isaiah that eunuchs and foreigners and other outcasts would be reincorporated in the end days: "To the eunuchs who keep my sabbaths, who choose the things that please me and hold fast my covenant, I will give, in my house and within my walls, a monument and a name better than sons and daughters; I will give them an everlasting name that shall not be cut off" (Isa 56:4–6). But rather than provide hope for the eunuch, it stands as a cruel reminder of the gulf that stood between this vision of inclusion in the temple cult and the harsh social reality of exclusion from temple worship the eunuch had just experienced (see 8:27).

The eunuch had just come from his trip to Jerusalem for worship, and no doubt was forbidden from entering the temple (Deut 23:1). When Luke shows that nothing hinders the eunuch from being baptized, ritually cleansed and incorporated into the body of Christ, he undoubtedly intends a thinly veiled anti-temple polemic. What is held out as a promise in the (distant?) future but is denied by the current practices of the temple cult, is offered freely by the Way's representative, whose founder and community had radically redrawn the Jewish purity map not only of places (see the preceding passage on the Samaritans in Acts 8:4–8), but now also of persons. The status of the socially despised and ritually polluted eunuch is ritually transformed by the act of Christian baptism.

But the passage from Isaiah, as understood by Luke, does not limit its vision to a description only of the servant's debased status. Rather, there are allusions, albeit ambiguous, to a radical reversal of social status. The first hint of reversal may come in the phrase in Acts 8:33 often translated "justice was denied him," while some prefer the translation "judgment was removed from him" (on Luke's use of "judgment," see Luke 10:14; 11:31–32). The next phrase is likewise ambiguous: "Who can describe his generation?" Is this a lament over the fact that the servant is cut off from his descendants or a note rejoicing the "indescribable generation" too many to number? The case for the last phrase in the Scripture citation, "for his life is taken up from the earth" (8:33), having a double meaning is much stronger. Here again, the reference may be either to the figure's death or his "lifting up" in exaltation, symbolized in Jesus' ascension in Acts 1:9.[53]

This double entendre of "lifting up" as both death and exaltation may sound on first hearing as distinctly Johannine. But Luke also understands the death and exaltation of Jesus as inextricably tied up into one event, despite the fact that he narrates the death, crucifixion, and ascension separately. The death, resurrection, and ascension, however, are not separate, unrelated episodes for Luke, but rather three aspects of one event. Two key texts justify this conclusion. In the Lukan transfiguration scene, Jesus is depicted as conversing with Moses and Elijah about "his departure (ἔχοδος, echodos), which he was about to accomplish in Jerusalem" (Luke 9:31). Now either this singular "exodus" refers to the entire death-exaltation transit, or it refers to only one of those events. If it refers only to the final departure in Luke 24:50–53, then one is left with the tension created by the passion predictions which clearly speak of his "death" as the event which must be "fulfilled in Jerusalem" (see Luke 18:31–32), while Acts 9:31, on this reading, claims that what "must be accomplished" in Jerusalem is Jesus' final departure.

On the other hand, if the "exodus" refers only to his death, then the final departure scene in 24:50–53 is superfluous, and there is tension between this passage and 9:51 where we are told that "the days drew near for him to be taken up." In fact, I have argued elsewhere that the word "taken up" (ἀνάλημψις, analēmpsis) used in Luke 9:51 is itself a word that carries a double entendre in the semantic currency of late antiquity and is best seen as a reference to the entire death/resurrection/exaltation of Jesus.[54] Thus it is not difficult to imagine that a writer who has already closely aligned the death and exaltation of Jesus (see Luke 9:31, 51; Acts 1:2), and for whom the larger theological pattern of reversal is well-known in Luke and Acts (see Luke 1:48; 3:5–6; 14:11; 18:9–14; Acts 2:32–33), would see a double entendre in the Greek of Isa 53 and end his quotation by reversing the despised status of the servant with reference to his exaltation through death, his "being lifted up from the earth"!

It becomes clear, upon close reading, that the specific citation of Isa 53 in Acts 8, rather than being a kind of place-holding proof-text (in whose place nearly any Old Testament prophetic text could stand), accomplishes two critical points for Luke. The eunuch is attracted to this figure described in Isa 53:7–8. To have included references to the servant's vicarious suffering would have served as an obstacle to the eunuch's identification with the sufferer's social location. Thus, for historical verisimilitude, these verses are cited.[55] Furthermore, these verses allow Luke to recapitulate the suffering/vindication of Jesus the servant in a very economical space. To have gone beyond the reference, "and his life is taken up from the earth," would have destroyed the death/exaltation schema.

Intertextual Echoes in Acts 8

We can now present an alternative to Hooker's view that Luke began and ended the Isaiah quotation where he did to avoid references to vicarious suffering. Luke may have wished to avoid these references, not because he was reticent to contemplate or uninterested in the suffering vocation of the servant; but rather, Luke avoids citing those parts of the passage because he would have repelled the passage's "attraction" in drawing the eunuch to identify with the servant, and he would have disrupted the humiliation/exaltation schema that he found in the rhetorical ambiguity of the Greek of Isa 53:7–8.

The allusion to vindication, to be sure, is implicit, and so the ambiguous nature of the Scripture requires a Christian interpreter. The eunuch asks: "About whom, pray, does the prophet say this, about himself or about someone else?" So Philip "opened his mouth (see 8:32b!) and beginning with this Scripture he told him the good news of Jesus" (8:34–35). This good news, no doubt, included the vindication as well as the suffering of Jesus (see Acts 2:23–24; 3:13–15) and what may have been ambiguous in the Scripture is now made clear in its Christian exposition. If the reference were left simply to the kerygmatic "good news" of the death and resurrection, however, then Hooker's objection would still hold true:

> These early chapters of Acts speak only of the historical fact of Christ's death; they do not dwell on his sufferings, or point out the parallel with the Servant Songs. Nor do they trace any connection between Christ's death and the forgiveness of sins, which we would expect if an identification of Jesus with the servant were intended: for while the forgiveness of sins was proclaimed as part of the kerygma from the very beginning, it is not suggested that this forgiveness was dependent upon Christ's death. . . . [56]

Philip's interpretation, however, does not stop simply with an appeal to the general kerygmatic "good news" of Jesus' death and exaltation. There is an important intertextual echo which takes the reader back to the last chapter of Luke's first volume. The phrase in Acts 8:35, "beginning from" (ἀρξάμενος ἀπὸ, *arxamenos apo*) this Scripture is a verbatim verbal echo of the same phrase in Luke 24:27, "beginning from (ἀρξάμενος ἀπὸ, *arxamenos apo*) Moses and from all the prophets."

Let me begin here by applying Richard Hays' criteria for determining allusions and echoes in Acts 8:35 to Luke 24.[57] Though Hays's criteria were crafted in terms of Old Testament citations and allusions in NT writings (specifically Paul), I think this intertextual echo between Acts 8 and Luke 24 meets all of his criteria: (1) The Gospel of Luke was *available* to the author and his original readers; (2) given the verbatim repetition of (ἀρξάμενος ἀπὸ, *arxamenos apo*) and the rhetorical stress placed on both passages in their narrative context, the volume is quite explicit; (3) the *recurrence* of parallels and patterns from Luke in Acts are well-known; (4) the *thematic coherence* is likewise strong—Luke 24 is an amplification of the shorthand of Acts 8; (5) it is *historically plausible* that Luke intended this intertextual echo and that his readers, at least upon subsequent readings, would have recognized it; (6) in terms of the *history of interpretation*, modern scholars, at least, have consistently pointed out the parallels between the stories of the road to Emmaus and the Ethiopian eunuch and suggested interpreting the two passages in light of each other;[58] (7) the suggested intertextual echo does illuminate the surrounding text and fits well within Luke's rhetorical argument about the Gentile mission, thus providing an aesthetically *satisfying* fit.

But what specifically is the context of the phrase in Luke 24? In this story, the resurrected Jesus has joined two disciples on their journey home. Cleopas and his companion have complained that the crucifixion of Jesus, "a prophet mighty in deed and word," had left them in utter despair: "we had hoped that he was the one to redeem Israel" (24:21). The resurrected, but as of yet unrecognized, Christ chastises them: "'O foolish ones, and slow of heart to believe all that the prophets have spoken! Was it not necessary that the Christ should suffer these things and enter into his glory?' And beginning with Moses and all the prophets, he interpreted to them in all the Scriptures the things concerning himself" (24:25–27). Here clearly, Jesus' exposition of Scripture, beginning with Moses and all the prophets, exposes the divine necessity of the Christ's suffering. But what was the purpose of this suffering?

This point is made clear a little later in Luke 24, in a passage which parallels 24:25–27. Here the risen Christ commissions his disciples: "'These are my words which I spoke to you, while I was still with you, that everything written about me in the law of Moses and the prophets and the psalms must be fulfilled.' Then he opened their minds (see Philip opening his mouth in 8:35) to understand the Scriptures and said to them, 'Thus it is written that the *Christ must suffer* and on the third day rise from the dead, and that *repentance and forgiveness of sins should be preached in his name to all nations*'" (24:44–47). For Luke the divine necessity of Christ's suffering was both for the redemption of Israel (24:21) and so that the gentiles (ἔθνη, *ethnē*, "nations") might hear the good news of repentance and forgiveness of sins!

Through the use of an intertextual echo, Philip's preaching the good news, beginning with this Scripture (Acts 8:35), is given content by the precursor text in Luke 24. Isaiah 53 is part of those Scriptures that give testimony to the divine necessity of Christ's suffering for the redemption of Israel and for the sake of the repentance and the forgiveness of sins of the Gentiles. Hooker is certainly right (in opposition to

Betz) that Isa 53 does not hold any unique place in the preaching of Acts about the suffering of Christ. But Isa 53, contrary to Hooker's position, is indeed *one* of the texts that Luke had in mind when he referred to Christ's suffering according to the Scriptures. In fact, it is the only one he explicitly cites!

What then are we to say about the use of Isa 53 in Acts 8? Over against Hooker, who, remember, argues that in Acts 8, Luke carefully avoids making reference to the vicarious suffering of the servant, we have argued that the citation begins and ends where it does in a way that is appropriate to the argument: The eunuch identifies with the humiliated and polluted servant and Luke has found in this particular passage, especially in the double entendre, "he was lifted up," a useful humiliation/exaltation schema, and one that is re-enacted when the eunuch is baptized by Philip.

Further, over against Hooker's insistence that the citation of Isa 53 in Acts 8 is nothing more than a "proof-text," I have argued that the intertextual echo back to Luke 24 gives the "theological exposition" of Christ's suffering, which Hooker claims is missing. With rhetorical subtlety, Luke gives both the *fact* and *significance* of Christ's suffering. To be sure, Isa 53 is not the only text Luke has in mind in Luke 24:25–27 and 24:44–46, but Isa 53 *is* part of the prophetic pattern of suffering that informs the early church's (or at least Luke's) understanding of the significance of Christ's suffering.

The conclusion of the Acts 8 passage comes, then, as no surprise. Convinced of the truth of Philip's message, the eunuch lets forth with the refrain of an unhindered gospel that runs throughout Acts: "Look here is water! What hinders me from being baptized?" (see Acts 10:47; 28:31). Until now, everything about the eunuch prevented him from undergoing religious initiation rites; he could not be circumcised and could not be a proselyte to Judaism. But now because of the "good news about Jesus" proclaimed to him by Philip, nothing prohibits his transformation being ritualized through Christian baptism. The suffering of Christ, the humiliated, polluted, yet exalted Servant, continues to bear fruit!

Conclusion

We have seen in this chapter that Luke is an interpreter of the Jewish tradition. First, we have seen that Luke has appropriated and redefined the tradition of Jerusalem as the center of the world, instead showing that the Christian mission moves well beyond the confines of

Judaism to encompass the entire Gentile world. Second, we have seen Luke reinterpret the Jewish Scriptures in the case of the Ethiopian Eunuch in such a way that the "unhindered gospel" is made clear. In both cases we have seen that Luke employs existing Jewish attitudes, traditions, and arguments in order to stake a claim for the existence of the Christian sect among the other Jewish sects.

Notes

1. The interpenetration of Hellenism and Judaism was decisively established by Martin Hengel in his monumental work, *Judaism and Hellenism: Studies in Their Encounter in Palestine During the Early Hellenistic Period* (trans. John Bowden; Philadelphia: Fortress, 1974). See also Gabriele Boccaccini, *Middle Judaism: Jewish Thought, 300 B.C.E.–200 C.E.* (Minneapolis: Fortress, 1991), especially chapter one, in which he demonstrates that there was no unified "Judaism" but rather "Judaisms," of which Christianity and Pharisaism were but two.

2. This point, of course, is not altogether true of some pagan traditions either. While our examples of friendship and physiognomy in the last chapter tended to cut across specific religious and philosophic traditions, certainly other ideas and social scripts had particular meaning within specific traditions. For example, cynic and stoic philosophy had well-developed and coherent notions of a variety of concepts and practices. See Troels Engberg-Pedersen, *Paul and the Stoics* (Edinburgh: T&T Clark, 2000).

3. On this see Chapter 1.

4. On the history of cartography in antiquity, see vol. 1, *Cartography in Prehistoric, Ancient, and Medieval Europe and the Mediterranean* of the encyclopedic six volume work, *History of Cartography* (ed. J. B. Harley and David Woodward; Chicago: University of Chicago Press, 1987).

5. Catherine Delano Smith, "Cartography in the Prehistoric Period in the Old World: Europe, the Middle East, and North Africa," *History of Cartography,* 1:85.

6. A. R. Millard, "Cartography in the Ancient Near East," *History of Cartography,* 1:111. The largest dimensions of the original clay tablet are 12.5 × 8 cm. It is currently housed in the British Museum.

7. Though see the medieval texts, *Midras Konen* and *Seder Rabba diBeresit,* which belonged to the rabbinic cosmographical tradition; see N. Sed, *La mystique cosmologique juive.* Ecole des Hautes Etudes en Science Sociales: Etudes Juives (Paris, 1981); cited by Philip S. Alexander, "Geography and the Bible (Early Jewish)," *ABD,* 2:977–88.

8. Daniel J. Boorstin, *The Discoverers* (New York: Random House, 1983), 100.

9. On the various types of medieval *Mappaemundi,* see David Woodward, "Medieval *Mappaemundi,*" *History of Cartography,* 1:286–370. Of special interest is the chart (p. 298) that shows that of the maps from the eighth to the fifteenth centuries; the tripartite maps account for over 50 percent of those extant, reaching a high of over 90 percent in the ninth century.

10. Boorstin, *The Discovers,* 101.

11. Boorstin, *The Discovers*, 101.

12. The extant map is 5 × 10.5 meters, but originally the mosaic may have been as large as 24 × 6 meters and composed of more than two million pieces of colored cubes, preserved in a church in Madaba, Jordan.

13. O. A. W. Dilke, "Cartography in the Byzantine Empire," *History of Cartography*, 1:265.

14. On the problems associated with "verbal maps," see Alexander, "Geography and the Bible (Early Jewish)," 977–88.

15. Strabo, *Geography* (LCL; trans. by Horace Leonard Jones; Cambridge: Harvard University Press, 1917; repr., 1989), 1.1.2.

16. Strabo, *Geography*, 1.2.9.

17. In their *Greek-English Lexicon of the New Testament Based on Semantic Domains*, vol. 1 (2d ed.; New York: United Bible Societies, 1989), Johannes P. Louw and Eugene A. Nida list "Geographical Objects and Features" as the first Semantic Domain. A frequency analysis of its various sub-domains demonstrates that, even after adjusting the results to take into account the fact that Luke and Acts are much longer than any other NT document, the Lukan writings demonstrate a higher rate of frequency for spatially related terms than any other NT document. In many cases, the subdomains of Domain 1 were represented by terms which are found only in Luke-Acts among the NT documents. Similar results were found in analyses of domains 80 ("space"), 81 ("spatial dimensions"), 82 ("spatial orientations"), and 83 ("spatial positions"). I wish to thank my former graduate assistants, Stanley Harstine and Mark Proctor, for their help in conducting these analyses.

18. Hans Conzelmann, *The Theology of St. Luke* (trans. Geoffrey Buswell; New York: Harper, 1961), 70.

19. Johnson, *The Gospel of Luke*, 11.

20. Fitzmyer, *The Gospel according to Luke I–IX*, 1:168.

21. W. D. Davies, *The Gospel and the Land: Early Christianity and Jewish Territorial Doctrine* (Berkeley: University of California Press, 1974), 255.

22. W. D. Davies, *The Gospel and the Land*, 255–56.

23. On the definition of "authorial audience" see chapter 1.

24. I have modified the terminology from Elizabeth Struthers Malbon in *Narrative Space and Mythic Meaning in Mark* (San Francisco: Harper & Row, 1986), who also speaks of architectural space.

25. Talbert, *Reading Luke*, 113.

26. Johnson, *The Gospel of Luke*, 14–15.

27. On the importance of the Table-of-Nations tradition for Luke, see James M. Scott, "Luke's Geographical Horizon," in *The Book of Acts in Its First Century Setting*, vol. 2, *Graeco-Roman Setting* (ed. David W. J. Gill and Conrad Gempf; Grand Rapids: Eerdmans, 1994), 483–544. I do not, however, follow Scott (530–41) in his argument that the entire book of Acts is organized around the missions to Shem (Acts 2:1–8:25), Ham (8:26–40), and Japheth (9:1–28:31).

28. Talbert, *Reading Luke*, 122.

29. I am not suggesting that the implied reader necessarily had knowledge of these *specific* texts, but rather was generally familiar with the positions they articulated.

30. See Alexander, "Geography and the Bible (Early Jewish)," 980–82. All translations of Second Temple Jewish texts, unless otherwise noted, are taken from the *OTP* translations.

31. On the *omphalos* tradition in Old Testament studies, see Brevard S. Childs, *Myth and Reality in the Old Testament* (SBT 27; Naperville, Ill.: Alec R. Allenson, 1960); Samuel Terrien, "The Omphalos Myth and Hebrew Religion," *VT* 20 (1970): 313–38.

32. Conzelmann, *Theology of St. Luke*, 132–36.

33. On the theme of suffering in Luke-Acts, see the various writings of David Moessner, esp. " 'The Christ Must Suffer,' The Church Must Suffer: Rethinking the Theology of the Cross in Luke-Acts," *SBLSP* 29 (1990): 165–95.

34. Jonathan Z. Smith, *Map Is Not Territory: Studies in the History of Religions* (SJLA 23; Leiden: Brill, 1978), 309.

35. Morna Hooker, *Jesus and the Servant: The Influence of the Servant Concept of Deutero-Isaiah in the New Testament* (London: SPCK, 1959), 163.

36. I think that only by combining a detailed passage-by-passage analysis and a coherent theory of early Christian use(s) of Jewish Scriptures can one begin to propose Hooker's thesis.

37. Hooker, *Jesus and the Servant*, 150.

38. Hooker, *Jesus and the Servant*, 150–51.

39. Hooker, *Jesus and the Servant*, 151.

40. Hooker, *Jesus and the Servant*, 113.

41. Hooker, *Jesus and the Servant*, 113.

42. Hooker, *Jesus and the Servant*, 114.

43. Hooker, *Jesus and the Servant*, 113.

44. Hooker, *Jesus and the Servant*, 113.

45. For a discussion of the significance of Ethiopia both as a geographical and ethnic descriptor, see Clarice Martin, "A Chamberlain's Journey and the Challenge of Interpretation for Liberation," *Semeia* 47 (1989): 105–35.

46. See F. Scott Spencer, "The Ethiopian Eunuch and His Bible: A Social-Science Analysis," *BTB* 22 (1992): 156. This article sparked the idea of the importance of the eunuch's social status for understanding the function of the Isa 53 citation in Acts 8.

47. See Bruce J. Malina and Jerome H. Neyrey, "Honor and Shame in Luke-Acts: Pivotal Values of the Mediterranean World," in *The Social World of Luke-Acts: Models for Interpretation* (ed. Jerome H. Neyrey; Peabody, Mass.: Hendrickson, 1991), 41–44.

48. See Spencer, "The Ethiopian Eunuch and His Bible," 158–59; idem, *The Portrait of Philip in Acts: A Study of Roles and Relations* (JSNTSup 67; Sheffield: JSOT Press, 1992), 168–72.

49. See Jerome H. Neyrey, "The Symbolic Universe of Luke-Acts: 'They Turn the World Upside Down,' " in *The Social World of Luke-Acts*, 278–85.

50. Spencer, "The Ethiopian Eunuch and His Bible," 159.

51. This section's title is derived from Spencer's article cited above.

52. See Braun, *Feasting and Social Rhetoric in Luke 14*, 50.

53. Or as Luke Johnson puts it: "the LXX can be read by the Messianist who confesses a resurrected prophet as 'life is lifted from the earth' " (*The Acts of the Apostles*, 156).

54. See Mikeal C. Parsons, *The Departure of Jesus in Luke-Acts: The Ascension Narratives in Context* (JSNTSup 21; Sheffield: Sheffield Academic Press, 1987), 128–33. In these pages, I also argue for a similar understanding of ἀνελήμφθη (*anelēmphthē*)in Acts 1:2. For a reference to ἀνάλημψις (*analēmpsis*) meaning "death," see *Pss. Sol.* 4:18. For other examples from late antiquity on

the meaning of ἀνάλημψις (*analēmpsis*) as "passing away" and "taken up," see P. A. van Stempvoort, "The Interpretation of the Ascension in Luke and Acts," *NTS* 5 (1959): 32–33.

55. Ironically, Hooker does not explore explanations for why this text might be appropriate for the eunuch to be reading, but simply acknowledges that "behind this story there may lie a genuine recollection that this was the chapter which the eunuch happened to be reading" (113).

56. Hooker, *Jesus and the Servant*, 110.

57. Though some might object to referring to an echo to Luke in the book of Acts as "intertextual" because they form one continuous narrative, I have argued elsewhere that Luke and Acts are two independent, but interrelated works and thus intertextual echo is a fitting term; see Parsons and Pervo, *Rethinking the Unity of Luke and Acts*.

58. See, e.g., Joseph A. Grass, "Emmaus Revisited (Luke 24:13–35 and Acts 8:26–40)," *CBQ* 26 (1964): 463–67; and many of the commentaries.

CHAPTER 6

Interpreting Christian Traditions: Parables and Paul

Introduction

So far we have seen that Luke is an interpreter of both the pagan traditions pervasive in the ancient Mediterranean world as well as the Jewish traditions out of which Christianity was born. This chapter seeks to demonstrate that Luke is likewise an interpreter of Christian traditions. Certainly Luke did not write his two-volume narrative in a vacuum; rather, many Christian traditions already existed, some oral and some written.[1] This chapter will explore two examples of Luke's appropriation of existing Christian traditions. One example comes from Luke, the other from Acts; one example deals with the author, the other deals with the audience. We will first examine Luke's use of the so-called "L" parables in the Lukan travel narrative. Here we will see that Luke has taken existing material and reworked and reinterpreted that material in the service of his narrative. Our focus, then, is not on the pre-Lukan history of the parables, for this has been the work of the source critics. Instead, our attention will be given to the performance of these parables as they function in the Lukan narrative. In the second case, we will compare the portrayals of Paul in the letters of Paul with the portrayal of Paul as a character in Acts. Here again we will see that Luke has taken existing Christian material and used it in the service of his narrative.

Luke as Interpreter of Parables

Landmarks Along the Way: The Function of the 'L' Parables in the Lukan Travel Narrative

Influenced by the form-critical work of Joachim Jeremias and C. H. Dodd, most scholars more often than not have viewed the parables as the bedrock of the Jesus tradition, holding the most promise for recovering the authentic voice of Jesus (*ipsissima vox*), if not his very words (*ipsissima verba*).[2] The recent studies by B. B. Scott and Charles Hedrick have also taken this form-critical approach.[3] To be sure, certain interpreters have resisted the thoroughly historical approach of "excavating" the text for dominical "nuggets." Dan Via, for example, treated the parables as distinct literary objects.[4] But even he "lifted" the parables out of their immediate narrative and canonical contexts. So focusing on the canonical performance of the parables is an opportunity not only to hear them afresh within their narrative contexts but to experience them as part of the larger canonical witness as the church has done for nearly two thousand years.

This emphasis on the final, canonical form of the parables provides a helpful clue in terms of organizing the material. The interpreter interested in this canonical approach, however, will find little help from the scholarly literature on parables. As noted above, parable research has focused on the parables as a form-critical source for Jesus' teachings preserved in oral tradition or as discrete, aesthetic objects. In both cases, the narrative, canonical context is of secondary concern. Two examples will amply illustrate this point.

The classic form-critical study on the parables by Joachim Jeremias attempted to establish the original message of the parables in the teaching of Jesus. The conclusion Jeremias reached at the end of his study was that "all the parables of Jesus compel his hearers to come to decision about his person and mission. For they are all full of the secret of the Kingdom of God (Mark 4:11), that is to say, the recognition of an eschatology that is in process of realization."[5] Jeremias catalogues ten different strategies by which the reconstructed parables attempt to achieve this goal. Below is a list of those categories and the Lukan parables as Jeremias assigned them:[6]

1. Now is the Day of Salvation

2. God's Mercy for Sinners: The Two Debtors (7:41–43); The Lost Drachma (15:8–10); The Father's Love (The Prodigal Son, 15:11–32); The Pharisee and the Publican (18:9–14)

3. The Great Assurance: The Friend asked for Help at Night (11:5–8);
   The Unjust Judge (18:1–8)

4. The Imminence of Catastrophe: The Rich Fool (12:16–21)

5. It May Be Too Late: The Barren Fig-Tree (13:6–9)

6. The Challenge of the Hour: The Choice of Places at the Table
   (14:7–11); The Tower-builder and the King contemplating a
   Campaign (14:28–32); The Unjust Steward (16:1–8); The Rich
   Man and Lazarus (16:19–31); The Servant's Reward (17:7–10)

7. Realized Discipleship: The Good Samaritan (10:25–37)

8. The Via Dolorosa and Exaltation of the Son of Man

9. The Consummation

10. Parabolic Actions

Jeremias was concerned with a thematic organization of the parables. Of course, Jeremias was little interested in the final form of the parables; in fact, he spent the first half of his book detailing the procedure for stripping away these secondary accretions to Jesus' parables. And his study, while providing helpful comments on individual parables, does not assist in the organization of the parables in a way sensitive to their narrative function in the canonical, final form of Luke's Gospel.

Brandon Scott has recently published a major study on the parables, *Hear Then the Parable*. Like Jeremias, Scott was concerned to reconstruct the teachings of Jesus. Unlike Jeremias, however, Scott was also interested in the narrative context of the parables (though for Scott, that context was still clearly secondary),[7] as well as aspects of Mediterranean society and culture in which these parables were originally uttered and subsequently preserved. In fact, Scott employed "three of the elementary aspects of Mediterranean social life and culture as basic categories for the parables."[8] The first basis of social exchange moves from the basic social unit of the family outward in concentric circles to the village, city, and finally to those who are farthest away from the family, the "foreigner," which Scott referred to simply as "beyond." The second category, "Masters and Servants," embodies the client-patron model of the exchange of power. Finally, the third group of parables, "Home and Farm," invests the "artifacts of daily life with metaphorical and symbolic significance."[9] Below is a list of the categories along with Scott's classification of the Lukan parables.[10]

FAMILY, VILLAGE, CITY, AND BEYOND

Who Has a Friend? (Luke 11:5–8)

    Two Men Went Up to the Temple (Luke 18:10–14a)

    A Man Had Two Sons (Luke 15:11–32)

    A Rich Man Clothed in Purple (Luke 16:19–31)

    In a City There Was a Judge (Luke 18:2–5)

    From Jerusalem to Jericho (Luke 10:30–35)

MASTERS AND SERVANTS

    A Creditor Had Two Debtors (Luke 7:41–43)

    Who Has a Servant Plowing (Luke 17:7–9)

    A Rich Man Had a Steward (Luke 16:1–8a)

HOME AND FARM

    A Woman with Ten Drachmas (Luke 15:8–10)

    A Man Had a Fig Tree (Luke 13:6–9)

Scott's insights into the social and cultural setting of the parables are illuminating and are especially helpful in the exegesis of the individual parables. But again, for the interpreter interested in the final form of the parables and their function in the Lukan narrative, his classification is inadequate.

How then are the "L" parables to be approached if the interest is primarily in their canonical function? To attend primarily to the "canonical performance" of parables does not preclude examining the prehistory or reception history of the parables, but it does mean that the focus is on the canonical shape of the parables and their function within the narrative of Luke. To understand the parables in this way involves exploring three different contexts:

1. The Russian philosopher and literary critic Mikhail Bakhtin is reputed to have remarked: "Every text remembers where it has been." Though the focus is on the final form of the parables, the interpreter will be aided by a consideration of where these parables have been, that is, on the "pre-history" of these texts. I argue below that the writer of Luke had access to an "L" parable collection, which probably had been structured in a ring composition, and Luke preserved the structure as he incorporated the parable collection into his Gospel. By understanding

the major emphases of the parable collection, the interpreter may gain further insight into the canonical function of the parables.

2. It is important to note the narrative context into which these parables have been re-integrated, namely the journey of Jesus to Jerusalem in Luke 9–19. This framework provides an interpretive clue for the parables, and at the same time, the parables provide helpful landmarks in interpretating a section of Luke's Gospel that has been remarkably resistant to organization.

3. Finally, we must consider the immediate context and the large literary environment of the parable. These three strategies will serve as the outline for the rest of this chapter.

Grouping The Uniquely Lukan Parables: A Possible "L" Parable Collection

It is first necessary to identify which of the parables in Luke's Gospel are unique to the Third Gospel, that is, which parables may rightly be labeled as "L" parables. This task is not quite as easy as one might imagine, since interpreters do not always agree on what constitutes a "Lukan parable." Since all the interpreters do agree that all but one (the parable of the two debtors, 7:41–43) of the potential "L" parables are found within the so-called travel narrative, we will limit our search to Luke chapters 9–19. Thus, we begin by cataloguing all the parables located within the Lukan travel narrative (see Table 1).[11]

Table 1. All Parables in the Lukan Travel Narrative

10:30–35	*The good Samaritan*
11:5–8	*The shameless neighbor*
11:24–26	The return of the unclean spirit
12:16–21	*The rich fool*
12:36–38	The returning master
12:39–40	The thief in the night
12:42–46	The good and wicked servants
12:58–59	Going before a judge
13:6–9	*The barren fig tree*
13:18–19	The mustard seed
13:20–21	The yeast
13:24–30	The narrow door
14:7–11	*The choice of places at table*
14:16–24	The great supper

14:28–30	The fool at work
14:31–32	The fool at war
15:3–7	The lost sheep
15:8–10	The lost coin
15:11–32	*The lost sons*
16:1–9	*The dishonest steward*
16:19–31	*The rich man and Lazarus*
17:7–10	The servant
18:1–8	*The unjust judge*
18:9–14	*The Pharisee & the tax collector*
19:11–27	The entrusted money

The italicized parables represent what I have identified as the parables belonging to an "L" parable collection that was incorporated into the Lukan travel narrative.[12] By isolating these parables, it is possible to detect something of the overall structure of the parables collection.

Table 2. "L" Parables in the Lukan Travel Narrative

10:30–35	The good Samaritan
11:5–8	The shameless neighbor
12:16–21	The rich fool
13:6–9	The barren fig tree
14:7–11	The choice of places at table
15:11–32	The lost sons
16:1–9	The dishonest steward
16:19–31	The rich man and Lazarus
18:1–8	The unjust judge
18:9–14	The Pharisee & the tax collector

First, some observations about the selection of the "L" parables. Many would also identify Luke 14:28–30, 14:31–32, and 17:7–9 as uniquely Lukan parables.[13] I have excluded them from the "L" collection because they, like 11:5–8, contain the formula "which of you" but unlike 11:5–8 are embedded in a longer discourse of Jesus. The "which of you" formula of 11:5 prompted the Lukan creation of these other three parables (perhaps from traditional material) and were not part of the "L" collection itself Others have argued that the parable of the returning master (12:36–38) is not distinctively Lukan, but rather finds a parallel with Mark 13:34.[14] The parallels between the two parables are not that close, and this would be the only parable in the Synoptic tradition shared by Luke and Mark and not found in Matthew. Therefore, it is best to view the two parables as representing independent traditions. Finally, the parable of the lost coin, Luke 15:8–10, is clearly unique to Luke among the Synoptics, but is not taken to be part of the "L" parable collection. Rather, the parable of the lost sheep, Luke 15:3–7 (found also in Matt. 18:12–13 and *Gos. Thom.* 107), was part of the material available to Luke when he wrote his Gospel (see Luke 1:1–4), and the parable of the lost coin was probably appended at that point to form a bridge to the parable of the lost sons (which was in the parable collection) and to unify the three parables of the coin, the sheep, and the sons, around the theme of "that which was lost now being found."

Observations on the Overall Structure of the Parable Collection

Now we may offer some observations about the overall structure of the collection.

1. The "L" parable collection may be aligned in a chiastic or ring structure, in which the parables are paired (indicated below by the coordinating letters A/A'; B/B' etc.). This "L" parable collection also consists of two sub-groups of five parables. The first parable of each group, the parable of the good Samaritan (10:30–35) and the parable of the lost sons (15:11–32), are no doubt the two most memorable parables, judging from the subsequent history of interpretation. A sixth parable, Luke 14:3–11, lies at the heart of the collection, between the two subgroups. This parable and the last parable of the second subgroup (18:9–14, also the last in the collection), each contain the saying: "For all who exalt themselves will be humbled, and those who humble themselves will be exalted" (4:11; 18:14). This theme of reversal seems to be the overarching theme of the "L" parable collection (a point to which we shall return again in the detailed discussion of 14:3–11).

2. The reversal contrast is embedded in the very structure of the parable collection which, in the paired parables, alternates in its narrative audience.[15]

A 10:30–35/A' 18:9–14: OUTSIDERS (lawyer 10:25; those who trusted in themselves 18:9)
B 11:5–8/B' 18:1–8: INSIDERS (disciples, 11:5; disciples 17:22)
C 12:16–21/C' 16:19–31: OUTSIDERS (multitudes, 12:13 Pharisees, 16:14)
D 12:36–38/D' 16:1–9: INSIDERS (disciples, 12:22; disciples 16:1)
E 13:6–9/E') 15:11–32: OUTSIDERS (multitudes, 12:54; Pharisees and scribes, 15:2)

This structure suggests that the collection and also the final form of Luke aimed at addressing the issue of who was "in" and who was "out" in relationship to Jesus and what behaviors were characteristic of those two groups. As we shall see, however, the boundary between the insiders and outsiders was not absolute. It was possible for outsiders to become insiders, and it was even possible for insiders to become outsiders!

3. Another interesting feature is that of the eleven "L" parables, only six are designated as a parable in the introductory frame. In each case, it is one (and only one) of the twinned parables which is so introduced.

The cumulative effect of these observations is to suggest that this collection of parables was carefully organized to emphasize their rhetoric of reversal, a theological theme, which was preserved in the final form of the text, even though the tightly knit structure itself was not.

Observations on Common Elements in the "Twinned" Parables

The phenomenon of "twinned" parables allows further insight into the "L" parable collection. The similarities between each pair of parables are examined below.[16]

A. 10:30–35 The good Samaritan/A' 18:9–14 The Pharisee and the tax collector. The Jewish religious establishment is negatively depicted in both parables. In both, the religious leaders are explicitly identified (priest/Levite; Pharisee), a phenomenon unparalleled in the other parables in Luke. The protagonist in each case is an unlikely hero, a Samaritan and a tax-collector. The contrast between the negatively portrayed religious leaders and the unexpected heroes highlights the theme of the reversal of expectations. Verbally the parables are linked by the important theological theme of justification (δικαιόω, *dikaioō*). The parable of the good Samaritan addresses the lawyer's concern that he be justified, while the Pharisee and publican both receive Jesus' verdict on whether or not they went home justified. Since δικαιόω (*dikaioō*) occurs in no other parable in Luke's travel narrative, this verbal link is noteworthy. Closely related is the conceptual (though not verbal) link of mercy: the good Samaritan shows mercy; the publican prays, "God be merciful to me . . ."

B. 11:5–8 The shameless neighbor/B' 18:1–8 The unjust judge. The similarities between the parables of the shameless neighbor and the unjust judge are even more striking. Each has two main characters, a petitioner and a granter of petitions. In each, the second character is reluctant to grant the request and does so for improper reasons. Both parables illustrate that God will answer the prayers of his people. This idiom, "to be bothered" (παρέχω κόπος, *parechō kopos*) occurs in no other parable, but is here the focus of both; neither the one roused from his sleep nor the unjust judge wishes to be bothered. Nonetheless, if such audacity or persistence is successful with the recalcitrant, how much more will such audacity or persistence be rewarded by a God willing to grant his people's request.

C. *12:16–21 The rich fool/C′ 16:19–31 The rich man and Lazarus.* The parables of the rich fool and the rich man and Lazarus both begin with the verbal parallel, "a certain man" (ἄνθρωπος τις πλούσιος, *anthrōpos tis plousios*—found elsewhere only in the parable of the unjust steward). The rich fool and the rich man of Luke 16:19–31 parallel each other not only in the fact that they are rich, but each seems unconcerned with anyone except himself. As Blomberg notes: "The rich fool ignores God; the rich man ignores Lazarus. Both die; no other parables of Jesus relate the death of one of their characters. Both parables continue by recounting the tragic consequences of the rich men's deaths."[17] Again, the note of reversal is struck; this time it is economic.

D. *12:36–38 The returning master/D′ 16:1–9 The dishonest steward.* Both accounts are servant parables; and in both, the servants must prepare for an uncertain and potentially tragic future encounter with their master. The setting of both parables is the house: in the one, the house of the servants preparing to receive the master, in the other, the houses of the master's debtors that the servant is preparing to visit. Admittedly the verbal links between the two are rather weak, though in both the master is referred to as "Lord" (κύριος, *kurios*).

E. *13:6–9 The barren fig tree/E′ 15:11–32 The lost sons.* On the surface these two parables seem to have little in common with each other. Both do deal with repentance but more importantly, both parables are open-ended. We do not know whether the gardener's plea to spare the fig tree will be heeded by its owner nor whether the elder brother will accept the gracious invitation of the father to join the banquet. This open-endedness is necessary to prevent the theme of reversal, so prominent in the rest of the collection, from being taken as dividing insiders and outsiders absolutely. There is the possibility for reversing the reversal!

When the parable collection is introduced into the travel narrative, this point of open-endedness is reinforced by the story in Luke of the rich ruler in Luke 18. He asks, "Good teacher, what must I do to inherit eternal life?" (8:18). This question takes the reader back to the beginning of the travel narrative (and the parables collection) to the lawyer who asks the same question in Luke 10. In neither case, that of the rich man in Luke 18 (contrary to Mark) nor the lawyer in Luke 10, does Luke record their response. The potential for repentance for transformation is still held out as a possibility.

Integrating the "L" Parables Collection into the Canonical Text

John Nolland has argued that there is a

> very strong case for the view that Luke has used a parables source as core source for the construction of his journey narrative. He has retained the parables in the original chiastic order of that source, but he has heavily expanded with other materials and seems to have made no attempt to use as his own the structure of his source. . . . [18]

While it is true that the parallelisms of the "L" parable collection are not maintained when Luke introduces them into the final form of the Third Gospel, this is not to suggest that the form and function of the collection did not affect the shape and theme of the Lukan travel narrative. In other words, though scholars have not agreed on the details, many have sensed that the travel narrative is held together by an overarching chiastic structure,[19] a structure that may have been encouraged by the chiastic structure of the parable collection. The theme of reversal, so prominent in the "L" collection, is likewise a crucial feature retained in the travel narrative itself.

One may ask why Luke has broken apart this tight rhetorical unit. First we may observe that the most significant element of the ring composition, its center, is, in fact, preserved. Luke 14:7–11 retains its place of prominence in canonical Luke by its location at the "heart" of the parables in the travel narrative (12 parables come before it, 12 after it), suggesting that Luke has retained the reversal motif as a major theme of the travel narrative (see Table 1 above). Further, the outermost ring is also partially preserved as the parable of the good Samaritan (Luke 10:30–35) is still the first parable in the travel narrative and the parable of the Pharisee and the tax collector (18:9–14) is next to last, followed only by the parable of the entrusted money (19:11–27).[20]

The Narrative Framework: The Journey to Jerusalem

The central section of Luke's Gospel is set within the framework of a journey narrative. But the way of Jesus is not expressive of his physical arrival in Jerusalem nor of his progress toward his passion. At the outset, the journey is described as Jesus' ἀνάλημψις (*analēmpsis*), literally his

"taking up" (9:51). As noted earlier (in chapter 5), this "taking up" refers
to the entire complex of events that forms Jesus' transit to the Father: his
passion, death, burial, resurrection, and ascension/exaltation. Jesus'
journeying along the way is also depicted in Luke as an "exodus." In
the transfiguration scene in Luke 9:28–36, only Luke of the Synoptic
Gospels reports that Jesus, Moses, and Elijah were speaking of Jesus'
"departure" or "exodus" (author's translation), "which he was about to
accomplish at Jerusalem" (9:31). So the journey to Jerusalem is a new
Exodus by which Jesus forges a redemptive path to the glory of the
Father. The way of Jesus becomes paradigmatic for Jesus' followers:
"The didactic material given in the context of a journey fits Luke's conception of the life of faith as a pilgrimage, always on the move."[21]

In this context, the "L" parables become landmarks for instructing
the disciples along this way. They serve to remind the reader that the
journey of Jesus is also their journey, and that journey is filled with unexpected twists and turns. Along the way, outsiders can become insiders
and insiders can become outsiders. Along the way, the exalted can be
humbled and the humble exalted

This theme of reversal is important not only in the "L" parable collection or the Lukan travel narrative; it is an important overall motif in
the Gospel of Luke (see, for example, Luke 1:53–55; 6:20–26; 9:24). And,
indeed, it is a point that would have been well understood by a first-
century Mediterranean audience for whom "the attribution of human
reversals of fortune . . . would have been common."[22]

Consider, for example, these comments by Plutarch:

> But, in spite of this condition of affairs, some persons, through their
> foolishness, are so silly and conceited, that when only a little ex-
> alted, either because of abundance of money, or importance of of-
> fice, or petty political preferments, or because of position and
> repute, they threaten and insult those in lower station, not bearing
> in mind the uncertainty and inconstancy of fortune, nor yet the fact
> that the lofty is easily brought low and the humble in turn is ex-
> alted, transposed by the swift-moving changes of fortune.[23]

Luke, of course, credits God, not *Tyche/Fortuna* (fortune), with
this power to effect reversals in human affairs. As York noted: "For the
person in Luke's audience still living under the value system of the
world, enjoying honor and prestige and despising the outcast, Luke's
message was one of harsh warning. For the societal misfits and poor
who had believed in Christ, Luke's Gospel offered a message of confirming hope."[24]

So far we have seen that Luke had access to a collection of parables that he incorporated into his Gospel. What is significant is not the mere fact that there was a pre-Lukan source; instead, what is significant is the *way* in which Luke appropriated that material in the service of the larger narrative. Thus it is the way in which those parables are performed in the Gospel context that is significant. We now shift our attention from the Gospel to Acts. In Acts we will see a similar interpretive scheme at work in the Lukan narrative.[25]

Hearing Luke's Story of Paul in the Context of the Corpus Paulinum

Since Philipp Vielhauer's influential 1950 essay "Zum 'Paulinismus' der Apostelgeschichte," the dominant critical position has been that there is little connection between the Paul of Acts and the Paul of the epistles. [26] In the areas of natural theology, the Jewish law, Christology/ redemption, and eschatology, Vielhauer found irreconcilable contrast between the two. That position, however, has not gone unchallenged. Peder Borgen, for example, argues for a continuity of theological development between Paul and the author of Acts, and more recently, William O. Walker Jr. defends and expands arguments made in 1938 by Morton S. Enslin that Luke knew and was influenced by Paul's letters, and, moreover, that there were reasonable explanations concerning why Luke did not mention the letters or even that Paul wrote letters.[27]

We continue the discussion from the theoretical approach of the authorial audience. How would an audience familiar with Paul through his letters "hear" Luke's story of Paul in Acts? We will examine points of contact between the Paul of Acts and of the letters in the areas of Paul as rhetor, miracle-worker, apostle, and theologian. We will demonstrate that while the Paul of the letters and the Paul of Acts are not identical, there is plenty of continuity between them.

As we noted in chapter 2, the practice of ancient rhetoric pervaded the Hellenistic world in which Luke and Paul lived.[28] Despite serious challenges, a spate of studies exploring various rhetorical dimensions of Paul's writings have appeared over the past two decades.[29] Stanley Porter has observed: "In the study of rhetoric and the New Testament, in recent times more attention has been given to the Pauline letters than to any other part of the New Testament."[30] Beginning with the publication of Hans Dieter Betz's commentary on Galatians, a number of studies have explored the rhetorical genre and the arrangement of the constituent parts of individual Pauline letters.[31] These studies rarely agree in

their rhetorical analysis, generating some skepticism regarding the usefulness of applying rhetorical theory to epistolary material in general
and to Paul's epistles in particular. [32] Nonetheless, these studies do represent progress in our understanding as a comparison of Betz's rather
blunted rhetorical analysis of Galatians with the more subtle treatment
of 1 Corinthians by his student, Margaret Mitchell, demonstrates.

Furthermore, the study of Paul's rhetorical style, in light of the
handbook tradition, while in its infancy in comparison to the question
of genre and arrangement, provides further confirmation that Paul was
familiar with rhetorical practice, even if he may not have known all the
technical nomenclature for the various tropes and figures that he most
clearly (even if unconsciously) utilizes. At various places, Paul uses
metonymy (Quintilian, 8.6.23, Ps-Cicero, *Ad Her.*, 4.32.43; "by his
blood" is a metonymy for death in Rom 5:9–10), synecdoche (Quintilian,
8.6.19–22, 9.3.58–59, Ps-Cicero, *Ad Herennium* 4.33.44–45; "Moses" is
used to refer to the whole Pentateuch in 2 Cor 3:15), antonomasia
(Quintilian, 8.6.29–30, Ps-Cicero, *Ad Herennium* 4.31.42; the descriptive phrase "the one to come" is substituted for the name of Christ in
Rom 5:14), hyperbole (Ps-Cicero, *Ad Herennium* 4.33.44; Paul claims
even if an angel preaches "another gospel," it should be rejected in Gal
1:8), litotes (Alexander, *Fig.* 2.23; Paul says he is "not ashamed of the
gospel" in Rom 1:16), anadiplosis (Alexander, *Fig.* 2.2; "but if children,
even heirs; heirs of God and joint heirs of Christ" in Rom 8:17), anaphora (Demetrius, *Eloc.* 141; phrases beginning with ἐν [*en*] nine times
in 2 Cor 6:4–10), polyptoton (Quintilian, 9.1.34), use of the same word
in multiple cases and/or number in Gal 1:1), paronomasia (Quintilian,
9.3.66–67, Ps-Cicero, *Ad Herennium* 4.21.29–32), play on homonyms
κρίνω (*krinō*) ["judge"] and κατακρίνω, *katakrinō*, [condemn] in Rom
2:1), and polysyndeton (Quintilian, 9.3.51–54; repetition of the negative
οὔτε [*oute*] in Rom 8:38–39; see also repetition of καί, *kai*, in Rom 9:4),
to name a few. [33] Of course, the evidence is too slender to argue conclu-
sively that Paul received formal rhetorical training. Nonetheless, even
within the context of the passage where Paul claims that his "speech and
proclamation were not with plausible/persuasive words of wisdom"
(1 Cor 2:4), Paul uses a variety of rhetorical strategies—antithesis (1 Cor
1:17), anaphora and litotes (1:26), antistrophe (1:26–28), accumulation
(2:1–5), and enthymemes (2:10). [34] A survey of the available literature
that explores the rhetoric of Paul's letters then leads us to agree with
Stanley Porter's conclusion that "so long as one is aware of the limits of
claims made for Pauline rhetoric, rhetorical categories can be profitably
used to interpret Paul's letters." [35]

Pauline Rhetoric in Acts

How would an audience familiar with Paul's rhetorical strategies in his letters respond to the speeches of Paul in Acts? Again, though recent works have marked differences in detail, the cumulative effect of these studies (noting in various speeches the use of major components of rhetorical speech), in our opinion, has been to demonstrate that the narrator and characters of Acts were familiar with the devices and strategies of ancient rhetoric as practiced during the Hellenistic period.[36] Much of the narrator's familiarity is communicated through the speeches of various characters in Acts, and of these characters in Acts, Paul is preeminent in his knowledge of rhetorical conventions.[37]

Recently, Derek Hogan has shown convincingly that Paul's defense speech in Acts 24 shows remarkable affinity with the component parts of a forensic speech as outlined by Quintilian.[38] For Quintilian the forensic speech consists of an *exordium* (introduction), *narratio* (statement of facts), *probatio* (proof), *refutatio* (refutation), and *peroratio* (conclusion) (see 3.9.1).[39] According to Hogan, Paul's speech before Felix (Acts 24:10b–21) contains several of these parts: *exordium* (10b); *narratio* (11–18a); and *probatio* (18b–21).[40] The speech lacks a *peroratio* (conclusion) because Felix interrupts Paul.[41] It also lacks, in Hogan's analysis, a *refutatio*, though this part of a forensic speech was not always recognized as a discreet element (see Aristotle, *Rhetoric*, 2.26). Furthermore, according to Ben Witherington,[42] Paul's speech before Agrippa (26:2–29) conforms even more closely to the rhetorical pattern: *exordium* (2–3); *narratio* (4–21); *probatio* (22–23); *refutatio* (25–26); and *peroratio* (27–29).[43]

What one may reasonably conclude from these and other studies is that Paul is no less skilled in rhetoric in Acts than he is in his letters; and, on the issue of Paul the rhetor, a first-century audience would have seen basic continuity between the letters and Acts. Furthermore, the audience would be led to conclude both from the epistles and from Acts that Paul's skill in rhetoric contributes to an understanding that Paul was a well educated man of high social status and impeccable moral virtue.[44]

Paul the Miracle-Worker

Miracles in the Ancient Mediterranean World

What does the authorial audience bring to the text concerning miracles? In the ancient Mediterranean world, miracles could be employed to demonstrate divinity and, therefore, win converts to a religious cult.[45] To cite only one example, in Apuleius's *Metamorphosis*, the protagonist Lucius is changed from a donkey back into a man by the goddess Isis, and thereafter becomes her follower and is initiated into her cult (*Metam.* 11). Miracles could also serve to encourage and strengthen the devotion among the members of the cult, as seen in the collection of miracles cited by Strabo for the Serapeum at Canopus.[46] The healing testimonies written in shrines of Asclepius may also have functioned in this manner. The term "signs" (σημεῖα, *sēmeia*) is typically used for these events, as is the stock phrase "signs and wonders" (σημεῖα καὶ τέρατα, *sēmeia kai terata*), a phrase that will particularly concern us. In the Greek world, the phrase "signs and wonders" generally referred to "portents which presaged important events."[47]

In the Jewish environment, miracles functioned in three ways: (1) to attest to a divine legitimating of a position, a person, or God; (2) to prove a person's innocence or righteousness, and (3) to win acknowledgment that the God of Israel was superior to other deities.[48] In the Jewish environment, both Philo and Josephus use the phrase "signs and wonders" in the Greek manner as portents of future events; however, as Leo O'Reilly points out, they also employ an Old Testament meaning, which will be more immediate to the New Testament usage, in which the miracles function to "show the divine origin of a word or revelation which accompanied them," as seen particularly in the Deuteronomic history.[49]

Miracles in the Pauline Corpus

In the New Testament, the phrase "signs and wonders" was often combined with "power" (δύναμις, *dynamis*) as evidence of the Holy Spirit's action in a legitimating and encouraging function, drawing on the Old Testament notion of God's spirit as creative power in action.[50] In Hebrews 2:1–4, for example, the audience is encouraged to pay close attention to the gospel message so as to adhere firmly to it, since the message of salvation was declared by Jesus, attested to by those who heard him, "as God also witnessed by signs and wonders and various powers and by gifts of the Holy Spirit according to his will." P. J. Gräbe argues for the pneumatological emphasis of δύναμις (*dynamis*) in Paul's letters, placing particular emphasis on Paul's understanding in Rom 15:19 that his ministry, his apostolate, is accomplished by God, but with the emphasis on the action of the Holy Spirit.[51]

Paul is somewhat cryptic in his references to his own miracles, but he refers to these phenomena in five of the undisputed letters. In 1 Thess

1:5, the word is shown true by the power of the Holy Spirit, which Paul uses to remind the community what kind of people "we were among you," so that the miracles are being employed both to evoke faith and to legitimate Paul's own position. The same kind of emphasis occurs in Gal 3:1–5, in which Paul reminds the community that their faith was elicited by the demonstrated power of the Spirit, and therefore that they received the faith through his efforts rather than those of his opponents. Paul recalls for the Corinthian community that his word came not in wisdom but "in demonstration (ἀποδείξει, *apodeixei*) of the Spirit and power (δυνάμεως, *dynameōs*) . . . that your faith may rest in the power of God" (ἐν δυνάμει θεοῦ, *en dynamei theou*; 1 Cor 2:4–5); again, miracles once helped to evoke faith and now serve to support his position. All the terms come together for the same purposes in 2 Cor 12:12: "The signs of the apostle were worked among you in all endurance, by signs and wonders and powerful deeds (σημείοις τε καὶ τέρασιν καὶ δυνάμεσιν, *sēmeiois te kai terasin kai dynamesin*)." In his letter to the Romans, Paul relates the ministry of Christ's words through him to win the Gentiles, "by word and deed, by the power of signs and wonders, by the power of the Spirit" (ἐν δυνάμει σημείων καὶ τεράτων, ἐν δυνάμει πνεύματος, *en dynamei sēmeiōn kai teratōn, en dynamei pneumatos*; 15:18–19).

From the wider environment and from Paul's letters, then, the authorial audience brings a concept of signs and wonders, especially combined with power and the action of the Holy Spirit, as God legitimating his own word, and, by extension, the word and action of carrier of the true tradition, all to induce saving faith.

Paul the Miracle-Worker in Acts

One of the ways Luke shows the legitimation of the true Jesus tradition as it is passed on from Jesus, to the Twelve, to Paul is by the occurrence of miracles.[52] Miracles evoke faith, legitimate one's positions or words, and demonstrate one's innocence or righteousness.[53] O'Reilly notes that Acts deliberately invokes the Old Testament use of signs and wonders.[54] In Acts, this theme begins in the second chapter. In 2:18–19, Peter quotes Joel 3:1–5, "In those days I shall pour out my spirit, and they shall prophesy. And I shall show wonders (τέρατα, *terata*) in the heaven above and signs (σημεῖα, *sēmeia*) on the earth below."[55] Immediately Peter argues the fulfillment of the prophecy is in Jesus, who was "attested (ἀποδεδειγμένον, *apodedeigmenon*) to you by God with powers and wonders and signs (δυνάμεσι καὶ τέρατα καὶ σημείοις, *denamesi kai terata kai sēmeiois*) which God worked through him"

(2:22). The audience, bringing 1 Cor 2:4–5 to the table, now hears the demonstration of the spirit and power of God through signs and wonders taken back to the core of the true tradition with Jesus, a tradition which builds upon the Old Testament and its witness to the power of God for salvation.

"Signs and wonders" quickly becomes a stock phrase in Acts to show the continuation of the legitimate tradition from Jesus to the apostles (2:43; 4:30; 5:12; 6:8).[56] Stephen invokes Moses as a performer of signs and wonders (7:36), reminding the audience of the legitimating tradition that began in the Old Testament narrative of the power of salvation in history. The audience is specifically drawn into the story of Paul and Barnabas as legitimate authorities of the tradition beginning in Acts 13:4–12, when the proconsul believes the word when he sees Paul blind Elymas. This story is the first of many satisfying expansions of Paul's cryptic description of "signs and wonders." The audience soon hears the Lord in the narrative witness to the legitimacy of Paul and Barnabas as they preached his word, "giving signs and wonders to be done by their hands" (14:3); immediately, a specific example is portrayed to the audience as Paul heals a lame man (14:8–10). The narrative emphasis builds as the audience hears the assembly at Jerusalem told by Paul and Barnabas about the "signs and wonders God worked through them among the Gentiles" (15:12), then hears the council's favorable judgment on the Gentile mission as an extension of the true Jesus tradition. Paul's insistence in the letters that such signs and wonders show legitimacy is here given powerful support and expanded for the audience within the larger narrative of the early church. The point now made, the audience continues to hear support and specific examples of the miracles they heard about in general terms in the Pauline epistles (Acts 16:18; 19:11; 20:10); moreover, Luke also expands the use of miracles to include the proof of innocence or righteousness (Acts 28:5–10).

Peder Borgen points out that Paul uses "signs and wonders" as proof of his apostleship, and that a similar spectrum of meaning is found in Acts, so that Luke considers Paul a miracle-worker, though not an apostle.[57] We suggest that Luke's use of signs and wonders supports his reference to Paul and Barnabas as apostles (Acts 14:13); in other words, the audience hears the expansion of Paul's cryptic references, an expansion that legitimates him as bearer of the true tradition that originated with Jesus by placing his miracles in the context of those of other disciples and emphasizing the role of the Spirit. This legitimation leads us into the next topic for consideration, Paul the Apostle.

Paul the Apostle

Paul, the Epistolary Apostle

An intriguing topic is the profound silence of Acts on the fact of Paul's letter-writing itself; surely, one would think, an audience would wonder why Luke puts forth no explicit evidence of letters as part of Paul's missionary efforts.[58] The expectations of the audience, however, may have been different than we initially anticipate. Consider, for example, Sallust's *The War with Catiline*. Despite the plethora of evidence Cicero left on the dramatic events of 64–63 B.C.E. (speeches, personal correspondence, and poetry), as well as the fact that the statesman Cicero was known primarily as an orator, Sallust spends only one line on one of the greatest speeches of Cicero's career, the "First Oration against Catiline": "Then the consul Marcus Tullius . . . delivered a brilliant oration beneficial to the state, which he later wrote out and published."[59] Philostratus' *Lives of the Sophists* offers another example. In his section on Favorinus, Philostratus reprints only one brief statement and one line of a letter by the philosopher, and both examples are offered only to illustrate certain personal relations (8.490). While Philostratus includes a brief section on the style of Favorinus, singling out his dissertation on philosophy for particular praise, he grants a very small amount of space, relative to the whole, to this consideration of the philosopher's writing, and that in a biography devoted only to this man. [60]

Furthermore, if we consider the reason for Paul's letter writing, we also find no reason for the audience to expect its mention. In "The Apostolic Parousia: Form and Significance," Robert Funk discusses the Aristotelian and Hellenistic motif of the presence of parties to one another through letters and argues that the same structural elements in Paul's letters reveal a similar understanding; the letters, in fact, substitute for Paul's apostolic presence.[61] For Paul, the significance of his presence is more profound than was the case in Greek examples. Passages such as 1 Cor 5:3–5 show that "Paul must have thought of his presence as the bearer of charismatic, one might even say, eschatological power."[62] An audience familiar with the Pauline letters, therefore, would not necessarily expect a narrative placing Paul in a larger context to discuss the epistolary aspect of his ministry. There is no need in the logic of the Acts narrative to record Paul's absence and thus the need to mention his letter writing activity is eliminated. Acts, rather, expands the audience's knowledge of Paul to other aspects of his ministry (speeches, for example), highlighting similarity to other disciples. The focus on Paul as epistolary author is a modern preoccupation.

Paul, Apostolic Laborer and Athlete

Paul uses examples of his own suffering endurance in his letters to legitimate his claim as carrier of the true apostolic tradition. Two aspects of Paul's conception of his ministry as a struggle of endurance are: (1) his material self-support, and (2) his use of athletic imagery. In 1 Corinthians, part of Paul's defense of his true apostleship is the fact that he earns his own way. In 1 Cor 9:1–18, Paul insists that he has not claimed the right of material support for the work of his ministry: "We have not used (ἐχρησάμεθα, echrēsametha) this right, but we endure everything lest we place any obstacle against the gospel of Christ" (9:12); repetition emphasizes his point: "I have used (κέχρημαι, kechrēmai) none of these rights" (9:15). One of the many sufferings of the true apostles, in fact, is working with their own hands (1 Cor 4:12).[63] In Acts, Paul reminds the elders in Ephesus that his own hands took care of his needs (χρείαις, chreiais), a reminder that provides a leadership model for them (20:33–34). The reference is brief but comes in a crucial speech, his farewell address to believers. The audience of Acts, then, receives a consistent picture of the place Paul's material independence can play in his understanding of his ministry.

Paul employs athletic metaphors for his self-understanding of his role a total of four times in three of the undisputed letters, almost exclusively in the image of his mission as a race to run, adhering to the "course prescribed for him by God."[64] In Gal 2:2, Paul relates how he traveled to the apostles in Jerusalem to describe the message he preached to the Gentiles, "lest I somehow should be running (τρέχω, trechō) or had run (ἔδραμον, edramon) in vain."[65] Training is an element in the imagery as well. In Phil 2:16, Paul encourages the community to live faithfully the Christian life "so that in the day of Christ I may boast that I did not run (ἔδραμον, edramon) in vain or labor (ἐκοπίασα, ekopiasa) in vain," where "labor" in this context should be taken as a metaphor of athletic training.[66] Paul uses the metaphor for the Christian lives of other believers as well, showing that it is not only his own apostolic mission that he sees in these terms of endurance (Gal 5:7; 1 Cor 9:24).

In Acts, Paul first applies the metaphor of a racecourse to the mission of John the Baptist: "And as John was completing the course (δρόμον, dromon), he said, 'Who do you suppose that I am?'" (13:25). Although this instance differs from applying it to a Christian community, he is nonetheless applying the metaphor to a mission other than his own. In Acts 20:24, Paul asserts that his only desire is to "finish my course (δρόμον, *dromon*) and the ministry which I received from the Lord Jesus." A reminder of the training aspect of the metaphor appears in Acts 24:16, in which Paul asserts, "I always train (ἀσκῶ, *askō*) to have a clear conscience." [67] The use of the athletic imagery by Paul in Acts is too infrequent to argue for a substantial expansion of that metaphor found in his letters. But enough echoes appear at important points to assure the audience that this is the Paul they know from the letters. This is the Paul who teaches that the only way to live a call from God is with the self-discipline, exertion and endurance of an athlete, whether the call is a prophetic one like John's, an apostolic one like his own, or one to the Christian life in general. Neither the insistence on his material independence nor the use of athletic metaphors is, of course, decisive on its own, but they have a cumulative effect of assuring the audience that this figure is indeed the Paul they hear in the epistles.

Paul, the Suffering Apostle

Ernst Haenchen contends that while Paul is a great miracle-worker in Acts, Paul in the letters did not "overcome all obstacles by miraculous means—an apostle must plunge into the depths of suffering and *there* experience the help of Christ."[68] As we have seen, the narrative of Acts did not describe Paul using miracles magically to "overcome all obstacles" but rather to evoke faith and to legitimate his position, as Paul does in the letters. In the case of suffering, as well, we shall hear from the audience's perspective a confluence of the author of the letters with the figure in Acts.

Paul employs forms of πάσχω (*paschō*, Rom 8:17–18; Gal 3:4; 1 Cor 12:26; 2 Cor 1:3–8; Phil 2:9, 3:10; 1 Thess 2:2, 14) and, more often, θλῖψις (*thlipsis*, 2 Cor 1:3–8; 6:4; 7:4; 8:2; Phil 1:17; 4:14; 1 Thess 1:6; 3:3; 3:7; Rom 5:3; 8:35; 12:12) for suffering.[69] The latter term was commonly used in the LXX for various types of affliction, but "its theological significance arose from the fact that it predominantly denotes the oppression and affliction of the people of Israel or of the righteous who represent Israel."[70] The term is always used in the New Testament for people of the church, members of the body of Christ, who therefore share in the sufferings of his body, and sometimes explicitly in the sense of eschatological tribulation.[71] This eschatological sense it shared with Judaism (Dan 12:1; *As. Mos.* 8:1; *4 Ezra* 13:16–19; *2 Bar.* 25:1ff.).

In his letters, Paul describes his suffering in some detail. "Ill-clothed, buffeted and homeless" are only a few of his struggles (1 Cor

4:11); he is also in danger from the Jews, from the Gentiles, and at sea (2 Cor 11:23–33). One interpretative option for Paul's "thorn in the flesh" (2 Cor 12:7) has been his apostolic sufferings at the hands of his enemies.[72] These trials are crucial to and expected in apostleship, and Paul does not discuss this suffering outside the topic of his service to God (2 Cor 6:4–10). The afflictions are necessary because they are part of the suffering of Christ, to the point that Paul can say that the missionaries carry in the body the death of Jesus (2 Cor 4:10; see Phil 1:17). The true followers, then, will share in the apostolic sufferings as well:

> Blessed by God the Father of our Lord Jesus Christ . . . who comforts us in all our affliction (θλίψει, *thlipsei*); for as we share abundantly in Christ's sufferings (παθήματα, *pathēmata*), thus through Christ we share abundantly in comfort . . . If we are afflicted (θλιβόμεθα, *thlibometha*), it is for your comfort and salvation; and if we are comforted, it is for your comfort, which you experience when you patiently endure the same sufferings (παθημάτων, *pathēmatōn*) that we suffer (πάσχομεν, *paschomen*) . . . you share in our sufferings (παθημάτων, *pathēmatōn*; 2 Cor 1:3–8; Cf. 1 Thess 1:6).

Paul himself, moreover, connects closely in his own letter the active power of the Holy Spirit with suffering as proof of apostleship that is worthy of imitation:

> Our gospel came to you not only in word, but also in power (δυνάμει, *dynamei*) and in the Holy Spirit and in full conviction, for you know what kind of men we proved to be among you for your sake. And you became imitators of us and of the Lord, receiving the word in much affliction (θλίψει, *thlipsei*) with joy from the Holy Spirit, so that you became a model to all the believers in Macedonian and in Achaia. (1 Thess 1:5–7)

Not only apostles, then, but also all believers will suffer and must remain firm in faith. Paul sent Timothy to Thessalonica to establish the believers in their faith, "that no one be moved by these afflictions (θλίψεσιν, *thlipsesin*). You yourselves know that this is to be our lot. For when we were with you, we told you beforehand that we were about to suffer (θλίβεσθαι, *thlibesthai*); just as it has happened and as you know" (1 Thess 3:3–4). Suffering has the positive role of producing endurance for the path (Rom 5:3), but can never separate the believer from the love of Christ (Rom 8:35). The believers, therefore, must be "patient in affliction (θλίψει, *thlipsei*) and constant in prayer" (Rom 12:12). Suffering is necessary and the true followers follow models and become models themselves.

Listening to Acts, the audience quickly receives a picture of suffering apostleship within which to understand the Paul of the epistles. Not only does Jesus proclaim that he must suffer and die (Lk 9:22; 19:31–33, etc.), but, for Jesus' followers in Acts, suffering for the gospel is established as necessary long before the account of Paul begins to dominate the narrative (Acts 4:1–3; 5:17–18; 6:12; 7:54; 8:3; 12:1–5). The audience is, in fact, introduced to Paul in the midst of the profound suffering of Stephen, and is repeatedly reminded of Paul's role in the suffering of the church (7:60–8:3; 9:1–2; 22:4–5; 26:9–11).

The narrative of Acts fills out Paul's experiences of suffering and expands the knowledge of the audience with specific examples of his endangerment by Gentiles (14:5; 16:19–24, etc.), Jews (13:50; 14:2, 19, etc.), and his travels at sea (27:13–44). The terms Paul employs in the epistles move through Acts in an intriguing way. Forms of πάσχω (*paschō*) are used in reference to the necessity of Christ's suffering, first proclaimed by Peter (3:18), then twice by Paul (17:3; 26:23). In between, God applies the term to the necessity of Paul's suffering in his instructions to Ananias (9:16).[73] Though this reference is almost mysteriously cryptic at this point in the narrative, the audience who knows Paul's letters already understands its crucial importance to Paul's discipleship.

The audience hears the term θλῖψις (*thlipsis*) first in Stephen's speech, concerning Joseph: "but God was with him and rescued him from all his afflictions" (ἐκ πασῶν τῶν θλίψεων, *ek pasōn tōn thlipseōn;* 7:9–10). The fathers suffered great affliction (θλῖψις μεγάλη, *thlipsis megalē*) as well by the famine in Egypt and Canaan (7:11).[74] Later, they hear that those believers "who were scattered because of the persecution (θλίψεως, *thlipseōs*) that arose over Stephen traveled as far as Phoenicia and Cyprus and Antioch, speaking the word to none except Jews" (11:19).[75] Soon, θλῖψις (*thlipsis*) recurs with reference to the next "questionable" inheritors of the true tradition, Paul and Barnabas. Paul is stoned and left for dead outside the city; then, with near-miraculous strength and courage, he gets up and reenters the city. When Paul and Barnabas "had preached the gospel to that city and had made many disciples," they returned to Lystra, Iconium, and Antioch, "strengthening the souls of the disciples, exhorting them to continue in the faith, and saying that through many tribulations (διὰ πολλῶν θλίψεων, *dia pollōn thlipseōn*) we must enter the kingdom of God. And when they had appointed elders for them in every church, with prayer and fasting they committed them to the Lord in whom they believed (14:19–23)." Later, the term recurs on Paul's own lips in his farewell address to depositors of the tradition, the Ephesian elders: "the Holy Spirit testifies to me in each city that imprisonment and afflictions (θλίψεις, *thlipseis*) await me"

(20:23). He continues immediately with the importance of accomplishing his ministry, using an athletic metaphor (20:24).

In Paul's final recounting of his call in Acts 26, moreover, his apostolic vocation as the apostle who suffers for Christ has strong parallels with his own self-understanding in Gal 1. In both accounts, he recounts his life in Judaism with focus on his own persecution of the church (Gal 1:13; Acts 26:10–11) and his zeal for Jewish traditions (Acts 26:4; see Phil 3:5–6).

In Acts, he was "set apart" (26:15), in Galatians, "appointed" (1:15). In Acts, Christ says that he is appearing to Paul for his mission to the Gentiles (26:16–18); in Galatians, Paul describes Christ as revealed to him for his mission to the Gentiles (1:16). In Galatians, Paul goes on to describe his persecution by the Jews who seized and tried to kill him (1:21), events already related in Acts that have led Paul to this situation. The Acts narrative, then, develops for the audience what they already know in part from the letters: Paul was right that afflictions are a necessary part of his vocation as an apostle. The expansion in areas of detail shows that Paul fits the pattern of the suffering ones who belong to the suffering messiah.

The above consideration of the importance of suffering to apostleship leads us directly into Paul the theologian.

Paul the Theologian

Atonement

When Paul discusses atonement, he is clear that the death of Jesus has salvific significance. In 1 Cor 15:3–11, Paul reports the saving tradition he received, that "Christ died for our sins in accordance with the scriptures, that he was buried, that he was raised on the third day" (15:3–4). Quickly, however, Paul says, "If Christ has not been raised, your faith is futile and you are yet in your sins" (15:17), placing both death and resurrection in tandem to effect the release of sins for the believer. The entire context, of course, is Paul's mission to the Gentiles. In 15:20, Paul goes on to describe Christ risen from the dead as "first fruits of those who have fallen asleep." In 2 Cor 5:14–15, Paul says "we are convinced that one died for all; therefore, all have died. And he died for all so that those who lived might live no longer for themselves but for him who for them died and was raised." Romans 8:17–18 connects the sufferings of Christ and the believers with the glorification of Christ and the future glorification of the believers (see Phil 3:10–11). The death and resurrection of Christ are preached in the context of Paul's sense of his own mission to the Gentiles (Gal 1).

The idea that the death of Jesus realizes atonement in Luke-Acts has often been dismissed.[76] David Moessner, however, examines the movement of plot in Luke-Acts to show how the narrative develops a picture of God's salvific plan that has three steps: (1) the rejection/suffering/death of Jesus → (2) the raising of Jesus → (3) the preaching of this light to Israel and the Gentiles.[77] Moessner shows that the emphasis in the narrative is on the death of Jesus for atonement, though Luke's characteristic phrase for atonement is "the release/forgiveness of sins."[78] Heard in this light, the suffering of Paul and his proclamation that Jesus must suffer (26:23) illuminates Luke's understanding of God's plan. The close connection in God's plan between the death and resurrection, that together result in the believer no longer living in his or her sins (1 Cor 15:3, 17), belongs both to the Paul of the letters and the narrative of Acts. Surely, then, the audience would hear the association and would not be especially surprised to hear Paul in Acts say that Christ must suffer, be first to rise from the dead (1 Cor 15:20, 23), and would proclaim salvation to the Gentiles (Paul's entire ministry in his letters). Note as well in Acts 26, which we already discussed as being readily comparable to Paul's self-understanding in Gal 1, that the persecution of Paul is followed closely by his declaration that the Christ must suffer.[79] Likewise, in Paul's speech in Acts to the Ephesian elders, a speech filled with references to his own suffering as well as the future suffering of the church (20:22-23, 29-30), the audience would hear the justification of the believer by God through Christ's blood (Rom 3:35; 5:8-9), echoed when Paul encourages the leaders to care for the church God obtained "through the blood of his own" (Acts 20:28).[80]

What, then, would auditors hear in Acts if they knew Paul's preaching of the Christ who died for us and was raised, and that we, whether apostles or believers, would share in those sufferings and hope to be raised as well, since the light of salvation was preached by Paul to the Gentiles? The audience has this teaching confirmed in Acts but placed in the larger salvific plan that the messianic light to Israel is the same light being preached to the Gentiles.

Natural Theology

Commentators have seen an irreconcilable difference between the Paul of the letters and of Acts in the area of so-called "natural theology," revealed by a comparison of Romans 1 with the Areopagus speech of Acts 17.[81] Actually, a comparison of the two chapters reveals striking similarities:

1. Acts 17:16 relates that Paul was provoked by the idols in Athens, and Rom 1 is a blanket condemnation of idolatry, so, despite Paul's accommodating tone in the Areopagus speech, the underlying reason is of the same content and character as in the Paul heard in the letters (see 1 Thess 1:9–10).

2. Natural theology is admitted in both passages: God the creator can be known in some manner from his works.

3. The kindness and generosity of God is assumed (Rom 2:4; Acts 17:30).

4. The command now is to repent (Rom 2:4; Acts 17:36).

5. The climax to both passages is eschatological (Rom 2:16; Acts 17:31).

The substantive difference comes primarily with the understanding of humans' and God's actions. In Romans, people are "without excuse" and, therefore, God responded by handing them over to their passions (repeated three times for emphasis). In Acts, people are led to the truth, and God has overlooked their ignorance to this point (17:30). Human responsibility is great in Romans, but not as great in Acts.

Commentators attempting to reconcile these two passages generally do so on the basis of the divergent contexts of the pagan, philosophically-minded audience of Acts 17 and the committed Jewish and Gentile Christian audience of Romans. [82] Do the dissimilar contexts so alter the message that the audience hears a profound disjuncture? The shaping of the Areopagus speech to the theme of ignorance is not surprising, since ignorance is a theme in Luke-Acts (Luke 23:34; Acts 3:17; 13:27), but the ignorance is subsumed to greater divine will. [83] The context in Romans is the explanation of why all people, Gentiles and Jews, are guilty and in need of redemption. The point of both is, of course, salvation. In both Romans and in Acts, then, Paul is provoked by idolatry and emphasizes natural theology within an eschatological framework; the Areopagus speech, however, is meant to expand the audience's knowledge of Paul into different situations and contexts, while Romans is explicatory of a substantially different concern. Given the strikingly different contexts, the similarities are more remarkable than the tensions. Hearing the common components, the audience would probably hear the difference as primarily one of context, and, having heard the Areopagus speech and Romans, they would have samples of the Paul who could be all things to all people in hopes of winning as many as possible.

Law

Some commentators point out that Paul's strict attitude toward the Jewish law in his letter is simply not found in Paul's speeches in Acts.[84] While it is certainly true that the role of the law is not nearly so developed as in Galatians and Romans, is there no echo of the epistles in Acts, enough that the audience recognizes the Paul of the epistles? Acts 13:38 is commonly recognized as the closest parallel to Paul's thought on the law in Luke-Acts, in which Paul in Antioch of Pisidia states that through belief in Jesus through whom forgiveness of sins is proclaimed, one can be justified from everything from which they were "not able to be justified in the law of Moses" (οὐκ ἠδυνήθητε ἐν νόμῳ Μωϋσέως, *ouk ēdynēthēte en nomōi Mouses*).[85] In Romans 8:2–3, Paul says that God has done "what was not possible by the law" (τὸ γὰρ ἀδύνατον τοῦ νόμου, *to gar adynaton tou nomou*). Vielhauer points out major differences between Acts 13 and Paul's letters; most commentators concur that Luke is simply not clear about the gist of Paul's thought here.[86] In so doing, however, they implicitly admit Luke is attempting to evoke Paul's actual words.

In his important monograph *Luke and the Law*, Stephen Wilson points out that the law is a major issue for Luke only in relation to Stephen and Paul and becomes the central theme with Paul.[87] Luke, Wilson argues, is intent on defending Paul's innocence against charges that he abandoned the law and encouraged others to do so, profaned the temple, and generally caused trouble. When he closely examines the three major problematic pericopes concerning Paul and the law in Acts, the circumcision of Timothy (16:1–3), the Nazirite vow (21:17–27), and the appearance before the Sanhedrin (22:30–23:5), Wilson finds tension with Paul's letters only in the circumcision of Timothy, and even then he considers that such an incident could have caused the rumors of Gal 5:11.[88] From the perspective of the ancient audience, we would contend, the circumcision of Timothy could have provided a full context for an allusion in Galatians, a context that explained that the circumcision was based on expediency rather than theology; hence, there would be few grounds for contradiction between Acts 16 and Gal 5. The audience, moreover, could come away from a hearing of 1 Cor 9:19–23 with the impression that Paul would go to this great a length to win converts. So the circumcision of Timothy would not provide enough tension to make the audience consider that this was a quite different Paul than the man who wrote the epistles.

Wilson concludes that it is not the law *per se* that interests Luke, but rather, Paul himself and the rehabilitation of Paul's "contentious reputation."[89] As I. H. Marshall maintains, the difference in the attitude of Paul's letters toward the law and that in Acts is one of emphasis.[90] The letters emphasize Gentile freedom, while Acts portrays Paul as not opposed to Jewish Christians continuing a basically Jewish way of life.[91] The audience would hear in Acts a defense of Paul's actions little concerned with the theological aspect of an issue already settled for them.

Summary

What then may we conclude about what an authorial audience, familiar with some of Paul's letters, would have heard in Luke's story of Paul? Peder Borgen points out that in 1 Cor 15:1–11, Paul expands the traditions of the earliest church to include his own life and missionary activity. Borgen draws a parallel between this expansion and Luke-Acts, arguing that it is therefore not necessarily a delay of the Parousia that prompted in Luke-Acts a combination of tradition and missionary activity.[92] This provides one piece of evidence for Borgen that the Pauline letters "illustrate the background for the theology of Luke."[93] We suggest a further parallel between Paul's recitation in 1 Cor 15:3–10 and Acts: Acts, by cryptically evoking broader themes in Paul and by expanding some of Paul's cryptic references, demonstrates that Paul is exactly who he claims to be in that passage:

> Last of all, as to one born abnormally, he appeared also to me. For I am the least of the Apostles, who is not fit to be called an apostle, because I persecuted the church of God. But by the grace of God I am what I am, and his grace to me was not in vain. But I worked harder than any of them, though it was not I but the grace of God which is with me. Whether, therefore, it was I or they, thus we preach and thus you believed.

Luke's story of Paul recorded in Acts, expanding and condensing the story of Paul recorded in his epistles, would have been recognized by the authorial audience as essentially the same story. To reach this conclusion, one must assume that the author of Luke was familiar with Paul's thought. But is this familiarity derived from personal experience, oral tradition, or acquaintance with some unknown number of Paul's letters? Again, against critical consensus, our findings lead us to eliminate Luke's general familiarity with some amorphous, oral Pauline tradition. On the one hand, there is too much parallelism between Acts and the Epistles with regard to the use of rhetorical convention, the role and function of miracles in Paul's ministry, the understanding of the nature and shape of Paul's apostleship, and key elements of Paul's theology, to limit Luke's knowledge of Paul in this way. On the other hand, it would seem to us impossible to decide on the basis of the evidence presented whether Luke's knowledge of Paul was from personal acquaintance with him (taking the "we" passages as evidence of the narrator's first-hand knowledge of at least some of the events he records) or from an intimate knowledge of some of Paul's letters. If the former (personal acquaintance), then one would be led to conclude also that the Paul of the letters is essentially an accurate portrait of the "historical" Paul. We do not find this position particularly objectionable, but neither do we find it necessary. That is to say, if the authorial audience themselves knew Paul only through his letters, then the parallels would have been, strictly speaking, at a literary level—the authorial audience would have been comparing the character "Paul" portrayed in Acts with "Paul," whose narrative voice mediates the communication found in the letters. And at that level, we conclude that the authorial audience who knew Paul through his letters (and probably knew him *only* through those letters) would have recognized Luke's portrait of Paul as a reliable, though enriched and expanded, presentation of that same Apostle who through his rhetoric, miracles, suffering, and thought, proclaimed that "God was in Christ reconciling the world unto himself."

Conclusion

Luke was as adept in interpreting Christian traditions as he was in adapting pagan and Jewish concepts, conventions, and values. Whether modifying a parables collection to meet the needs of his narrative or constructing a portrait of Paul that was both coherent with the "Paul" known through his letters, Luke is sure-handed in his use of these materials to provide a "narrative of things fulfilled."

Notes

1. This chapter will not deal with the Synoptic problem of whether Luke used other written Gospels in composing his own, and if so, which ones and in what ways. Those questions have been well-worked already; see Thomas Longstaff, *The Synoptic Problem: A Bibliography, 1716–1988* (Macon, Ga.: Mercer University Press, 1988). Whatever model one may adopt for the relationship between the Synoptic Gospels, it is quite clear that some form of Christian traditions about the life of Jesus were already in existence—in whatever form— and Luke was not the first to write them (see Luke 1:1–4, the prologue to the Gospel).

2. Jeremias, *The Parables of Jesus;* and Dodd, *The Parables of the Kingdom.*

3. Scott, *Hear Then the Parable;* and Charles Hedrick, *Parables as Poetic Fictions: The Creative Voice of Jesus* (Peabody, Mass.: Hendrickson, 1994).

4. Dan O. Via, Jr., *The Parables: Their Literary and Existential Dimension* (Philadelphia: Fortress, 1967); also Robert W. Funk, *Parables and Presence* (Philadelphia: Fortress, 1982); and John Dominic Crossan, *In Parables: The Challenge of the Historical Jesus* (New York: Harper & Row, 1973).

5. Jeremias, *The Parables of Jesus,* 230.

6. Taken from his "Index of Synoptic Parables," in *The Parables of Jesus,* 247–48. Jeremias did not provide Lucan references for ##1, 8, 9, 10.

7. See Scott, *Hear Then the Parable,* 54–56, and passim throughout the commentary.

8. Scott, *Hear Then the Parable,* 73. Scott was well aware of the difficulties involved in categorizing the parables. After criticizing the categories of Adolf Jülicher (*Die Gleichnisreden Jesu* [Freiburg: J. C. B. Mohr, 1899]), Dodd, and Crossan, he commented (73): "These various organizational plans, by subordinating the parable to some scheme outside the parable, view the individual parable from the perspective of that scheme. Jülicher's instinct to treat the parables individually was correct, since such a method allows for a parable to develop its own polysemy [multiple meanings] without reference to an overall scheme. And yet an interpreter's mind recoils at a purely random arrangement of the parables. Is there no scheme or pattern that would at least help to organize them?"

9. Scott, *Hear Then the Parable,* 74.

10. Scott, *Hear Then the Parable,* vii–xi.

11. This list is adapted from Culpepper, "Luke," 297. It includes, in addition to parables unique to Luke, parables found in the so-called "triple tradition material" (Matthew, Mark, and Luke) and those shared in common between Matthew and Luke. Though Culpepper's list is representative of what may be called a critical consensus, there is, of course, disagreement about what constitutes a parable in Luke. Hedrick, for example, does not count 14:7–11 as a parable (see "Appendix B" in *The Parables as Poetic Fiction,* 252–53); see also the lists of parables in Jeremias, Dodd, Scott, and Via.

12. Here I am basically following Craig Blomberg, "Midrash, Chaismus, and the Outline of Luke's Central Section," in *Studies in Midrash and Historiography* (ed., R. T. France and David Wenham; Gospel Perspectives 3; Sheffield: JSOT Press, 1983), 240–44, though my assessment of the overall rhetorical effect of the "L" source differs significantly from his.

13. See, e.g., Jeremias, Hedrick, etc.

14. So, e.g., Hedrick, *The Parables as Poetic Fiction,* 252.

15. The narrative audience of the centerpiece parable, Luke 14:7–11, in the collection are also outsiders (dinner guests in the home of a Pharisee, 14:7).

16. I am especially indebted in the following paragraphs in this section to Blomberg, "Luke's Central Section," 240–44.

17. Blomberg, "Luke's Central Section," 241.

18. John Nolland, "Excursus: The Journey to Jerusalem," in *Luke 9:21–18:34* (WBC 35B; Dallas: Word Books, 1993), 2:530–31.

19. See, e.g., the chiastic structures proposed by Robert Morgenthaler, *Die lukanische Geschichtsschreibung als Zeugnis* (2 vols.; Zurich: Zwingli, 1978); Talbert, *Literary Patterns, Theological Themes, and the Genre of Luke-Acts;* Kenneth Bailey, *Poet and Peasant* (Grand Rapids: Eerdmans, 1976).

20. Culpepper ("Luke," 361–64) suggested that this last parable, which he called "the parable of the Greedy and Vengeful King," serves to contrast the behavior of wicked kings with that of Jesus who "is on his way to Jerusalem where he will be hailed as king" (363). As such, the parable, even though it falls at the end of the journey to Jerusalem, serves more as an introduction to the Passion Narrative, leaving the function of concluding the travel narrative to the parable of the Pharisee and the tax collector, which also concluded the L parable collection.

21. Talbert, *Reading Luke*, 113.

22. John O. York, *The Last Shall Be First: The Rhetoric of Reversal in Luke* (JSNTSup 46; Sheffield: Sheffield Academic Press, 1991), 181.

23. Plutarch, *Moralia* Vol. 2 (trans. F. C. Babbitt; LCL; New York: G. P. Putnam, 1928), 116–17. See York, *The Last Shall Be First*, 164–81, for other references.

24. York, *The Last Shall Be First*, 184.

25. The following section was co-authored with Pamela Kinlaw of Wheeling Jesuit University.

26. Originally published in *EvT* 10 (1950–51): 1–15. The English version was published as "On The 'Paulinism' of Acts," in *Studies in Luke-Acts: Essays Presented in Honor of Paul Schubert* (ed. L. E. Keck and J. L. Martyn; Nashville and New York: Abingdon, 1966): 33–50. See also John Knox, "Acts and the Pauline Letter Corpus," in *Studies in Luke-Acts,* 279–87; C. K. Barrett, "Acts and the Pauline Corpus," in *ExpT* 78 (1976–77): 2–5; Haenchen, *The Acts of the Apostles,* 112–16.

27. Peder Borgen, "From Paul to Luke: Observations Toward Clarification of the Theology of Luke-Acts," *CBQ* 31 (1969), 168–82; William O. Walker, Jr., "Acts and The Pauline Corpus Reconsidered," *JSNT* 24 (1985): 3–23; and Morton S. Enslin, "'Luke' and Paul," *JAOS* 58 (1938), 81–91. See also I. Howard Marshall, "Luke's View of Paul," in *SwJT* 33 (1990): 41–51; F. F. Bruce, "Is the Paul of Acts the Real Paul?" *BJRL* 58 (1976): 282–305; and William O. Walker, Jr., "Acts and the Pauline Corpus Revisited: Peter's Speech at the Jerusalem Conference," in *Literary Studies in Luke-Acts: Essays in Honor of Joseph B. Tyson* (ed. R. E. Thompson and T. E. Phillips; Macon, Ga.: Mercer University Press, 1998), 77–86. More recently, this topic has been addressed by Stanley E. Porter, *The Plot of Acts: Essays in Literary Criticism* (WUNT 15; Tübingen: Mohr/Siebeck, 1999); though we come to similar conclusions, our proposal differs both in terms of method and in specific points of argumentation.

28. See Clark, *Rhetoric in Greco-Roman Education.* See also the various works by George Kennedy: *The Art of Rhetoric in the Roman World* (Princeton: Princeton University Press, 1972); *Classical Rhetoric and Its Christian and Secular Tradition from Ancient to Modern Times* (Chapel Hill: University of North Carolina Press, 1980); *New Testament Interpretation through Rhetorical Criticism* (Chapel Hill: University of North Carolina Press, 1984); *A New History of Classical Rhetoric* (Princeton: Princeton University Press, 1994).

29. For bibliography on rhetorical analyses of Paul's writings, see D. F. Watson and A. J. Hauser, eds., *Rhetorical Criticism of the Bible* (Biblical Interpretation Series 4; Leiden: Brill, 1994), 178–202.

30. Stanley E. Porter, "Paul of Tarsus and His Letters," in *Handbook of Classical Rhetoric in the Hellenistic Period 330 B.C.–A.D. 400* (ed. Stanley E. Porter; Leiden: Brill, 1997), 533.

31. See Hans D. Betz, *Galatians: A Commentary on Paul's Letter to the Churches in Galatia* (Hermeneia; Philadelphia, Fortress, 1979). See, e.g., Robert Jewett, *The Thessalonian Correspondence: Pauline Rhetoric and Millenarian Piety* (FFNT; Philadelphia: Fortress, 1986); F. W. Hughes, *Early Christian Rhetoric and 2 Thessalonians* (JSNTSup 30; Sheffield: JSOT Press, 1989); Margaret Mitchell, *Paul and the Rhetoric of Reconciliation: An Exegetical Investigation of the Language and Composition of 1 Corinthians* (HUT 28; Tübingen: Mohr-Siebeck, 1991); A. Guerra, *Romans and the Apologetic Tradition: The Purpose, Genre and Audience of Paul's Letter* (SNTSMS 81; Cambridge: Cambridge University Press, 1995); Ira Jolivet, Jr. "The Structure and Argumentative Strategy of Romans" (PhD diss., Baylor University 1994).

32. See, e.g., Philip H. Kern, *Rhetoric and Galatians: Assessing an Approach to Paul's Epistle* (SNTSMS 101; Cambridge: Cambridge University Press, 1998); for a brief reply to Kern, see the review by Mikeal C. Parsons in *RelSRev* 26 (2000): 268.

33. These examples are drawn from the list compiled by Porter, "Paul of Tarsus and His Letters," 578–83, who in turn draws on the work, among others, of M. R. Cosby, "Paul's Persuasive Language in Romans 5," in *Persuasive Artistry: Studies in New Testament Rhetoric in Honor of George A. Kennedy* (ed. E. F. Watson; JSNTSup 50; Sheffield: JSOT, 1991), 209–26, and D. A. Campbell, *The Rhetoric of Righteousness in Romans 3:21–26* (JSNTSup 65; Sheffield: JSOT, 1992). For a critique of earlier style analyses, see J. E. Botha, "Style in the New Testament: The Need for Serious Reconsideration," *JSNT* 43 (1991): 71–87.

34. Porter, "Paul of Tarsus and His Letters," 537, citing J. R. Levison, "Did the Spirit Inspire Rhetoric? An Exploration of George Kennedy's Definition of Early Christian Rhetoric," in *Persuasive Artistry,* 36–37. See also S. M. Pogoloff, *Logos and Sophia: The Rhetorical Situation of 1 Corinthians* (SBLDS 134; Atlanta: Scholars Press, 1992).

35. Porter, "Paul of Tarsus and His Letters," 585.

36. For this argument and supporting bibliography, see chapter 3.

37. Satterthwaite, "Acts against the Background of Classical Rhetoric," 378, concludes: "At point after point Acts can be shown to operate according to conventions similar to those outlined in classical rhetorical treatises." Furthermore, we suggest, that, given the "rhetoric in the air" of antiquity, Luke's authorial audience, while no doubt unable themselves to reproduce these rhetorical devices in composition, were nevertheless able to respond to their effects.

38. See Hogan, "Paul's Defense."

39. The point is not, of course, that Luke (or Paul) borrowed directly from Quintilian, but rather that Quintilian represents a convenient summary of the typical rhetorical conventions associated with forensic (and other types of) speech. As Hogan notes ("Paul's Defense," 84), these speeches (and those in the ancient novels he also examines) are not "perfect specimens," but they nonetheless "manifest a basic reliance on the rhetorical tradition as preserved in Quintilian" (arguing against the conclusion of H. Stephen Brown, "Paul's Hearing at Caesarea: A Preliminary Comparison with Legal Literature of the Roman Period," in *SBLSP* 35 [1996]: 326).

40. Hogan ("Paul's Defense," 81) also conveniently catalogues other attempts to analyze Paul's defense speech in Acts 24, summarizing the analyses of W. R. Long, "The Trial of Paul in the Book of Acts" (PhD diss., Brown University, 1982), 231; Kennedy, *New Testament Interpretation Through Rhetorical*

Criticism, 136; Neyrey, "The Forensic Defense Speech," 221; Winter, "Official Proceedings," 322–27; and Witherington, *Acts,* 709–10.

41. As Hogan ("Paul's Defense," 83) notes this is a common feature in Acts with eight of the ten longest speeches being interrupted or concluded with a note by the narrator to the effect that the speaker had more to say.

42. Witherington, *Acts,* 739–53. Again, Hogan ("Paul's Defense," 83–84) has summarized various rhetorical analyses of this speech, including Frank Crouch, "The Persuasive Moment: Rhetorical Resolutions in Paul's Defense Before Agrippa" *SBLSP* 35 (1996): 333–42; Kennedy, *New Testament Interpretation Through Rhetorical Criticism,* 137; Neyrey, "The Forensic Defense Speech," 221, Winter, "Official Proceedings," 329–31. Hogan himself sees the *exordium* in vv. 2–3 and an extended *narratio* in 4–23, with the speech again being interrupted in v. 24.

43. In addition to using conventional elements of forensic speech, we might also expect to find the Lukan Paul using elements of rhetorical style as we found to be the case in his letters. In addition to the examples of inflection in Paul's speeches already mentioned in chapter three, we might note also Morgenthaler, *Lukas und Quintilian,* 331–34, who, among others, asserts Paul's Areopagus speech (Acts 17:22–31) is peppered with alliteration, hyperbaton, litotes, and a carefully crafted period, all elements of style according to the handbook tradition. See also Satterthwaite, "The Background of Classical Rhetoric," 367–75. Cadbury, *The Making of Luke-Acts* (London: SPCK, 1958; repr., Peabody, Mass.: Hendrickson, 1999), 120–21, has a short, but illuminating discussion of litotes in Acts (with several examples drawn from Paul's speeches in Acts). Of course, examples of rhetorical convention are not limited to Paul's speeches in Acts. The narrator, Peter, Stephen, and Tertullus, to name just a few, employ various rhetorical strategies. The standard work on Lukan style remains Henry J. Cadbury, *The Style and Literary Method of Luke* (Cambridge: Harvard University, 1920). See also Cadbury, *The Making of Luke-Acts,* 113–39.

44. See Hogan, "Paul's Defense," 85–87; Lentz, *Luke's Portrait of Paul,* 171.

45. Talbert, *Reading Luke,* 241–42.

46. Talbert, *Reading Luke,* 242.

47. Leo O'Reilly, *Word and Sign in The Acts of The Apostles: A Study in Lucan Theology* (Rome: Editrice Pontificia Università Gregoriana, 1987), 170–74.

48. Talbert, *Reading Luke,* 242–44.

49. O'Reilly, *Word and Sign,* 170–74. See also F. Stolz, "Zeichen und Wunder: Die prophetische Legitimation und ihre Geschichte," *ZTK* 69 (1972): 125–44.

50. P. J. Gräbe, "Δύναμις as a Pneumatological Concept in the Main Pauline Letters," *BZ* 36 (1992): 228–29.

51. Gräbe, "Δύναμις," 231. See also 1 Cor 2:1–5; 2 Cor 4:7; 6.7.

52. Talbert, *Reading Luke,* 3.

53. Talbert, *Reading Luke,* 242–43.

54. O'Reilly, *Word and Sign,* 174.

55. Σημεῖα (*sēmeia*) is not found in any extant version of the Old Testament, and most commentators assume that Luke has added it to conform to typical Christian usage. For us, the important point is that this is the text the audience heard.

56. The order "wonders and signs" in Acts 2 appears to follow Luke's edition or his own editing of the Joel text. Robert Sloan, "'Signs and Wonders': A Rhetorical Clue to the Pentecost Discourse," *EvQ* 63 (1991): 225–40.

57. Borgen, "From Paul," 176. See also Colin J. Hemer, *The Book of Acts in the Setting of Hellenistic History* (WUNT 49; Tübingen: J. C. B. Mohr, 1989), 435–37.

58. For other speculations on Luke's possible reasons for not mentioning or more obviously quoting from Paul's letters, see M. S. Enslin, "Once Again, Luke and Paul," *ZNW* 61 (1970): 268–71; and Walker, "Acts," 7–12. For the major opposing opinion, see Barrett, *Acts*, 3–4.

59. Delivered Nov. 8, 63 B.C.E.; Sallust, "The War With Catiline," 31.6 (LCL). Sallust refers to no other speeches of Cicero.

60. T. Hillard, A. Nobbs, and B. Winter, "Acts and The Pauline Corpus I: Ancient Literary Parallels," in *The Book of Acts in Its Ancient Literary Setting,* 183–214, consider parallel evidence between Sallust and Cicero in considering how the diverse approaches of ancient historiography might shed light on how the author of Acts may have used his sources.

61. Robert Funk, "The Apostolic *Parousia*: Form and Significance," in *Christian History and Interpretation: Studies Presented to John Knox* (ed. W. R. Farmer; Cambridge: Cambridge University, 1967), 249–68.

62. Funk, "Apostolic Parousia," 264–65.

63. See also 1 Thess 2:9. In 2 Cor 11:7–11; however, Paul admits he received assistance from the Macedonian believers while in Corinth, though his point is still the subsuming of his material rights as proper apostolic behavior in the particular situation.

64. David J. Williams, *Paul's Metaphors: Their Context and Character* (Peabody, Mass.: Hendrickson, 1999), 268–71.

65. See also 1 Cor 9:26 and Phil 3:14.

66. Williams, *Metaphors,* 268.

67. Williams, *Metaphors,* 270.

68. Haenchen, *Acts,* 113–14 (citing 2 Cor 12:10).

69. Paul can also use the term in a more general sense, as in 1 Cor 7:28.

70. H. Schlier, "θλῖψις," *TDNT* 3:139–48.

71. Schlier, "θλῖψις," 143–44. The article is probably correct in extending the eschatological meaning to most NT texts.

72. Although this interpretation is not the majority opinion, the option has had supporters from Chrysostom to the present. See especially Michael L. Barré, "Qumran and the Weakness of Paul," *CBQ* 42 (1980): 216–27, who points out that Paul otherwise uses κολαφίζειν (*kolaphizein*) only in 1 Cor 4:11, which, as we see above, refers to those who slander and persecute him, and that the described hardships preceding and following Paul's mention of the thorn in the flesh include references to persecution (11:23–29; 12:10). For convenient summaries of the copious secondary literature on Paul's thorn, see Victor Paul Furnish, *II Corinthians* (AB 32A; Garden City, N.Y.: Doubleday, 1984), 547–51 and Margaret E. Thrall, *The Second Epistle to the Corinthians* (ICC; 2 vols.; Edinburgh: T&T Clark, 2000), 2:809–18.

73. As C. K. Barrett points out, the rest of Acts describes Paul's sufferings that are introduced here; he also notes that Luke is caught in the narrative "between two motivations, on the one hand to show how much Paul was prepared

to suffer for Christ, on the other to show the power of God to deliver him from suffering," *Acts*, 1:457.

74. As Barrett notes that θλῖψις μεγάλη (*thlipsis megalē*) is Luke's own summarizing phrase, which does not occur in the text of Genesis: "in the relevant context in Genesis, θλῖψις (*thlipsis*) occurs only at 42:21, and does not refer to the famine" (*Acts*, 348). We see, then, Luke's shaping of the narrative with a pattern of this vocabulary.

75. Joseph Fitzmyer, *The Acts of the Apostles* (AB 31; NY: Doubleday, 1998), 475.

76. See, e.g, Haenchen, *Acts*, 90–92; Hans Conzelmann, *The Theology of St. Luke*, 201; Bart D. Ehrman, "The Cup, the Bread, and the Salvific Effect of Jesus' Death in Luke-Acts," *SBLSP* 30 (1991): 576–91.

77. David Moessner, "Christ," 165–95.

78. Moessner, "Christ," 167.

79. Moessner, "Christ," 188.

80. The Greek text διὰ τοῦ αἵματος τοῦ ιδίου (*dia tou aimatos tou idiou*) could also be translated "his own blood;" the echo would be present regardless.

81. Vielhauer, "Paulinism," 36–41; Haenchen, *Acts*, 528–30; Werner Georg Kümmel, *Introduction to the New Testament* (rev. and enl. English ed.; trans. H. C. Kee; Nashville: Abingdon, 1973), 182–83.

82. For example, Marshall, "Luke's View," 48; Hemer, "Speeches," 250–55.

83. Moessner, "Christ," 168.

84. Haenchen, *Acts*, 112–13; Vielhauer, "Paulinism," 38–43.

85. Walker ("Acts," 15–17) cites this instance as "more-or-less unconscious echoes of Pauline terminology and thought." He maintains that while this passage shows Luke is familiar with Paul's doctrine of justification through faith, "it is evident that the doctrine holds little real interest for him."

86. Stephen G. Wilson, *Luke and the Law* (SNTSMS 50; Cambridge: Cambridge University, 1983), 61–63. Vielhauer, "Paulinism," 41–42.

87. Wilson, *Luke*, 61–63.

88. Wilson, *Luke*, 64–65. Wilson finds that the Nazirite vow has historical problems when compared to knowledge of such vows in first-century Judaism, but such an action by Paul would be defensible on the grounds of 1 Cor 9:19–23. Wilson finds problems in historical plausibility with Paul's appearance before the Sanhedrin within the Acts narrative itself, but no obvious tension with Paul's letters.

89. Wilson, *Luke*, 68.

90. Marshall, "Luke's View," 41–51.

91. Marshall, "Luke's View," 49.

92. Borgen, "From Paul," 180.

93. Borgen, "From Paul," 169.

PART THREE

LUKE THE EVANGELIST

CHAPTER 7

Reconstituting the People of God: The Examples of Peter, Cornelius, and Others

The last section of this book deals with "Luke the Evangelist." Early in the Christian tradition, the writers of the four canonical Gospels were designated as "evangelists." The term, of course, derives from the Greek *euangelion*, "good news," and hence the evangelists were those who wrote of the "good news of Jesus Christ." Part of that good news had to do with the radically reoriented lifestyle early Christians associated with those who chose to identify with this new movement. The subject of this chapter is Luke's role as evangelist—the proclaimer of a gospel that seeks to convert its hearers. That conversion led, in Luke's mind, to a redefinition and a reconstitution of the people of God that made room for Gentiles and made new demands on the people of Israel.

Numerous studies have been written that focus on conversion in Acts and related issues.[1] Rather than rehashing those arguments, we shall examine what Luke considered to be the scriptural basis for reconstituting the people of God, namely his understanding of the Abrahamic covenant. We shall then consider one of the key conversion scenes in Acts.

Luke and the Covenant(s)

Luke is often referred to as "the Gentile Gospel," in contrast to Matthew, which is known as the "Jewish Gospel." There is, of course, some truth to these labels. Matthew, for example, begins his Gospel with a genealogy that details the Davidic lineage of Jesus. Furthermore, Matthew uses a fulfillment formula throughout his Gospel (especially in the infancy narrative) to show how certain events from Jesus' life fulfill prophecies found in Israel's Scriptures.[2] He also notes that Jesus' public ministry was confined to "the lost sheep of the house of Israel" (Matt 10:5–6; cf. 15:24). Finally, many think that Matthew has presented Jesus as a "new Moses" and has collected the speeches and parables of Jesus into five discourses (chs. 5–7; 10; 13; 18; 24–25) that parallel the five books of Moses.[3] Of course, Matthew's Gospel is also interested in the role of Gentiles in salvation history. From the non-Israelite women mentioned in the genealogy (Tamar, Rahab, Ruth, and Bathsheba) to the Gentile Magi who venerate the newborn King to the Great Commission at the end of the Gospel, where Jesus commissions his disciples to "make disciples of all the nations/Gentiles," Matthew has an eye toward the Gentiles' place in the people of God. Thus it would be a mistake to infer from its label as the "Jewish Gospel" that Matthew has no interest in things that are Gentile.[4]

Likewise, it would be a mistake to think that Luke, the "Gentile Gospel," has no interest in things Jewish. The Gospel begins in the vicinity of the temple and refers to the Jewish piety of Zechariah and Elizabeth. The Gospel also ends with expressions of Jewish piety (Luke 23:50–56; 24:52–53). In between these accounts, we find Jesus preaching, teaching, and healing in the synagogue (Luke 4:16–30; 6:6, 13:21). Furthermore, Luke understands that the "plan of God" (boulē tou theou) includes a mission to the Gentiles, a mission grounded in the Scriptures of Israel, which specifically fulfills the Abrahamic covenant (cf. Acts 3:25).

That is not to say that Luke is unaware of other covenants between God and his people in Israel's scriptures. In fact, in addition to the Abrahamic covenant, Luke mentions or alludes to the Noahic, Mosaic, and Davidic covenants and to the "new covenant" of Jeremiah. It is helpful to explore briefly the roles these other covenants play in Luke's narrative before turning to Luke's use of the Abrahamic covenant.

Noahic Covenant

In addition to God's promise not to destroy the earth again by means of a flood, the Noahic covenant imposes certain dietary restrictions on God's people:

> Then God blessed Noah and his sons, saying to them, "Be fruitful and increase in number and fill the earth. The fear and dread of you

will fall upon all the beasts of the earth and all the birds of the air, upon every creature that moves along the ground, and upon all the fish of the sea; they are given into your hands. Everything that lives and moves will be food for you. Just as I gave you the green plants, I now give you everything. But you must not eat meat that has its life-blood still in it." (Gen 9:1–3; cf. Lev 17:13 NIV)

This dietary restriction to avoid meat with blood in it seems to be echoed in the Apostolic Decree of Acts 15, and provides a compromise between the sect of the Pharisees and the advocates of the Gentile mission: "Instead we should write to them, telling them to *abstain* from food polluted by idols, from sexual immorality, *from the meat of strangled animals* and from blood" (Acts 15:20 NIV; cf. v. 29). While Gentiles do not have to be circumcised they should follow (among other things) the Noahic prohibition to abstain from eating the meat of strangled animals. Otherwise, the Noahic covenant is given little attention in the pages of Luke-Acts.

Mosaic Covenant

The Mosaic covenant is central to Israel's understanding of her relationship with Yahweh, and likewise holds an important, if ambiguous, place in Luke's writings.[5] Exodus 34:26–28 briefly summarizes the covenant with Moses:

> Then the LORD said to Moses, "Write down these words, for in accordance with these words I have made a covenant with you and with Israel." Moses was there with the LORD forty days and forty nights without eating bread or drinking water. And he wrote on the tablets the words of the covenant—the Ten Commandments (Exod 34:27–28 NIV).

We find a number of references to the law of Moses in Luke-Acts, some positive, others less so. In Jesus' response to the rich ruler's question, "What must I do to inherit eternal life?" (Luke 18:18 NIV), Jesus responds, "You know the commandments: 'Do not commit adultery, do not murder, do not steal, do not give false testimony, honor your father and mother'" (Luke 18:20 NIV; see also Luke 1:6; Luke 10:25–27). Presumably here Jesus endorses following the Mosaic law, though he points out that in the case of the rich ruler, one thing is still missing.

Of course, in the debate with Jewish leaders, the Christians were accused of ignoring, or worse, abrogating the law of Moses. This was one of the charges brought against Stephen, and later Paul: "For we have heard him say that this Jesus of Nazareth will destroy this place and change the customs Moses handed down to us" (Acts 6:14 NIV; cf. Acts 21:21). The Lukan Paul exposes what he considers to be the soteriological inadequacy of the law: "Through him everyone who believes is justified from everything you could not be justified from by the law of Moses" (Acts 13:39 NIV). Certainly, it would be fair to say that Luke (like Paul) had an ambivalent attitude toward the law. It clearly had a positive role in maintaining community boundaries, but seemed to have lost its soteriological function.

Davidic Covenant

As in much of early Christianity, the Davidic covenant was crucial for understanding Jesus' role in salvation history in Luke.[6] Isaiah 11 briefly summarizes of the expectations of David's heir:

> A shoot will come up from the stump of Jesse; from his roots a Branch will bear fruit. The Spirit of the LORD will rest on him—the Spirit of wisdom and of understanding, the Spirit of counsel and of power, the Spirit of knowledge and of the fear of the LORD—and he will delight in the fear of the LORD . . . with righteousness he will judge the needy, with justice he will give decisions for the poor of the earth. He will strike the earth with the rod of his mouth; with the breath of his lips he will slay the wicked. (Isa 11:1–4 NIV)

Luke's Gospel makes Jesus' Davidic pedigree known from the beginning. Zechariah proclaims: "Praise be to the Lord, the God of Israel, because he has come and has redeemed his people. He has raised up a horn of salvation for us in the house of his servant David" (Luke 1:68–69 NIV; see also 1:32). Furthermore, through his adopted father, Joseph, Jesus was of Davidic lineage (Luke 3:23–38; cf. 1:27). The blind man of Jericho recognizes Jesus to be the "son of David" (Luke 18:38, 39). The Lukan Jesus himself alludes to his Davidic lineage, when he asks, "How can they say that the Messiah is David's son? For David himself says in the book of Psalms, 'The Lord said to my Lord, "Sit at my right hand, until I make your enemies your footstool."' David thus calls him Lord; so how can he be his son?" (Luke 20:41–44).

Later in Acts, Peter will cite this same psalm passage (110:1) in support of his argument that Jesus is the Messiah, the Christ; he is both David's descendant and his Lord:

> God has raised this Jesus to life, and we are all witnesses of the fact. Exalted to the right hand of God, he has received from the Father

the promised Holy Spirit and has poured out what you now see and hear. For David did not ascend to heaven, and yet he said, "The Lord said to my Lord: Sit at my right hand until I make your enemies a footstool for your feet." Therefore let all Israel be assured of this: God has made this Jesus, whom you crucified, both Lord and Christ. (Acts 2:34–36 NIV)

Luke's fundamental understanding of Jesus as the Christ is through the lens of the Davidic covenant and its concomitant messianic expectations.

New Covenant of Jeremiah

Finally, I must mention Jeremiah's "new covenant":

"The time is coming," declares the LORD, "when I will make a new covenant with the house of Israel and with the house of Judah . . . This is the covenant I will make with the house of Israel after that time," declares the LORD. "I will put my law in their minds and write it on their hearts. I will be their God, and they will be my people." (Jer 31:31, 33 NIV)

This covenant does not receive much attention in Luke-Acts, but Jesus does allude to it in a key passage: "In the same way, after the supper he took the cup, saying, 'This cup is the new covenant in my blood, which is poured out for you'" (Luke 22:20 NIV). Though the language of "new covenant" is not prominent in the rest of Luke-Acts, the concept is certainly present, especially at Pentecost in Acts 2. Charles Talbert has commented insightfully about this text:

Sound, fire, and speech understood by all people were characteristic of the Sinai theophany. The same ingredients are found in the Pentecostal events. The Sinai theophany and the establishment of the Mosaic covenant were brought to mind as surely as would Elijah by the description of John the Baptist's dress in Mark 1:6. The typology of Acts 2:1–11, then, is that of making a covenant.

The Pentecostal events of Acts 2:1–11, however, are not just a Messianist renewal of the Sinai covenant. Luke-Acts thinks in terms of a new covenant. The Lukan Jesus said, "This cup is the new covenant in my blood, which will be shed for you" (Luke 22:20; cf. Exod 24:8). Luke's Bible speaks of a new covenant in Jer 31:31–34. In Ezek 11:17–20, God says about the new covenant: (a) "I will assemble you out of the countries where you have been scattered, and I will give you the land of Israel"(v. 17); (b) "I will give them a new heart and put a new spirit within them" (v. 19); and (c) I will "give them one heart" (v. 19). At Pentecost in Acts 2, this promise is ful-filled. A new spirit is given, the Holy Spirit! The promise of the Father has been fulfilled in the presence of those who have been as-sembled out of the countries to which they have been scattered. The gift of the Spirit will produce a people with one heart (vv. 41–47).[7]

Thus, Jeremiah's "new covenant" is important in understanding Lukan ecclesiology. But by far, the most important covenant for understanding Luke's view of the church, especially its mission, is the Abrahamic cove-nant to which we now turn our attention.

Abrahamic Covenant

The Abrahamic covenant (Gen 12:2) is explicitly cited in Peter's speech in Acts 3, in the context of the story of the healing of the lame man: "And you are heirs of the prophets and of the covenant God made with your fathers. He said to Abraham, 'Through your offspring all peoples on earth will be blessed'" (Acts 3:25 NIV). But the covenant is also alluded to throughout Luke-Acts.[8] The Abrahamic covenant was *foretold* in the coming of Christ. Consider Simeon's speech: "For my eyes have seen your salvation, which you have prepared in the sight of all people, a light for revelation to the Gentiles and for glory to your people Israel" (Luke 2:30–32 NIV). The Abrahamic covenant was *inaugurated* in Jesus' sermon in Nazareth:

> I assure you that there were many widows in Israel in Elijah's time, when the sky was shut for three and a half years and there was a se-vere famine throughout the land. Yet Elijah was not sent to any of them, but to a widow in Zarephath in the region of Sidon. And there were many in Israel with leprosy in the time of Elisha the prophet, yet not one of them was cleansed—only Naaman the Syr-ian. (Luke 4:25–27 NIV)

The Abrahamic Covenant was *declared* by Peter in his Pentecost ser-mon (Acts 2:39): "The promise is for you and your children and for all who are far off—for all whom the Lord our God will call" (NIV). Fi-nally, the Abrahamic Covenant *undergirds* Paul's Gentile mission (Acts 9:15–16; cf. Acts 8): "But the Lord said to Ananias, 'Go! This man is my chosen instrument to carry my name before the Gentiles and their kings and before the people of Israel. I will show him how much he must suf-fer for my name'" (NIV). The Abrahamic Covenant included not only Gentiles but those who had been marginalized by the temple cult (the bent woman [Luke 13:10–17], Zacchaeus [Luke 19:1–10], the lame man [Acts 3:1–26]). The Abrahamic covenant provides for Luke the scriptural warrant for the Gentile mission and Luke's understanding of conversion and the reconstitution of the people of God must be read in light of this covenant.

This point becomes all the more important when we realize that the book of Acts presents the "Christian" movement (known variously in Acts as the "Way" [9:2; 19:9, 23; 24:14], the "sect of the Nazarenes" [24:5], the "Christians" [11:26]) as one Jewish movement among several (see 5:17 on the use of "sect" [*hairēsis*] in Acts). This view of Christianity as a movement within pre-70 C.E. Judaism is the perspective of Christian, Jewish, and Roman characters in Acts, as well as the narrator himself.

Christian perspective

That members of the "Way" or Christians were still practicing Jews is demonstrated through their actions (Peter and John go up to the temple to worship in Acts 3), as well as their speeches. Twice, Paul makes the claim "I am a Jew" (21:39; 22:3). Later, he claims that he has "belonged to the strictest sect of our religion and lived as a Pharisee" (26:5; cf. also 24:14).

Jewish perspective

Tertullus, the Jewish advocate for the high priest before Felix claims: "We have, in fact, found this man a pestilent fellow, an agitator among all the Jews throughout the world, and a ringleader of the sect of the Nazarenes" (24:5).The Jews in Rome say to Paul: "But we would like to hear from you what you think, for with regard to this sect we know that everywhere it is spoken against" (28:22).

Roman perspective

Festus reports to Agrippa about Paul: his "accusers . . . did not charge him with any of the crimes that I was expecting. Instead they had certain points of disagreement with him about their own religion . . ." (25:18–19). In his letter to the governor Felix, the tribune, Claudius Lysas writes: "I found that he [Paul] was accused concerning questions of their law, but was charged with nothing deserving death or imprisonment" (23:29).

Narrator's perspective

The narrator or storyteller portrays the Christians as Jews: "But some believers who belonged to the sect of the Pharisees stood up and said, 'It is necessary for them to be circumcised and ordered to keep the law of Moses'" (15:5).

Therefore, the view that at its earliest stages the Christian movement was a discrete religion, separate from Judaism, is inaccurate and anachronistic. (For this reason, some scholars prefer to speak of these earliest Christians as "Messianists"—a term that has its own problems, since other groups also expected a Messiah.) It is important, however, when speaking about the Christian "Way" in the first few decades to understand that the conflicts with other Jewish groups (Pharisees, Sadducees) were part of intra-Jewish debates about which Jewish group was the "true Israel." Nonetheless, these first Christians, at least some of them, redrew the "maps of purity," arguing for the inclusion of people, places, and foods that otherwise fell "outside" the boundaries on most (though not all—think of the God-fearers) Jewish symbolic maps of purity. For Luke, the reconstitution of the people of God to include Gentiles was done under the authority of the Abrahamic covenant and for the purpose of presenting the Christian movement or way as the true heirs of Israel.[9] With this background in place, we now consider Acts 10–11.

The Conversion of Peter, Cornelius, and Others

Several of the best known stories of conversions to the movement known as the "Way" are found in the Lukan writings: the Ethiopian Eunuch (Acts 8), Saul (Acts 9),[10] Sergius Paulus (Acts 13), Lydia (Acts 16), the Philippian jailor (Acts 16), and others.[11] Within Luke's writings, however, pride of place for such stories surely belongs to the conversion of Cornelius, recorded in Acts 10–11. What follows is an exegesis of Acts 10–11, with an eye toward how Luke the evangelist presented responses to the Christian gospel by those who stood both within and without the early Christian community. Running beneath the surface of this story is Luke's conviction that the conversion of Peter and Cornelius (and his household) fulfills the Abrahamic promise that God's people will be a blessing to the nations. Peter needs to be radically transformed to this point of view.

Acts 10:1–11:18 is part of a larger unit comprised of three scenes that begin in Acts 9:32. These three scenes, the healing of Aeneas (9:32–35), the raising of Tabitha (9:36–43), and the conversion of Cornelius and his household (10:1–11:18), may all be grouped under the larger heading, "the acts of Peter." Theologically, all three stories serve to reveal further

Peter's complex character, as well as to underscore the inclusive nature of the gospel. Here Peter fulfills Jesus' commission (Acts 1:8) to be a witness in all Judea (9:32–35; 9:36–43) and to the end of the earth (10:1–11:18). Peter's acts parallel the earlier three stories in Acts of members of the Seven, who also obey Christ's commission to be witnesses in Jerusalem (6:8–7:60—Stephen), Samaria (8:14–25—Peter and John), and the end of the earth (8:26–40—Philip).[12]

Further, joining two shorter stories (8:4–25; 8:26–40//9:32–35; 9:36–43) with a longer third one (6:8–8:3//10:1–11:18) to make basically the same point is not uncommon in the Gospel of Luke. In fact, these stories are similar to Luke 15, in which we have the two briefer stories of the lost sheep (15:3–7) and the lost coin (15:8–10) standing alongside the much longer story of the lost sons (15:11–32)—with all three describing the joy in the kingdom, which occurs when that which was lost is found. And as with these three parables, readers can also detect the movement in these three stories in Acts to open the gospel to all persons.

In this story, many readers focus on the significance of the conversion of Cornelius and his household for the spread of the gospel to the Gentiles in Acts. And this is justifiable because this episode represents a critical turning point in the narrative of Acts. Equally as important, though, is Peter's "conversion" to a new point of view, namely, that salvation knows no human boundaries and that "God shows no partiality" (1:34). The chapter divisions here (as in many other places in Scripture) are misleading. The episode actually divides into seven scenes, interlinked by much repetition (the vision of Cornelius is reported four times; Peter's vision is thrice-related; and all of ch. 11 is basically a summary of ch. 10).[13]

This story is the fourth conversion story in Acts, following the conversions of the Samaritans (8:4–25), the Ethiopian Eunuch (8:26–40), and Saul (9:1–31), all of which prepare the audience for this conversion story, the conversion of Cornelius, and ultimately for the inauguration of the Gentile mission by Paul. But Cornelius is not the only one converted in this story. The narrator clearly notes that the entire household of Cornelius is saved (see 11:14). Thus the story is also the first of four "household conversion" stories in Acts (see also 16:11–15; 16:25–34; 18:1–11). This corporate aspect of conversion is sometimes neglected by readers.[14] We will return to this subject in our discussion of the sixth and seventh scenes of this unit.

Scene 1: 10:1–8. Cornelius's Vision in Caesarea

At the conclusion of the raising of Tabitha (9:43), the narrator leaves Peter in Joppa "for many days with one Simon, a tanner" (9:43) until he was summoned by Cornelius's men (10:17–18). While some commentators downplay the significance of the occupation of Peter's host,[15] the fact that Simon is a tanner does not seem insignificant. In almost every other instance where the narrator of Acts mentions a character's occupation, that occupation figures prominently in the story (see Simon the magician, 8:9, 26; Cornelius the centurion, 10:1; Bar-Jesus the magician, 13:6–7; Lydia, dealer in purple, 16:14, 16; Priscilla and Aquila, tentmakers, 18:3; Demetrius, a silversmith, 19:24). Furthermore, the fact that Peter had taken lodging with Simon, a tanner, is mentioned twice more in the narrative (10:6, 32), indicating its significance for the narrator.

A tanner was one who participated in a "trade which required the use of urine for processing leather, hence an unclean or mean trade."[16] While not, strictly speaking, a "chronically unclean" occupation,[17] later rabbis did despise the occupation as "dirty" and "smelly";[18] in other words, it was a socially ostracized trade (Dio Chrysostom 38; Artemidorus 4, 56). This particular tanner lived by the seaside (Acts 10:6). Simon's geographical location may be explained by the fact that tanners used sea water in their trade or that the sea breeze helped ameliorate the odor of the hides.[19] On Acts' social map of places, however, Simon's locale on the literal edge of town by the sea may also symbolize his liminal and marginalized place on the social map of persons. Peter has, then, taken a first step by taking up lodging with an ostracized tanner. We should not miss the irony of Peter's reticence to receive the vision of what is ritually clean and unclean in the very home of a socially marginalized tanner. Only a conversion of the most radical sorts will allow Peter's attitude to catch up with his setting!

At the beginning of chapter 10, the scene shifts from Joppa to Caesarea, from a primarily Jewish center to a city populated by mostly Gentiles. Caesarea has already been mentioned in the narrative of Acts: Philip had been left there, preaching (8:40), and Paul had stopped there on his journey to Tarsus (9:30). And the city would figure prominently again in Acts' story (see 12:19; 18:22; 21:8, 16; 23:23, 33; 25:1, 4, 6, 13). Our inferred audience would have recognized Caesarea as a coastal town which had been built on the site of Straton's Tower (Pliny the Elder, *Hist. Nat.*, 5.69; Strabo, *Geography,* 16.2.27), rebuilt by Herod the Great (with some stunning buildings, including a new port (see Josephus, *Ant.* 15.331–341), and a Roman military headquarters under Vespasian during the Jewish War (Josephus, *J.W.* 3.409–413).

Living in Caesarea were Cornelius, "a centurion of the Italian Cohort, as it was called," (10:1) and his household. Centurions, unlike higher ranking Roman military leaders (see Claudius Lysias at Acts 23),

Table 1. Cornelius's Vision

Acts 10:1–8 *Perspective: Narrator of Acts*	Acts 10:22 *Perspective: Cornelius' Messengers*	Acts 10:31–33 *Perspective: Cornelius*	Acts 11:13–14 *Perspective: Peter*
and saying to him, "Cornelius," 4He stared at him in terror and said, "What is it, Lord?" He answered, "Your prayers and your alms have ascended as a memorial before God.		31He said, 'Cornelius, your prayer has been heard and your alms have been remembered before God.	and saying,
5Now send men to Joppa for a certain Simon who is called Peter;	to send for you	32Send therefore to Joppa and ask for Simon, who is called Peter;	'Send to Joppa and bring Simon, who is called Peter;
6he is lodging with Simon, a tanner, whose house is by the seaside."		he is staying in the home of Simon, a tanner, by the sea.'	
7When the angel who spoke to him had left, he called two of his slaves and a devout soldier from the ranks of those who served him, 8and after telling them everything, he sent them to Joppa	to come to his house	33Therefore I sent for you immediately, and you have been kind enough to come. So now all of us are here in the presence of God	
	and to hear what you have to say."	to listen to all that the Lord has commanded you	14he will give you a message by which you and your entire household will be saved.'

Double underlining = verbatim agreement in the Greek; single underlining = near verbatim agreement (e.g., same Greek verb but different tense); broken underlining = conceptual, but not verbal, agreement are favorably depicted in Luke and Acts (see Luke 7:1–10; Acts 27:43, 44). Centurions were commanders of 100 men (a century), a sub-unit of a cohort (composed of six centuries), which in turn was a unit of a legion (composed of ten cohorts, approximately 6,000 soldiers).[20] Centurions were drawn from the ranks of the enlisted soldiers, were Roman citizens, were well-paid, and most importantly for Luke, were Gentiles. Given the presence of his "household," it is possible that Cornelius had retired in Caesarea, though this is certainly inconclusive from the evidence of the narrative (on this line, the "devout soldier" in 10:7 would likewise be retired). Like the centurion in Luke 7, Cornelius had both wealth at his disposal and subordinates under his authority.

More importantly for Luke, Cornelius is given a rather full and favorable characterization reminiscent of Tabitha. Cornelius and his house are described by Luke as devout and God-fearing, and Cornelius, specifically, is depicted as one who practiced traditional Jewish piety and "gave alms generously . . . and prayed constantly to God" (10:2; see Tob 12:8; cf. Tabitha who was "devoted to good works and acts of charity," 9:36). Much like the centurion in Luke 7 (who loved the Jewish nation and had built a synagogue for them, 7:5), the Gentile Cornelius had a piety that led to material benefits for the Jews: "he gave alms liberally to the people."

Despite being depicted as a benefactor of the Jews and a practitioner of Jewish piety, the opening characterization of Cornelius as "devout" and "God-fearing" has universalizing overtones as well. There has been much debate about the status, and even existence, of the God-fearers in the first century; in Luke's narrative world, it is quite clear that they did exist and that they were Gentiles (cf. Acts 11:18).

This notion of "fearing God" had deep roots in the traditions of the Old Testament. The concept of "fearing God" was originally linked to the cult of Israel; that is, the one who feared Yahweh would have participated in the cultus of this particular God. But in post-exilic Judaism, especially in the book of Proverbs (see 9:10; 1:7; 3:7), the notion of "fearing God" had lost its cultic associations, and wisdom teachers "universalized the concept of allegiance to Yahweh."[21] "The fear of God is the beginning of wisdom" (Prov 9:10). Ronald Clements has observed: "In a context where Jews found themselves living in political and social environments where they were beyond the range of either the earlier state-centered laws of Judah and Israel or the jurisdiction of the priest of the Jerusalem temple there was a practical need for defining Jewish morality and piety in terms drawn from creation itself."[22] In this context, "fearing God" "described the requisite attitude of life in which a truly Jewish morality and piety could flourish in a Gentile setting."[23] As a

"God-fearer," Cornelius was associating with the tradition of Jewish piety, which already had universalizing tendencies (see below on Acts 10:34–35).

Further, the description of Cornelius as "devout" lends support to this view. While εὐσεβής (*eusebēs*) and its cognates denote Jewish reverence (see Sir 11:17; 13:17; 27:11; 2 Macc 12:47), the verb form occurs in Acts 17:23, in which Paul seeks to convince the Athenians that the "unknown god" they worship (εὐσεβεῖτε, *eusebeite*) is the God of Israel. Paul also appeals here to the wisdom tradition of creation ("The God who made the world and everything in it," 17:24). This description of Cornelius as "devout," then, also affirms that Cornelius is a Gentile attracted to the universalizing stream of first-century Judaism, most commonly found in wisdom traditions.

Following this extended description of his character, Cornelius has a vision (10:3). Again, the elements reinforce Cornelius's piety. The vision occurs at the ninth hour of the day, which Luke has already identified as "the time for prayer" (see Acts 3:1). In this vision, an "angel of God" reinforces the view of Cornelius's piety: "Your prayers and your alms have ascended as a memorial before God" (10:4). Though the time of prayer remains the same in Acts, the setting has changed from the temple (in Acts 3:1) to a house (implied here at 10:3, but made explicit at 10:30). The shift from temple to house reinforces the characterization of Cornelius as one who can engage in traditional acts of piety quite apart from a traditional cultic context. The shift also contributes to Luke's argument that the house and not the temple (or the synagogue) is the appropriate socio-religious institution for expressing piety to God.

The vision is reported in the form of a commissioning (see also Acts 9:10–17a). The story has most of the traditional elements:

Introduction: (1–2)   "In Caesarea there was a man named Cornelius"

Confrontation: (3)   ". . . he had a vision in which he clearly saw an angel of God"

Reaction: (4a)   "And he stared at him in terror and said, 'What is it, Lord?'"

Reassurance: (4b)   "'Your prayers and your alms have ascended as a memorial before God.'"

Commission: (5–6)   "Now send men to Joppa for a certain Simon who is called Peter. . . .'"

Conclusion: (7–8)   "When the angel who spoke to him had left, he
called two of his slaves and a devout soldier . . .
and after telling them everything, he sent them
to Joppa."[24]

Two variations in the commissioning type scene are noteworthy.
First, the commission in vv. 5–6 is incomplete. Cornelius is not told why
he should send for Peter, only that he should. Peter's vision (in the next
scene) is likewise incomplete (see below). These visions "are best called
divine promptings because they are incomplete in themselves. They re-
quire human action or reflection. The message to Cornelius is that he
must send for a certain Simon Peter. Only sufficient information to locate Peter is given, and apart from human response to this prompting
nothing would be accomplished."[25] Throughout the narrative the activities are directed from above (cf. ch. 9), but that does not mean that
there is no human response to this divine activity. Rather the divine
"promptings" of both Cornelius and Peter are incomplete and are only
understood after further reflection and interaction with other human
characters. Revelation here is depicted in contextual and interrelational
terms, which means that both Cornelius and Peter have to respond to
the divine promptings before they can receive further illumination.

The incompleteness of the commission makes the other variation
even more striking. Despite the fact that Cornelius is given only the bar-
est of details about Peter, he does not resist the vision; the traditional
element of "protest" is entirely missing (see comments on 9:10–17a).
Without further question, Cornelius complies by dispatching from his
household two personal servants and a "faithful" soldier to fetch Peter
(10:7–8). Cornelius's unquestioning obedience stands in sharp contrast
to Peter resistance in the next scene (and Ananias's earlier objections at
9:13). His loyalty, from Luke's perspective, is due less to being a "good
soldier" and more to his genuinely pious character.

Scene 2: 10:9–16. Peter's Vision in Joppa

The temporal change to "noon the following day" (10:9) notes a
change in scene. Further, there is a change in participants as the focus
shifts from the messengers from Cornelius's house, who "were on their
journey and approaching the city," to Peter, who "went up on the roof to
pray" (10:9b). The sixth hour (noon) was not the usual time for Jewish
prayers or meals. It was a common time in Luke's narrative world for divine guidance (see Acts 22:6; possibly 8:26). It may also indicate Peter's
piety in praying at an undesignated time. Likewise, roofs were a typical

site for prayer in the biblical tradition (see 2 Kgs 23:12; Neh 8:16; Jer 19:13; Zeph 1:5).

For the modern Western audience, it is not surprising that Peter should become hungry during his prayer since noon is a common meal time. At the discourse level, however, the narrator makes it clear from the use of δέ (*de*) instead of καί (*kai*) that Peter's hunger is an unexpected twist to the story.[26] The audience is left to fill the gap left by the narrator's brief note that "while they were preparing [it], Peter fell into a trance." Did Peter call out from the roof to his host about his hunger? Does the "they" include Simon and his servants or fellow Christians? While the audience ponders the understated hospitality of Simon and his household, the narrator moves on to what is more important: Peter's vision.

Peter, like Cornelius, experiences a vision while at prayer (10:10), and so we have an example of a "double vision." In this vision, Peter sees the heaven opened, recalling the scene at Jesus' baptism (Luke 3:21) and more recently Stephen's vision (7:56). The opened heaven is a typical element in visions (see LXX Isa 63:19; 3 Macc 6:18; *2 Bar.* 22:1; John 1:51; *Corpus Hermeticum* 13:17). Peter sees "something like a large sheet coming down, being lowered to the ground by its four corners" (10:11). The word translated here "something" (σκεῦος, *skeuos*) often refers to a container, and some have seen symbolic value with the "four corners" of the sheet perhaps representing the four corners or ends of the earth (see Isa 11:12; Ezek 7:2; Rev 7:1; 20:8), thus pointing to a worldwide mission.[27] If this symbolism is intended, it is not close to the surface of the text.

More important are the sheet's contents: "In it were all kinds of four-footed creatures and reptiles and birds of the air" (10:12). The passage echoes Gen 1:24, as well as 6:20, 7:14, and 8:19. It also reflects the divisions of the animal world, including from a Jewish perspective, presumably clean and unclean animals (though Noah is given permission to eat both clean and unclean animals). A voice (see the baptism of Jesus in Luke 3) issues a command: "Get up, Peter; slaughter and eat" (Acts 10:13; my translation). This phrase violates Jewish food laws (see Lev 11:47), but echoes Deut 12:15 ("Whenever you desire you may slaughter and eat meat . . . the unclean and the clean may eat of it . . ."). The word for slaughter (θύω, *thuō*) is used in Luke and Acts in reference to religious or cultic "sacrifice" (see Luke 22:7; Acts 14:13; 15:18), but may also have a more general meaning of "kill," though even then retaining at least ritualistic overtones of "slaughter" (see Luke 15:23, 27, 30). One must not miss the significance of the command to perform ritual "slaughter" not in the temple, but on the roof of a house.

Table 2. Synopsis of Peter's Vision

Acts 10:9–21 *Perspective: Narrator of Acts*	Acts 10:28–29 *Perspective: Peter before Cornelius and his household*	Acts 11:4–12 *Perspective: Peter before the Jerusalem believers*	Acts 15:8–9 *Perspective: Peter before the Jerusalem Council*
14But Peter said, "By no means, Lord; for I have never eaten anything	28and he said to them,	8But I replied, 'By no means, Lord; for	"My brothers, you know that in the early days God made a choice among you, that by my mouth the Gentiles would hear the message of the good news and become believers.
that is profane and unclean."	"You yourselves know that it is unlawful for a Jew to associate with or to visit a Gentile; but God has shown me that I should not call anyone profane or unclean.	nothing profane or unclean has ever entered my mouth.'	
15The voice said to him again, a second time,		9But a second time the voice answered from heaven,	
"What God has made clean, you must not call profane."		'What God has made clean, you must not call profane.'	And God, who knows the human heart, testified to them by giving them the Holy Spirit, just as he did to us; and in cleansing their hearts by faith
19While Peter was still thinking about the vision, the Spirit said to him, "Look, three men are searching for you.	29So when I was sent for I came without objection.	12The Spirit told me	
20Now get up, go down, and go with them		to go with them and not to make a distinction between them and us.	
without hesitation;			
for I have sent them."			he has made no distinction between them and us.

Double underlining = verbatim agreement in the Greek; single underlining = near verbatim agreement (e.g., same Greek verb but different tense); broken underlining = conceptual, but not verbal, agreement

If the divine voice intends that Peter's ritual slaughtering of the animals in his vision will render them fit for consumption (see Deut 12:21–22), Peter misses those allusions altogether, hearing only a command to disobey dietary regulations: "By no means, Lord; for I have never eaten anything that is profane and unclean" (10:14). The negative is emphatic and is used only here in the New Testament (see Gen 18:25; Jonah 1:14; Ezek 4:14). Though the audience might wonder why Peter could not have chosen one of the "clean" animals from the sheet, the narrator does not address that issue. As the narrative unfolds, the audience (as well as Peter) will be led to conclude that the clean animals were polluted by their association with the unclean animals and will apply that insight to social interaction among persons. At this point in the narrative, though, the point is simply that Peter thinks he knows what is clean and unclean, and he refuses to eat what is unclean.

The voice addresses Peter, now for a second time: "What God has made clean, you must not call profane" (10:16). This declaration is repeated twice more in the course of the narrative and though the words are the same, the statement accrues in meaning and nuance over the larger narrative stretch from 10:1–11:18. Here, it is simply a statement that Peter should not call any animal unclean because God has cleansed it. The scene concludes: "This happened three times, and the thing was suddenly taken up to heaven" (10:16). The ambiguous referent, "this," must surely refer to the exchange between Peter and the voice, with Peter thrice refusing to eat. The sheet is finally taken up into heaven from whence it came, and the vision is over.

This vision may be over, but it is still very much incomplete. Three times Peter is shown a sheet with all kinds of animals on it and is commanded to eat. Three times Peter refuses, claiming, "By no means, Lord, for I have never eaten anything that is profane or unclean" (10:14). The issues are by no means clear. Echoes of Jesus' baptism scene may recall for the audience the subsequent temptation of Jesus who was hungry but refused to turn stones to bread. Perhaps Satan has not finished sifting Peter like wheat (Luke 22:31) and is now tempting him to disobey Torah regulations (as he did Jesus). Or is Peter thrice resisting temptation, not of Satan, but of the Lord? Peter's reference to Lord does not rule out a divinely planned temptation. After all, the disciples themselves were taught to pray by Jesus himself, "Do not bring us to the time of trial . . ." (Luke 11:4).

While a first encounter with this narrative might cause the audience to entertain such a reading, the rest of the story and subsequent rereadings through retrospective patterning will cause the audience to revise these initial impressions. By the end of the story it is clear that Peter is not nobly resisting temptation but once again thrice denying his Lord (see Luke 23). His resistance stands in sharp contrast to Cornelius's unquestioning obedience. What remains unclear is the subject of this vision: Is Peter to disregard Jewish dietary laws or is something else at stake?

Scene 3: 10:17–23a. Cornelius's Men in Joppa

The audience is not the only one left wondering about the vision. Scene 3 begins with Peter "greatly puzzled about what to make of the vision that he had seen" (10:17). At that moment, Cornelius's emissaries arrive in Joppa. After having inquired about the specific location of Simon the tanner's house (they had been told only that it was "by the seaside," 10:6), the messengers stand by the gate (πυλών, pylōn; used also of a residential abode in Luke 16:20; Acts 12:13). Perhaps they do not enter because they are aware that as Gentiles they would contaminate a Jewish home, even the home of a tanner. Or perhaps the smell of the tanner's trade, infamous in antiquity (see Pliny, Hist. Nat. 23.140) encouraged them to observe Jewish purity codes! At any rate, from this position beside the gate, Cornelius's messengers cry out and ask, "Is Simon Peter lodging here?" (10:18; my translation).

The narrator leaves the messengers there and returns to Peter who is still "pondering over the vision" (10:19). The word "ponder" is a hapax in the New Testament and is one of several words in this scene which use the intensive prefix διά (διαπορέω, diaporeō—"puzzle"; διερωτάω, dierōtaō—"find out by inquiry"; διενθυμέομαι, dienthumeomai—"ponder"; διακρίνω, diakrinō—"discriminate" or "hesitate") to heighten the drama of the encounter.[28] The Spirit directs Peter in his next action: "Look, three men are searching for you. Now get up, go down, and go with them without hesitation; for I have sent them" (10:19b–20). Luke does not distinguish among the angel directing Cornelius, the voice in Peter's vision, or here the Spirit—all three represent the divine guidance of God.[29] There is interesting rhetorical ambiguity in the word translated "without hesitation" (διακρίνω, diakrinō). In the active voice, the word means to "make a distinction" (see Acts 15:9). In the middle or passive (as it is here), it may mean "doubt" or "hesitate." The meaning here is ambiguous; probably the primary connotation is for Peter to go "without hesitation." But the sense of "without discrimination" cannot be far from the surface; it is certainly the way Peter understands the word later in his retelling of this event in 11:12 (see below)! The puzzled Peter, then, is still obedient enough to respond to the Spirit's call to go with these men "without hesitation" and "without discrimination" (10:20).

Peter descends from the roof and speaks to the men, saying, "I am the one you are looking for; what is the reason for your coming?" (10:21b). The reply of Cornelius's messengers begins to unlock for Peter and the reader Peter's puzzling vision and is the first of three times when Cornelius's vision will be repeated. The messengers reinforce the characterization of Cornelius as a devout God-fearer that the audience encountered at the beginning of the unit (10:1): "Cornelius, a centurion, an upright and God-fearing man, who is well spoken of by the whole Jewish nation" (10:22). Still, there are some subtle variations between this version and the earlier one that begin to reduce the role of Cornelius.[30] No reference is made to Cornelius's practices of alms-giving or prayer, and the "angel of God" (10:3) has become simply a "holy angel."

Furthermore, the messengers add a dimension to their version of the vision that was entirely missing from the narrator's telling of the vision, namely that Cornelius is sending for a certain Simon Peter "to come to his house and *to hear what you [Peter] have to say*" (10:22). This change "more clearly places the role of Cornelius as a passive receiver of a message which Peter is to bear."[31] This reduction of Cornelius's role will continue in the third and fourth repetitions of the vision (see below) and is similar to the fading of Ananias in the subsequent retellings of Paul's conversion (see chs. 22, 26).

Peter responds by extending hospitality to these Gentile visitors and giving them a night's lodging.[32] Hospitality has already played a significant role in this unit: Simon the tanner is Peter's host; Peter (and Simon) are hosts to Cornelius messengers; Cornelius will be host to Peter and his companions. Though table fellowship was less of a problem when Jews entertained Gentiles,[33] this act of hospitality to Gentiles by Peter already begins to blur the distinctions between "insider" and "outsider," which many observant Jews would wish to maintain (see *Jub.* 22:16; *Joseph and Asenath* 7:1). Cornelius is not the only one awaiting a conversion experience. The way for Peter's conversion is being gradually but thoroughly prepared, and this act of hospitality is a significant step in that direction!

Scene 4: 10:23b–33. Peter in Caesarea

Again, the scene change is marked by a temporal shift: "The *next day* he got up and went with them, and some of the believers from Joppa accompanied him" (10:23b). Typical of introductory statements, this one reflects an indefinite space ("he went with them") and an unspecified group ("some believers").[34] The presence of these "believers from Joppa" gives the following scenes a public, ecclesiastical context—this is no isolated encounter between two individuals—and they will become important validating witnesses later in the story (see 10:45, 11:12). Another temporal notice, "the next day" (10:24), ends the two-day journey from Joppa to Caesarea and pushes the story into its fourth day. The third person singular, "he entered (εἰσῆλθεν, *eiselthen*) Caesarea," keeps Peter on center stage and pushes his traveling companions into the background until they are needed.

The narrator reports that Cornelius was waiting for Peter to arrive, and in preparation had "called together his relatives and close friends" (10:24c). The extended household mentioned in 10:2 is brought back into focus and will be an important element in the subsequent narrative. These two sets of unfocused introductory statements (v. 23b and 24) serve to bring the two groups of participants together in a focused scene.

Finally, the two protagonists meet: "On Peter's arrival, Cornelius met him . . ." (10:25a). The "coming together" of Peter and Cornelius is emphasized by the cluster of words in this opening sub-scene (23b–27) formed with the prefix sun (*syn*, "with"): συνέρχομαι (*synerxomai*)— "accompany," vv. 23, 27; συγκαλέω (*sygkaleō*)—"call together," v. 24; συγγενεῖς (*syngeneis*)—"relatives," v. 24; συναντάω (*synantaō*)—"meet," v. 25; συνομιλέω (*synomileō*)—"talk with," v. 27.[35] In a reverential and subordinating gesture, Cornelius falls at Peter's feet and worships him (cf. Acts 4:35).

Lest Cornelius's action be mistaken as more than reverential respect (as in Xenophon's *The Ephesian Tale* 1.1.3; 1.2.7; 1.12.1), Peter raises him up and declares his own mortality: "Stand up; I am only a mortal" (cf. the similar response in Acts 14:15, though there the crowds are quite explicit in their identification of Paul and Barnabas as deities). For the second time, the narrator emphasizes that Peter has entered Cornelius's house: "And as he talked with him, he went in and found that many had assembled" (10:27). Luke is not bothered by the redundancy and rather than trying to explain the repetition as Peter's movement from gate to house,[36] it is better understood as underscoring the significance of the space in which the story occurs. Krodel's comments are on target: "This verb [enter] is found twice . . . in order to highlight the importance of this step of entering the home of a Gentile. By entering, Peter is blurring the distinction between Jew and Gentile (cf. vv. 15 and 20). On the other hand, Cornelius, by falling down at this feet and worshipping Peter is blurring the distinction between God and his creature (cf. 14:15; 28:6; 12:22)."[37]

Peter takes his next step toward conversion and correctly interpreting his vision when he sees the crowd of Gentiles gathered in Cornelius's house and says: "You yourselves know that it is unlawful for a Jew to associate with or to visit a Gentile, but God has shown me that I should not call anyone profane or unclean" (10:28). Peter's statement makes two moves toward interpreting his vision, one dramatic, one subtle. The dramatic move is that Peter perceives, both through reflection and subsequent interaction with these Gentiles, that his vision was about more than clean and unclean foods: It involves proper social interaction with persons: "I should not call anyone profane or unclean." In the Hellenistic period, "Gentile hostility toward Jews frequently involved suspicions that rooted in what appeared to them to be social isolation" and "the isolation was almost altogether a direct result of Jewish adherence to dietary regulations and laws of impurity."[38] This view is borne out by *Jub.* 22:16: "Separate yourself from the gentiles, and do not eat with them, and do not perform deeds like theirs, and do not become associates of theirs"[39] (for a Gentile's perspective on Jewish refusal to associate with Gentiles, see Juvenal, *Satire,* 14.96–106; Tacitus, *Hist.* 5.5). Thus, to move the discussion from food to persons would have seemed natural to the audience.

The other change from the original vision evident in Peter's statement is more subtle. It is forbidden, Peter says, for a Jew to associate with or visit an unclean Gentile (or foreigner ἀλλόφυλος, *allophylos*), because such contact would defile the Jew. Whereas Peter had equated "common" and "unclean" in the original vision ("By no means, Lord; for I have never eaten anything common *and* unclean"), here he distinguishes between the two, saying "God has shown me that I should not call anyone common *or* unclean" (my translation). The shift from "and" (καί, *kai*) in 10:14 to "or" (ἤ, *ē*) here at 10:28 is significant in extending Peter's understanding of the vision. There are two categories of defilement: defilement by lifestyle and defilement by association. The logic of his statement can be drawn out in the following parallelism: The Jew who is defiled by association with a Gentile is "common"; the Gentile is by diet and lifestyle "unclean." So, Peter claims God has revealed to him that he is to refrain from calling any Jew "common" for associating with Gentiles or any Gentile "unclean" because of diet.[40]

The distinction between "common" and "unclean" had first been made by the voice in the vision: "What God has made clean, you must not call common" (10:15; my translation). The voice does not address what Peter had called "unclean." In this current speech, Peter indicates that he now understands the reference to be to those "clean" animals that have been defiled by association with the unclean (see Lev 20:24–26). Even though the unclean animals should be unclean by their indiscriminate mixing with the unclean on the sheet, the voice declares that God has cleansed them. Peter, after subsequent reflection and interaction with the Gentiles from Cornelius's house, moves his thinking from food to persons. He understands that Jews are not polluted by contact with Gentiles, because God has cleansed them. This is the point he will make later to the circumcised believers at Jerusalem who are concerned about his table-fellowship with the uncircumcised (see 11:4–12). But here, Peter has pressed beyond the vision in another way. Not only has he extended the vision from food to persons, he has extended the statement of the divine voice to include Gentiles. Not only has God cleansed the Jew, who by all rights should have been defiled by association with Gentiles, so that Peter should no longer refer to them as "common," but God has also cleansed the Gentile, so that Peter should refrain from calling them "unclean." Just as it will be important for the Jewish believers to hear that they are not defiled by associating with Gentiles, Peter infers from his vision that neither are Gentiles unclean and makes this claim here before his Gentile audience. Later he will make the very bold move of declaring Gentiles clean before a Jewish audience (see 15:9).[41]

In other words, Peter understands that the vision of the sheet is not just about what can or cannot be eaten, a cultural "map of the body"; but more importantly the vision addresses the question of who is and is not clean, a radically new cultural "map of persons." Sociologists use the term "map" to designate "the concrete and systematic patterns of organizing, locating, and classifying persons, places, times, actions, etc. according to some abstract notion of 'purity' or order."[42] Just as Stephen proposed a new map of holy places (which did not limit "holy space" to the temple), so Peter is being directed to draw a new cultural map of people which was radically inclusive and gave Gentiles a place on the map. The issue is not whether Gentiles can be included in salvation: Peter has heard Jesus say as much (Luke 24:47) and has himself preached it (Acts 2:39; 3:25–26). The obstacle for the Jewish Christian to launch the Gentile mission is Gentile uncleanness "which prevents Jews from associating freely with Gentiles."[43] The vision of the sheet, Peter is being gradually led to understand, now removes that obstacle.

So Peter takes a great step forward toward understanding that his vision entails more than food; he has made it into an allegory about persons. Further, the vision has declared as "clean" not only Jews (like Peter) who were made "common" by association with Gentiles, but also includes God's cleansing of Gentiles, "unclean" because of diet. Still, Peter has not grasped its full import that he is to accept Cornelius as a Christian brother.

Peter concludes his address by affirming that he came with Cornelius's messengers "without objection" and now asks (for a second time, cf. 10:21): "Now may I ask why you sent for me?"(10:29). Cornelius responds by recounting (now for the third time) his vision (10:30–33). While the substance of the vision is the same, Cornelius introduces some interesting variations which the reader should note (see Table 1).[44] By functioning as an intradiegetic narrator, that is, as a character within the story, Cornelius adds weight to his observations. Yet even in this speech, the role of Cornelius is further reduced, continuing the pattern begun in the second report (see 10:22). Missing is any description of Cornelius's piety. Instead, Cornelius simply reports: "Four days ago at this very hour, at three o'clock, I was praying in my house" (10:30). No longer is the angel described as "an angel of God" (v. 3) or a "holy angel" but simply a "man in dazzling clothes" (10:30). The narrator's description matches almost word for word the earlier account (31–32; cf. 10:4–5), though there is a subtle shift in voice and tone. In the first account the angel says: "Your prayers and your alms have ascended as a memorial before God" (10:4), while Cornelius reports the words as follows: "Cornelius, your prayer has been heard and your alms have been remembered before God" (10:32). Cornelius's version strips the statement of any cultic or sacrificial connotation ("prayers and alms ascending as a memorial") and shifts the focus from the issue of which institution, house or temple, is the appropriate place for acts of piety to an emphasis, in Cornelius's version, on God's hearing and remembering, thus heightening the role of God's divine guidance in the episode. The remainder of the angel's instruction is essentially the same in both accounts, reinforcing Cornelius's reliability (see Table 1).

There is an additional comment from Cornelius, though, which also changes the emphasis of the scene: "So now all of us are here in the presence of God to listen to all that the Lord has commanded you to say" (10:33). The emphasis is on the *entire* household of Cornelius gathered to *hear all* that God has commanded. As Ronald Witherup has observed: "The role of Cornelius has become more passive as the role of Peter has become more active."[45] Further, Cornelius's speech serves to set the stage for Peter's kerygmatic declaration in Scene 5 by employing a variety of rhetorical devices: 1) the use of "now" (νῦν, *nyn*), which often marks major turning points in Acts (cf. 3:17); 2) the phrase "in the presence of God" identifies the group as being in audience with God; 3) the phrase "we are here . . . to listen" affirms that Cornelius's household is prepared to do what other speeches have demanded, e.g. "listen" (cf. 2:22); 4) the words "all that the Lord has commanded you to say" reinforce the notion that the following speech by Peter ultimately has God as its source.[46]

Scene 5: 10:34–43. Peter's Speech

After Cornelius recounts his vision, Peter responds to Cornelius's invitation to address the assembly. His speech falls into three parts, the introduction (34–35), the kerygma (36–42), and the conclusion (43). The speech begins with a solemn notice "when Peter opened his mouth, he said,"(my translation) indicating the importance of his speech (see also Acts 8:35; 18:14; also Exod 4:12; Num 22:28; Judg 11:36; Ezek 33:22; Dan 3:25; 10:16). Peter's conversion to this new perspective of Gentile cleanness is continued in the opening line of this speech: "In truth, I am understanding that God shows no partiality" (10:34; my translation). Each phrase is significant. Five of the seven occurrences of the phrase translated "in truth" or "truly" (ἐπ᾽ ἀληθείας, *ep᾽ alētheias*) are in Luke and Acts (Luke 4:25; 20:21; 22:59; and Acts 4:27; 10:34) and all occur in speeches confirming the truthfulness (theological or historical) of the statement which follows. Interestingly, in its last occurrence in the Gospel, the phrase is directed toward Peter by a stander-by in the high priest's courtyard who accuses Peter of knowing Jesus, "Truly this man was also with him, for he is a Galilean" (22:59; my translation), an accusation which is true despite Peter's protest (22:60). So also here in Peter's speech, the audience may trust that what follows is true. The verb "understand" (καταλαμβάνω, *katalambanō*) is in the present tense and is best understood as a "progressive present," that is, "I am understanding."[47] Peter's understanding continues to grow from his accepting hospitality from a tanner, a marginalized Jew, to extending hospitality to Gentile strangers, to entering the house of a Gentile, to expressing his understanding that he is not to call anyone "common or unclean."

Now Peter expresses his conviction that this understanding is ultimately rooted in God's own character: "God shows no partiality" (10:34). The phrase translated "partiality" (προσωπολήμπτης, *prosōpolēmptēs*) literally means "lifting up the face" and is related to several Greek terms (προσωπολημπτέω, προσωπολημψία, λαμβάνειν πρόσωπον), which are used to translate a Hebrew idiom, "lifting the face" (נָשָׂא פָנִים, *yisa᾽ panîm*) that "pictures God as an oriental monarch lifting the face of a petitioner," thus receiving him or her with favor.[48] Early Christian writers employ the image created by this semantic cluster to argue for the impartiality of God; that is, they argue, as Peter does here, that God does not discriminate (see Rom 2:11; Col 3:25; Eph 6:9; *1 Clem.* 1:3; *Letter of Barnabas* 4:12; Polycarp, *Letter to the Philippians* 6:1) and that it is wrong for humans to do so (Jas 2:1, 9). Though the arguments of these writers are subtly nuanced,[49] they are grounded in the Old Testament. Deuteronomy 10:17–18 provides conceptual background for Acts 10:34: "For the Lord your God is God of gods and Lord of lords, the great God, mighty and awesome, who is not partial [LXX θαυμάζει πρόσωπον, *thaumazei prosōpon*] and takes no bribe, who executes judgment for the [LXX προσηλύτῳ καί, *prosēlutō kai;* proselyte and] the orphan and the widow and he loves the stranger [LXX proselyte]. . . ."

Peter's understanding of God's impartiality now extends beyond the Jew and includes the Gentile; his view has not only been shaped by his vision of the sheet, but also by his perception of Cornelius. The speech continues: "in every nation anyone who fears him and does what is right is acceptable to him" (10:35). Peter has come to accept the pious characterization of Cornelius as "one who fears God" (10:2; 22) and "righteous" (10:22) and is now willing to generalize by saying "in every nation, anyone . . ." who may be characterized in these ways "is acceptable" to God. The use of the word "acceptable" (δεκτός, *dektos*) is interesting here. Originally associated with the sacrificial cult (LXX Exod 28:34; Lev 1:3–4; 17:4; 19:5; and passim), the wisdom traditions had extended its meaning to refer to a life pleasing to God.[50] For example, LXX Prov 12:22 asserts "the one who acts faithfully is acceptable [δεκτός, *dektos*] to him," and Prov 15:8 reads "the prayers of the righteous are acceptable to him" (see also Prov 10:24; 11:1; 16:5; Sir 2:5). Peter's speech continues to draw upon the same universalizing tendencies of the Jewish wisdom tradition that the narrator had made use of at the beginning of the unit (see comments on Acts 10:2 above).

The next two verses are grammatically obscure, giving rise to a variety of textual variants.[51] Perhaps the best way to understand these verses has been suggested by Harald Riesenfeld who proposed the following translation: "(34) Truly I perceive that God shows no partiality, (35) but in every nation anyone who fears him and practices righteousness is acceptable to him. (36) This [namely, that God shows no partiality] is the word which he sent to the children of Israel, preaching good news of peace through Jesus Christ—He is Lord of all."[52] This translation has the advantage of removing the phrase "He is Lord of all" from a disruptive and intrusive phrase (placed in parentheses in the RSV and separated from the sentence by a dash in the NRSV) to the centerpiece of the thought unit. Both God, who "shows no partiality," and Jesus, who is "Lord of all" (see Acts 2:36), support Peter's perspective on the radically inclusive nature of the gospel.

There are several allusions to Old Testament passages in 10:36. The "message which God sent" (τὸν λόγον ὃν ἀπέστειλεν, *ton logon hon apesteilen;* my translation) recalls the healing message of LXX Ps 106:20 ("he sent out his message [ἀπέστειλεν τὸν λόγον, *apesteilen ton logon*] and healed them" my translation); see the reference to healing later in

Peter's speech at 10:38). "Preaching good news of peace" (my translation) echoes LXX Isa 52:7, but is modified to state that this peace comes through Jesus Christ. Peace as a messianic blessing is thematic for Luke (cf. Luke 1:79; 2:14; 7:50; 8:48; 10:5–6; 19:38, 42; 24:36; Acts 7:26; 9:31). The pronouncement of salvific peace was also an essential element of protocol for the household mission established by Jesus in Luke 10:5–7.[53] Peter states that this good news of impartial peace conveyed through Jesus Christ was "sent to the children of Israel" (this phrase, τοῖς υἱοῖς Ἰσραήλ, *tois huiois Israēl*, literally "sons of Israel," also occurs at Luke 1:16; Acts 5:21; 7:23, 37; 9:15). Given this emphasis on the universalism of this message of peace, the audience might wonder why Peter begins his speech by casting both its content and rhetoric in such a specifically Jewish light.

First, we should remember that Luke (like Paul) knows that this gospel was given "to the Jew first and then the Greek" (Rom 1:16; 2:9, 10), thus even the message of radical inclusion begins as part of the larger narrative of Israel's story. Second, Robert Tannehill has made the interesting suggestion that this part of Peter's speech not only echoes the Old Testament passages cited above, but also (and primarily he argues) "the angel's annunciation of Jesus' birth to the shepherds in Luke 2."[54] In this case, the "children of Israel" who receive the message are the shepherds of Luke 2. He notes these parallels in language between Luke 2:10–14 and Acts 10:36: (1) The angel says, "I preach good news" (εὐαγγελίζομαι, *euangelizomai*) concerning the birth of (2) "Messiah Lord" (χριστός, *christos*, κύριος, *kyrios*). (3) The angelic chorus then proclaims "on earth peace" (εἰρήνη, *eirēnē*). The similarities to Acts 10:36 are striking: "preaching good news of peace through Jesus Christ" who is Lord. Peter, however, goes beyond the divine impartiality of the infancy narrative. There the angel proclaimed that Jesus would bring joy to "all the people" (παντὶ τῷ λαῷ, *panti tō laō*), normally understood to refer to the Jewish people. But Peter extends that understanding both theologically (God shows no partiality to neither Jews *nor* Gentiles) and christologically (Jesus is Lord of all, *both* Jews and Gentiles).

Third, the inclusiveness of Peter's message is shot throughout this speech, even in those parts that seem to refer to the specifically Jewish character of the gospel. This is achieved in part by employing two-edged rhetoric. The "preaching of good news" echoes not only the OT, but also the imperial birth of Augustus.[55] Likewise, "peace" would communicate not only to Jewish audience who expected "peace" as part of the messianic age (cf. Isa. 11:6–9), but "peace" was part of the benefits of the Roman imperial governance. Finally, the phrase "Lord of all" is found not only of Yahweh in Jewish documents of the Second Temple period

(*T. Mos.* 4:2; *The Letter of Aristeas* 16, 18; Wis 6:7; 8:9), but also describing the god Osiris in Plutarch (*Isis and Osiris* 12; see also Epictetus 4.1.12). This pattern of using language that communicates on several cultural levels here affirms the universality of divine impartiality and is typical of Lukan rhetorical strategy elsewhere.[56] As we shall see, it continues in the rest of the speech.

If Tannehill is correct in identifying Acts 10:36 as an echo of the Lukan birth narrative, then "the whole of vv. 36–43 presents a summary of Luke's Gospel in chronological order, from the birth of Jesus to the commission to the apostles at the end of Luke 24."[57] As such, it is the only outline of the life of Jesus outside the Gospels. The speech continues, "you know what took place throughout all Judea, beginning in Galilee after the baptism that John announced" (10:37, my translation; cf. 1:4–5, 22). Peter's use of "you know" is either a rhetorical gesture to endear the listener to the speaker (giving the auditors credit for knowing what in fact they do not) or assumes that these events are public knowledge and known even to a Gentile audience in Caesarea (see also Paul's comment that Agrippa must know about the suffering Messiah because "this thing was not done in a corner," 26:26).

Peter continues his speech by noting "how God anointed Jesus of Nazareth with the Holy Spirit and with power" (10:38a; see also the prayer of the Jerusalem congregation in Acts 4:27–28, which refers to God anointing Jesus).[58] This phrase recalls not only the baptism of Jesus, where the Holy Spirit descended upon Jesus (Luke 3:20–22), but also Jesus' inaugural speech at Nazareth where he claimed, "The Spirit of the Lord is upon me, because he has anointed me" (Luke 4:18; cf. 4:14, in which it says Jesus was "filled with the power of the Spirit"). Jesus is reading from Isa 61 and claims that this Scripture describes his prophetic role. The outline which follows in Peter's speech characterizes Jesus' ministry as one of benefaction: "how he went about doing good and healing all who were oppressed by the devil" (10:38b). This image of benefaction translates the passage from Isaiah in which the anointing is for preaching "good news to the poor," "release to the captives," "recovery of sight to the blind," and to free the oppressed (see Luke 4:18–20; Isa 61:1–2). Benefaction is a particularly appropriate image for an audience familiar with patronage and especially the, presumably, Gentile audience in Cornelius's house, who no doubt had personally enjoyed the benefits of Cornelius's benefaction (and readers who also were no doubt aware of self-serving benefactors; see Luke 22:25).

Luke has already described the apostle's healing ministry as a "benefaction" (see Acts 4:9) and placed the miracles of Christian missionaries in stark contrast to the magic practiced by the agents of Satan (see Acts 8:4–25). He now argues, through Peter's speech, that Jesus' healing ministry was itself the act of a generous benefactor engaged in a struggle against demonic forces by "healing all who were oppressed by the devil" (10:38b). The word "oppress" (καταδυναστεύω, *katadyna-steuō*) is found in the New Testament only here and at Jas 2:6 where it refers to the poor being oppressed by the rich, a connotation found also in the Greek Old Testament (see Exod 1:13; 21:17; Neh 5:5; Amos 4:1; 8:4; Jer 7:6, 22:3; Ezek 18:7). Thus, Luke employs the economic terminology of the Greco-Roman patronage system and also of the Jewish Scriptures to interpret Jesus' ministry as engaged in fulfilling Isaiah's vision.

Peter claims Jesus was able to engage in this ministry of healing and benefaction because "God was with him" (10:38c). Luke has already used this phrase in Stephen's speech to characterize Joseph, who was rescued from all his afflictions because "God was with him" (7:9). Similar words are used to depict the presence of God with Mary (Luke 1:28), John the Baptist (Luke 1:66), Christian missionaries in Antioch (Acts 11:21), and Paul (Acts 18:10). "They are all benefactors in the service of God, the supreme benefactor."[59] The phrase was also a favorite one in the Greek Old Testament to describe God's protection and empowerment of his servants (Gen 21:20, 22; 39:2; Exod 3:12; Isa 58:11). So, too, Jesus is empowered by God to fulfill his prophetic vocation (see also Acts 2:22).

In Acts 10:39–42, Peter returns to familiar themes of apostolic witness and the kerygma of Jesus' death and resurrection. In Acts 10:39, Peter asserts: "We are witnesses to all that he did both in Judea and Jerusalem." Apostolic witness is a Lukan theme (see Acts 1:8, 22; 2:32; 3:15; 5:32; 13:31; 22:15; 26:16), and the reference here to being witnesses of "all that he did both in Judea and Jerusalem" fulfills the first qualification Peter earlier claimed was necessary for anyone who was part of the circle of the Twelve: "one of the men who have accompanied us during all the time that the Lord Jesus went in and out among us" (see Acts 1:1, 21–22).

Peter then focuses attention on one particular aspect of all that Jesus did, namely his death and resurrection: "They put him to death by hanging him on a tree; but God raised him on the third day and allowed him to appear" (10:39b–40). This kerygmatic formula, "they put him to death/but God raised him," is found with some variation throughout the early speeches in Acts (see 2:23–24; 3:13–15; 4:10; 5:30–31), as well as some of the subsequent addresses by Paul (13:28–31; 26:22–23). The amplification that Jesus was put to death "by hanging on a tree" (κρεμάσαντες ἐπὶ ξύλου, *kremasantes epi xylou*) clearly recalls the language of LXX Deut 21:23, "Cursed by God is everyone who hangs on a tree" (my translation; κρεμάμενος ἐπὶ χύλου, *kremamenos epi xylou*) and occurs earlier in a Petrine speech at Acts 5:30. The shameful death of Jesus is in sharp contrast to God who "raised him on the third day."

There are two points in this part of the speech that share in the ideological perspective of the narrator of Acts. First, the death of Jesus is inseparable from his resurrection. Suffering is an integral part of exaltation; this is true not only for Christ but also for the church.[60] Second, from Luke's perspective, God is the one responsible for the resurrection of Jesus: Here as elsewhere, it is God who acts to raise him from the dead. Peter goes on to say that God was also responsible for the post-resurrection appearances; "and [God] allowed him [Jesus] to appear." The word, διδόναι (*didonai*), translated here "allow," is also used of God's active participation in Christ's resurrection in Acts 2:27 and 13:35, both of which are quotations of LXX Ps 15:10. Thus, while there are no explicit Old Testament quotations here in the speech, echoes and allusions to the Old Testament profoundly shape the rhetoric of Peter's address, a point to which we shall return in a moment.

In v. 41, Peter resumes the theme of witness: God allowed Christ to appear "not to all the people but to us who were chosen by God as witnesses, and who ate and drank with him after he rose from the dead." Noting that God chose the apostles to be "witnesses" is consistent with the theocentric focus of this speech. Luke sees no conflict with his comments elsewhere that Jesus had chosen and appointed the apostles as witnesses (Luke 6:13–16; 24:48) or that this election had taken place "through the Holy Spirit" (Acts 1:2); ultimately God is responsible. The reference to those witnesses who "ate and drank" with Christ after his resurrection fulfills Peter's second stipulated qualification for electing a replacement for the Twelve ("one of these must become a witness with us to his resurrection"; Acts 1:22) and calls to mind those passages where the resurrected Christ did, indeed, eat with his followers (Luke 24:30; 41–43; Acts 1:4). Perhaps equally important, the reference to "eating and drinking" recalls the third element of Jesus' instructions for a household mission of the seventy-two in Luke 10:5–7: "stay in that house, eating and drinking whatever they give you" (10:7a NIV). Peter is the first follower in Acts (but not the last; see 16:11–15, 25–34; 18:1–11) to enact the household mission and specifically to partake in table-fellowship with Cornelius and his household (see Acts 10:48; 11:3). More will be said about Peter's household mission in the comments on Scene 6 and 7.

The resurrected Christ "commanded us to preach to the people" (10:42; cf. 1:8). This note that the message must go first to the Jewish people (λαός, *laos*) has been struck before (Acts 3:26) and will be sounded again (Acts 13:46; see comments above). Once again Peter claims that the apostles have been called to bear witness, this time specifically to the fact that Christ "is the one ordained by God as judge of the living and the dead" (10:42b). The sovereignty of God is emphasized by the phrase "the one ordained [ὁ ὡρισμένος, ho hōrismenos] by God" and recalls the "set plan" [τῇ ὡρισμένῃ βουλῇ, tē hōrismenē boulē] of God in Acts 2:23 (cf. 4:28). The role of Christ as judge recurs in Paul's Areopagus speech in 17:31: "he [God] will have the world judged in righteousness by a man whom he has appointed" (κρίνειν τὴν οἰκουμένην ἐν δικαιοσύνῃ ἐν ἀνδρὶ ᾧ ὥρισεν, krinein tēn oikoumenēn en dikaiosynē en andri hō hōrisen). While the idea of Christ as eschatological judge may be grounded in the tradition of the Danielic Son of Man as judge (see Dan 7:13–14), here (as elsewhere in this speech) "Peter perhaps was interpreting the title in terms that would have been comprehensible to a Gentile."[61] That Christ is judge "of the living and the dead" makes the same universalizing point of Peter's earlier claim that Jesus is "Lord of all" (10:36) "and is part of the envelope structure."[62]

In the concluding element of his speech, Peter appeals to another common Lukan theme: the witness of the Old Testament prophets ("All the prophets testify about him"; 10:43a; see Luke 24:27, 44; Acts 3:24; 26:22). While it is true that Peter nowhere in this speech quotes the Old Testament directly, it would be a mistake to conclude that "in the Cornelius story scripture plays almost no role whatsoever."[63] While Peter may have avoided direct quotations from the Old Testament because of his Gentile audience (as will be the case later with Paul in Acts 13 and 17), our analysis above has demonstrated that the entire episode and specifically Peter's address are replete with Old Testament echoes and allusions. Further, the hermeneutic in those echoes and in this reference to the prophets may aptly be called a "messianic exegesis" at work here as elsewhere in Acts.[64]

Peter's conclusion recapitulates important concepts for Luke: "believing in Christ" (πιστεύω, pisteuō, with various prepositions: 5:14; 8:12; 9:42; 11:17; 13:39;16:34; 18:8; 19:4; 24:14; 26:27; 27:25), forgiveness of sins (2:38; 3:19; 5:31; 13:38; 22:16; 26:18), and the efficacy of Christ's name (2:38; 3:16; 4:10, 12; 21:13). Just as significant is the inclusio that the theme of universality forms with the beginning of the speech: "*everyone* who believes in him receives forgiveness of sins through his name" (10:43b). To be sure, there is nothing in the speech which indicates that the apostles are themselves responsible for a Gentile mission;[65] they are called to "preach to the (Jewish) people." Still, Luke knows that this proclamation is a necessary part of the Gentile mission (see Acts 13:46), and Peter is here affirming the fact that the story of the

Jewish Messiah has universal significance for Gentiles as well. The subsequent events in the next scene confirm Peter's insight and push him toward the last step in his "conversion" process to understanding that the story of Jesus is a word of salvation for Cornelius and his household.[66]

Scene 6: 10:44–48. *The Gentile Pentecost*

Before Peter could finish speaking, a second Pentecost occurs (10:44; the rhetorical technique of the "interrupted speech" occurs also at 2:36; 17:32; 22:22; 23:7; 26:24; cf. 11:15). Both the untimely nature of the Spirit's arrival (during Peter's speech and before baptism) and the amazement of the circumcised believers emphasize the surprising initiative of God, who is still directing these actions.

This "Gentile Pentecost" is the fourth outpouring of the Holy Spirit in Acts (2:1–4; 4:3; 8:17). The phenomenon is experienced by "all who heard the word" (10:44b), recalling Peter's address. The focus has now shifted from the individual character, Cornelius, to his household. "The reception of the Holy Spirit by the household at Acts 10:44–48 becomes the occasion for the disappearance of Cornelius from the story and, ultimately, from the pages of Acts."[67]

When this scene is recounted in Acts 15 by Peter and James, they relate the conversion of a group, not an individual. The corporate nature of the experience is continued in the next verse: "The circumcised believers who had come with Peter were astounded that the gift of the Holy Spirit had been poured out even on the Gentiles" (10:45). And as in the first Pentecost, the gift of the Spirit is confirmed for the "circumcised believers" when "they heard them [the Gentiles] speaking in tongues and extolling God" (10:46). So the scene which had focused on Peter and Cornelius now brings to the foreground those believers who had accompanied Peter to Caesarea (10:23) and the household of Cornelius (10:2, 24); both groups had remained silently in the background until this moment. This emphasis on the communal nature of the event continues until the end of the scene.

According to Philip Esler, speaking in tongues is an "irrefutable legitimation for the acceptance of the Gentiles into the community."[68] In light of this demonstrable evidence, Peter asks, "Is anyone able to *hinder* the water for baptizing these who have received the Holy Spirit just like us?"(10:47a; my translation). The answer for Luke is, of course, "No!" Just as earlier nothing could hinder the Ethiopian Eunuch from being baptized (8:36) and later not even prison could hinder Paul from preaching the gospel (28:31), so now the barrier of Gentile uncleanness could no longer hinder the inclusion of Gentiles into the kingdom though it would be subject of one more debate! (see ch. 15). Continuing the theme of the household's conversion, Peter, then, commands "*them* to be baptized in the name of Jesus Christ" (10:47b). The scene ends on the familiar note of hospitality ("Then they invited him to stay for several days," 10:48), though again the shift from first to third person is important in underscoring that "the household gradually supplants Cornelius as the primary focus of the narrative."[69] The conversion of this Gentile household occupies center stage in the conflict presented in the next and final scene of this episode.

Scene 7:11:1–18. Reporting to the Jerusalem Church

The change in scene is marked by a shift in locale and participants: "Now the apostles and the believers who were in Judea heard that the Gentiles had also accepted the word of God" (11:1). Word of these events at Cornelius's house travels back to Judea to the apostles and believers, who together comprise the entire Jerusalem congregation. Neither the leaders nor the rank and file evidently had any problem with the conversion and baptism of the household since the word "receive" (δέχομαι, *dechomai*) is used several times in conjunction with the word of God to mean "receiving and accepting it so as to become believers" (cf. Acts 8:14; 17:11).[70] Nor did they object to understanding that "what had happened at Caesarea was not an isolated exception but a new direction in the church's mission."[71]

But the Jerusalem church did have objections which they expressed when Peter returned to Jerusalem: "The circumcised believers criticized him" (11:2). The "circumcised believers" do not here refer to a specific "party" or "faction" but rather to the whole congregation of Jewish Christians who stand in contrast to the "uncircumcised" men with whom Peter has socially interacted. Luke makes full use of the polyvalence of the word translated here "criticized" (διακρίνομαι, *diakrinomai*). Earlier the same word had been used by the voice that instructed Peter to accompany Cornelius's messengers without doubt or discrimination, and later in this scene will be so used again. "What the Spirit forbade Peter to do toward the Gentiles, namely 'debate/make distinctions/ doubt,' these fellow Jews are now doing toward him!"[72]

The specific charges they level against Peter are two: "Why do you enter [into the house of] uncircumcised men and eat with them?" (11:3; my translation). Peter is accused first of entering, presumably the house[73] of uncircumcised men, itself an unclean space (cf. the charge leveled against Jesus in the Zacchaeus story : "He has gone [εἰσῆλθεν, *eisēlthen*] to lodge with a sinful man," Luke 19:7). Second, he is charged with eating with unclean Gentiles, another taboo (see 2 Macc 5:27; Luke 5:30). Peter's table-fellowship with Gentiles is not mentioned explicitly in the preceding narrative, but it can be inferred from Peter's stay in Cornelius's house "for several days" that he did share meals (see Acts 10:48). More to the point, Peter does not deny the charge in his defense speech. (Lost in both accusation and response is the point so important earlier in the story that Cornelius was a "God-fearer" and presumably would not have served unclean food to his kosher guests.)

Peter does have a response, however, which falls into four parts. First, he recounts his vision at Joppa (11:4–10), then he gives his version of Cornelius's vision (11:11–14); next he recounts the Pentecost experience, and finally he concludes his address with a question (11:17) that forces his audience to share in his conclusion (11:18). Peter's address contains certain elements typical of a defense speech (cf. Plato, *Phaedrus* 266D–E; Aristotle, *Rhetoric* 1345b): narration (*narratio*) which dominates the response; proof (*probatio*) in the form of witnesses (11:12) and signs (11:15); and a conclusion (*peroratio*) in the form of a rhetorical question (11:17).[74]

The narrator also notes that Peter began to explain "in order" or "step by step" (καθεξῆς, *kathexēs*). The modern audience expecting the story to be told in chronological sequence will be surprised to hear that Peter begins by reversing the order of presentation of the visions: His own vision precedes that of Cornelius (on this see chapter 2). But the word "in order" (which also occurs in the preface of Luke's Gospel and represents an ideal which the narrator himself would like to fulfill) has little to do with chronological or linear order. Rather, Peter (and in a larger sense the narrator) is seeking to present the events in a manner which his audience will find convincing.

Peter begins then by recounting his vision (11:5–10; cf. 10:9–16). As in our analysis of the retellings of Cornelius's vision (10:22, 30–33; and see comments below on 11:11–14), there are significant variations in the retelling (see Table 2).[75] This second version truncates the first: "I was in the city of Joppa praying and in a trance I saw a vision" (11:5). Any reference to Simon the tanner (cf. 10:5, 17, 32) is entirely missing, perhaps an effort on Peter's part to avoid further distressing his circumcised audience with news of his lodging with an objectionable Jew. Second, there is no reference to Peter's hunger or food being prepared, perhaps because he wishes to save his first explicit reference to eating until later in the vision when God instructs him to "eat." Further, though the report of the great sheet is nearly verbatim ("there was something like a large sheet coming down"), the direction emphasized changes from something "being lowered *to the ground* by its four corners" (10:11) to the sheet "being lowered *from heaven*" (11:5). This change allows Peter to streamline his presentation, omitting the reference to the "heavens being opened" (10:11), while maintaining that the vision did indeed originate in heaven.

Peter also adds several details of a personal and intimate nature: "It [the sheet] came close to me, and as I was staring at it . . ." (11:5b–6a; ἀτενίζω [*atenizō*] is a distinctly Lukan word—ten of the fourteen occurrences in the New Testament are in Acts, and two others are in Luke). These details not only add color, they draw the hearer into the account and form part of Peter's strategy in narrating his story "in order" (καθεξῆς, *kathexēs*), in a way that helps his hearers follow the logic of his thinking and ultimately convinces them to accept the truth of what he says.

The expansion from a three- to a four-fold classification introduces a variety of animals, "beasts of prey" or "wild animals" (θηρία, *thēria*), an expression that is used quite generically, especially in LXX Gen 1:25 which reports that "God made the wild animals of the earth of every variety" (ἐποίησεν ὁ θεὸς τὰ θηρία τῆς γῆς κατὰ γένος, *epoiēsen ho theos ta thēria tēs gēs kata genos;* cf. also LXX Ps 148:10). In some ancient literature, these "wild animals" are depicted as dangerous.[76] Near the end of the book, the viper (ἔχιδνα, *echidna*) that bites Paul on Malta (28:1–6) is twice called a θηρίον (*thērion,* for other places where the word is used of snakes, see Aretaeus 159.8; Galen 4.779). So, not only does the addition of "wild animals" make "the indiscriminate command to kill and eat even more radical,"[77] for the audience familiar with the rest of Acts, the presence of the "wild animals" may introduce a sinister element into the story.

The divine voice's words reported by Peter here are verbatim the same as those recorded earlier by the narrator: "Rise, Peter, slaughter and eat" (ἀναστάς, Πέτρε, θῦσον καὶ φάγε, *anastas, Petre, thyson kai phage;* 11:7; see 10:13). And the beginning of Peter's response is likewise verbatim the same: "By no means, Lord" (μηδαμῶς, κύριε, *mēdamōs, kyrie;* 11:8, see 10:14). But the remainder of his reply contains several interesting and important variations. First, there is a shift in subject. In 10:14, Peter claims, "I have never eaten anything common and unclean," but here in 11:8, he says, "Nothing common or unclean has ever entered my mouth." This change forefronts the words "common or unclean" and removes the specific reference to Peter eating.

There is also the change from the connective "common *and* unclean" to the disjunctive "common *or* unclean." This change had already occurred in Peter's earlier elliptical reference to his vision: "God has shown me that I should not call anyone profane or unclean" (10:28). Already here, Peter has begun allegorizing the vision from a focus on clean and unclean foods to a comment on the purity status of persons (see the full discussion on 10:28). And in doing so, he has differentiated between common and unclean in a way that he had not done in the initial vision where common and unclean were essentially synonyms. Here in Acts 11, Peter's subsequent reflection on the meaning of the vision has shaped his retelling of it.[78]

When Peter asserts, "Nothing common *or* unclean has ever entered my mouth," he is claiming that he has neither eaten any food made "common" by being mixed with unclean food (cf. 11:47) nor has he eaten anything "unclean" (cf. Lev 11). So when the voice responds at 11:9 (in verbatim agreement with 10:15), "That which God has cleansed, you must not call common," Peter intends his audience to come to the same conclusion that he eventually reached. The vision is not just about diet; it is about the very issue of Jew/Gentile associations with which these circumcised believers are so concerned. Further, the divine voice insists that Jews who associate with Gentiles have been cleansed by God and should not be called "common." Peter is able to make this point a bit more emphatically simply by changing the conjunction "and" to the disjunctive "or." By making this subtle change, Peter is able to reinterpret the vision in its retelling without having to offer explicit interpretation as he did in 10:28. This strategy also allows Peter to avoid for the moment the more objectionable conclusion for Jewish hearers that he had earlier shared with a Gentile audience, namely that Gentiles should not be called unclean either. (He will, of course, make that claim at the Jerusalem council, 15:9.) By employing these rhetorical strategies, his audience will hopefully reach the same conclusion, perhaps sooner than did Peter himself!

After reporting that the vision occurred three times before "everything was pulled up again into heaven" (11:10; cf. 10:16), Peter next recounts the visit of three men. References to Cornelius and the tanner are fastidiously avoided. They were sent "from Caesarea" (not Cornelius; see also 11:12 where Peter and the six brothers enter "the [unnamed] man's house"; see 10:17, 24–25) and "arrived at the house where we were" (11:11; not Simon's house, see 10:17). Nor are these messengers allowed in Peter's retelling to state why they have come or to give any of the favorable characterizations of Cornelius as a pious man. This fact is somewhat striking since a "God-fearing man, who is well spoken of by the whole Jewish nation" (10:22) would seem much less objectionable to the Jerusalem believers than some "uncircumcised" men they may have imagined. This omission may be Peter's way of pressing the issue of

Jew/Gentile relations; he is unwilling to take the edge off his point by characterizing Cornelius as a Gentile already attracted to Judaism.

Echoing 10:20 (but in diegetic rather than mimetic mode), Peter reports that "the Spirit told me to go with them and not to make a distinction between them and us" (11:12). The event in Caesarea was divinely prompted. Peter continues: "These six brothers also accompanied me, and we entered the man's house" (11:12). The audience already knows that these brothers are "circumcised believers" (10:45), though the number "six" is new information. While it is possible that the number is symbolically significant (Peter with the six brothers brings to seven the total number of Jewish Christians who enter the Gentiles house), more important is the fact that Peter includes these fellow circumcised believers as also "guilty" of the charge of entering the house of uncircumcised men, an accusation originally leveled against Peter alone (11:3; note the second person singular, εἰσῆλθες, eisēlthes). "Peter has not only made them witnesses to the events (in which capacity they are critical to his defense), but has also implicated them in his own actions; they were participants! They were with him, heard his speech, saw the result of the Spirit's outpouring, and made no objection *then* to the baptism."[79]

After entering the house, Peter recounts Cornelius's vision (though Cornelius is again left unnamed). "He told us how he had seen the angel standing in his house and saying, 'Send to Joppa and bring Simon, who is called Peter; he will give a message by which you and your entire household will be saved'" (11:13–15). The multiple layers of narration are interesting: "Luke says that Peter says that Cornelius says that the angel says" (see Luke 15; Acts 2). Still, the angel maintains an authoritative voice through "direct speech." "[E]ven at this remove, with two narrators intervening, what the angel said is reported in directly quoted speech. There is thus the semblance of mimesis."[80]

Again, the speech of the angel reported by Peter (summarizing Cornelius!) contains truncations and expansions. Missing, as was true in the preceding verses, are any references to Cornelius's pious acts; even his name is omitted again! Rather, the entire message focuses on Peter and his message of salvation for the household. "In this final version Cornelius's role has been reduced far into the background to allow the importance of Peter's role (and the action of the Holy Spirit) to come to the fore."[81] The significance of the entire event has been boiled down to the salvation of a Gentile household. The narrative "flow" from Jew-Gentile table-fellowship to the question of the salvation of the Gentiles is exactly opposite that of the flow of Acts 15 which moves from the soteriological question to the issue of table-fellowship (see comments on ch. 15). It is this message of salvific peace that is the crucial element of the household mission (see Luke 10:5–7), which until now had been implied but not explicitly stated.

That salvation, Peter argues, was confirmed by the gift of the Holy Spirit. Peter here connects this Pentecost experience ("And as I began to speak, the Holy Spirit fell upon them," 11:15) with the first Pentecost ("just as it had on us at the beginning") in which many in his audience had no doubt participated. He had made a similar connection earlier (see 10:47: "these people who have received the Holy Spirit just as we have"). Both Pentecosts take place in a house (οἶκος, *oikos*) and signal the replacement of the temple by the house as the sacred space which embodies "socially and ideologically the structures, values, and goals of an inclusive gospel of universal salvation."[82]

What is new here is found in the next verse: "And I remembered the word of the Lord, how he had said, 'John baptized with water, but you will be baptized with the Holy Spirit'" (11:16). The experience, Peter reveals (for the first time), prompted a memory of and a new application for a dominical saying (see Acts 1:5; cf. Luke 3:16): Not only did the Jerusalem church receive a baptism in the Holy Spirit, but that work continues. "In the light of his new experience Peter came to understand that the first Pentecost was only a partial fulfillment of this promise and that the Pentecost of the Gentiles completed it."[83]

The conclusion of Peter's defense is a sharply stated question: "If then God gave them the same gift that he gave us when we believed in the Lord Jesus Christ, who was I that I could hinder God?" (11:17). Familiar themes are sounded again: the Holy Spirit as a gift (Acts 2:38), the parallels between the first Pentecost in Jerusalem and this "Gentile Pentecost" ("God gave them the same gift he gave us . . ."; cf. 10:47; 11:15), and most notable, the motif of the "unhindered" gospel ("who was I that I could hinder God?" 8:37; 10:47; 28:31).

This question is not intended to be "merely rhetorical," and the silence is finally broken when these Jewish Christians from Jerusalem praise God saying, "Then God has given even to the Gentiles the repentance that leads to life" (11:18).

Conclusion

The issue of Gentile inclusion in the church is by no means resolved as Acts 15 demonstrates, but at least Peter's conversion is as complete as Cornelius's. For him, at least, as far as Jews and Gentiles were concerned, God "has made no distinction between them and us" (15:9). Further, these two individuals are joined in their conversion by two groups:

1) the Jerusalem church who desist from criticizing Peter ("they grew silent;" my translation) and rejoice with Peter that "God has given even to the Gentiles the repentance that leads to life," and 2) the household of Cornelius who increasingly become the focus of this story as the recipients of a message by which they shall be saved!

To view these "conversions" as being from one religion to another as though Christianity and Judaism were depicted in Acts as two discrete and separate entities is anachronistic. Nonetheless, this is what many scholars do. As we have already noted, "Luke's overall narrative" presents the "Christian" movement as one Jewish sect among several.

Furthermore, the view that in Acts Christianity is universal and superior and Judaism is particularistic and inferior is inaccurate, especially in view of the Cornelius passage. As we have seen, the category of "God-fearers" was closely related to the post-exilic Jewish wisdom tradition that universalized the concept of allegiance to Yahweh. "God-fearing" "described the requisite attitude of life in which a truly Jewish morality and piety could flourish in a Gentile setting."[84] So when Peter claims that "in every nation anyone who fears him and does what is right is acceptable to him" (10:35), Peter is continuing a universalizing tendency already found in Judaism (cf. LXX Prov 12:22; Sir 2:5), not asserting the triumph of a superior, universalizing Christian religion to a provincial, inferior Judaism. In Acts, the Christian sect moved in a universalizing Jewish current, a current that recognizes that through Christ, Gentiles are to be included as children of Abraham and are a vital part of the reconstituted people of God.

Notes

1. In addition to studies on conversion in antiquity and/or the New Testament, e.g., A. D. Nock, *Conversion* (London: Oxford University Press, 1933); Thomas M. Finn, *From Death to Rebirth: Ritual and Conversion in Antiquity* (New York: Paulist, 1997); and Beverly R. Gaventa, *From Darkness to Light: Aspects of Conversion in the New Testament* (Philadelphia: Fortress, 1986), which devote significant space to Acts, see also R. Michiels, "a conception lucanienne de la conversion," *ETL* 41 (1965): 42–78; Jacques Dupont, "Conversion in the Acts of the Apostles," in *The Salvation of the Gentiles* (New York: Paulist, 1979), 61–84; Charles H. Talbert, "Conversion in the Acts of the Apostles: Ancient Auditors' Perceptions," in *Literary Studies in Luke-Acts* (ed. Richard P. Thompson and Thomas E. Phillips; Macon, Ga.: Mercer University Press, 1998), 141–54; Joel B. Green, "'To Turn from Darkness to Light' (Acts 26:18): Conversion in the Narrative of Luke-Acts," in *Conversion in the Wesleyan Tradition* (Nashville: Abingdon, 2001), 103–18, 271–74.

2. See Krister Stendahl, *The School of St. Matthew, and Its Use of the Old Testament* (rev. ed.; Philadelphia: Fortress, 1968).

3. See John P. Meier, *The Vision of Matthew* (New York: Paulist, 1979) whose commentary is structured around these "five books."

4. David Garland has also noted, that in addition to this interest in the fate of Gentiles, that Matthew's "anti-Jewish" material (21:43; 23:32–35, 35; 27:25) prohibits one from concluding "too quickly that Matthew was primarily for Jews" (*Reading Matthew: A Literary and Theological Commentary on the First Gospel* [New York: Crossroad, 1995], 2).

5. See Stephen G. Wilson, *Luke and the Law* (Cambridge: Cambridge University Press, 1983).

6. See Mark L. Strauss, *The Davidic Messiah in Luke-Acts: The Promise and Its Fulfillment in Lukan Christology* (Sheffield: Sheffield Academic Press, 1995).

7. Talbert, *Reading Acts*, 43–44.

8. On the importance of Abraham in Luke, see N. A. Dahl, "The Story of Abraham in Luke-Acts," in *Jesus in the Memory of the Early Church* (Minneapolis: Fortress, 1976), 66–86; J. B. Green, "The Problem of a Beginning: Israel's Scriptures in Luke 1–2," *BBR* 4 (1994): 61–85; Robert Brawley, "Abrahamic Covenant Traditions and the Characterization of God in Luke-Acts," in *The Unity of Luke Acts* (BETL 142; ed. J. Verheyden; Leuven-Louvain: Leuven University Press/Presses universitaires de Louvain, 1999), 109–32; J. S. Siker, *Disinheriting the Jews. Abraham in Early Christian Controversy* (Louisville: Westminster John Knox, 1991); Turid Karlsen Seim, "Abraham, Ancestor or Archetype? A Comparison of Abraham-Language in 4 Maccabees and Luke-Acts," in *Antiquity and Humanity: Essays on Ancient Religion and Philosophy. Presented to Hans Dieter Betz on His 70th Birthday* (ed. Adela Yarbro Collins and Margaret M. Mitchell; Tübingen: Mohr Siebeck, 2001), 27–42.

9. Ultimately, with the success of the Gentile mission, the fall of Jerusalem, and the redefinition of Judaism by the "rabbis" (Pharisees), Christianity was, in fact, recognized by Jews, Christians, and Romans, as a separate religion, but not until sometime after 200 C.E.; see Alan F. Segal, *Rebecca's Children: Judaism and Christianity in the Roman World* (Cambridge, Mass.: Harvard University Press, 1986).

10. Though Krister Stendahl rightly challenged whether, based on a close reading of Paul's own writings, it is better to speak of Paul's call or Paul's conversion. In Acts, the call of Paul to be apostle to the Gentiles is clearly shaped by a narrative that must be dubbed his "conversion." See Stendahl, *Paul Among the Jews and Gentiles* (Philadelphia: Fortress, 1976), 7–23.

11. On these household conversion narratives in Acts, see David L. Matson, *Household Conversion Narratives in Acts: Pattern and Interpretation* (JSNTSup 123; Sheffield: Sheffield Academic Press, 1996).

12. Talbert, *Reading Acts*, 43.

13. Haenchen, *The Acts of the Apostles*, 357–59

14. Matson, *Household Conversion Narratives in Acts*.

15. See Hans Conzelmann, *Acts of the Apostles* (trans. James Limburg, et al. Hermeneia; Philadelphia: Fortress, 1987), 77; Haenchen, *Acts*, 340.

16. Bruce Malina and Jerome Neyrey, "First-Century Personality: Dyadic, Not Individualistic," in *The Social World of Luke-Acts: Models for Interpretation* (ed. Jerome H. Neyrey; Peabody, Mass: Hendrickson, 1991), 88.

17. Contrary to Johnson, *The Acts of the Apostles*, 179.

18. See Str-B 2.695.

19. So John Polhill, *Acts* (NAC 26; Nashville: Broadman, 1992), 248; 249 n. 63.

20. See T. R. S. Broughton, "The Roman Army," in *The Beginnings of Christianity* (5 vols.; eds. Foakes F. J. Jackson and Kirsopp Lake; Grand Rapids: Eerdmans, reprinted 1979) 5: 427–45.

21. Ronald E. Clements, "The Old Testament Background of Acts 10:34–35," in *With Steadfast Purpose: Essays in Honor of Henry Jackson Flanders, Jr.* (ed. Naymond H. Keathley; Waco, Tex.: Baylor University Press, 1990), 213.

22. Clements, "The Old Testament Background of Acts 10:34–35," 214–15.

23. Ibid., 215.

24. See B. J. Hubbard, "Commissioning Stories in Luke-Acts: A Study of Their Antecedents, Form and Content," *Semeia* 8 (1977): 118–22.

25. Tannehill, *The Narrative Unity of Luke-Acts*, 2:128–29.

26. Against Johnson, *Acts*, 183. On the adversative force of *de* in Acts, see Stephen Levinsohn, *Textual Connections in Acts* (SBLMS 31: Atlanta: Scholars Press, 1987), 91.

27. See Polhill, *Acts*, 254.

28. See Gaventa, *From Darkness to Light*, 115.

29. Polhill, *Acts*, 256.

30. On this, see Ronald Witherup, "Cornelius Over and Over and Over Again: 'Functional Redundancy' in the Acts of the Apostles," *JSNT* 49 (1993): 45–66, at 55.

31. Witherup, "Cornelius," 55.

32. On the importance of hospitality for understanding these scenes, see Andrew Arterbury, "The Ancient Custom of Hospitality, The Greek Novels, and Acts 10:1–11:18," *PRSt* 29 (2002): 53–72.

33. Polhill, *Acts*, 257.

34. See Robert Funk, *The Poetics of Biblical Narrative* (Sonoma, Calif.: Polebridge, 1988), 151.

35. Gaventa, *From Darkness to Light*, 116, 128; Witherup, "Cornelius," 52.

36. Haenchen, *Acts*, 350.

37. Krodel, *Acts*, 193.

38. Joseph B. Tyson, "The Gentile Mission and the Authority of Scripture in Acts," *NTS* 33 (1987): 619–31, at 627.

39. Translation from O. S. Wintermute, "Jubilees," in *The Old Testament Pseudepigrapha* (2 vols.; ed. James H. Charlesworth; Garden City, N.Y.: Doubleday & Co., 1985), 2:98.

40. C. House, "Defilement by Association: Some Insights from the Usage of *koinos/koinoô* in Acts 10 and 11," *AUSS* 21 (1983): 143–53, makes a similar argument for the meaning of "common" and "unclean," though he does not see any narrative development in this understanding.

41. For more on this argument see Mikeal C. Parsons "'Nothing Defiled AND Unclean': The Conjunction's Function in Acts 11:14," *PRSt* 27 (2000): 263–74.

42. Neyrey, "The Symbolic Universe of Luke-Acts: 'They Turn the World Upside Down,'" in *The Social World of Luke-Acts*, 278.

43. Tannehill, *Narrative Unity*, 2:135.

44. Tables 1 and 2 are arranged in a fashion similar to a synoptic parallel, where similar material is placed side by side. In both tables, verbatim and near-verbatim materials are indicated with double underlining and single underlin-

ing, respectively (material that is similar conceptually but not linguistically is indicated by a broken line). The differences, discussed above, then become significant for our understanding of the tracing Luke's train of thought.

45. Witherup, "Cornelius," 57.

46. Soards, *The Speeches in Acts*, 71.

47. Johnson, *Acts*, 191.

48. Polhill, *Acts*, 260.

49. On the differences between Luke and Paul's ideas of divine impartiality, see J. M. Bassler, "Luke and Paul on Impartiality," *Bib* 66 (1985): 546–52.

50. Johnson, *Acts*, 191.

51. See Barrett, *A Critical and Exegetical Commentary on the Acts of the Apostles*, 1:521–22.

52. Cited by Krodel, *Acts*, 196; for alternative understandings see Tannehill, *Narrative Unity*, 2:139–41 and Johnson, *Acts*, 191

53. See Matson, *Household Conversion Narratives in Acts*, 44–47, 111.

54. Tannehill, *Narrative Unity*, 2:138.

55. For the Greek text of the inscription, see W. Dittenberger, ed., *Orientis Graecae Inscriptiones Selectae* (2 vols.; Leipzig: S. Hirzel, 1903–05; repr. Hildesheim: Olms, 1960), 2.48–60 [= *OGIS* 458].

56. See Danker, *Jesus and the New Age*.

57. Tannehill, *Narrative Unity*, 2:140.

58. See Soards, *The Speeches in Acts*, 74.

59. Krodel, *Acts*, 197.

60. See David Moessner, "The Christ Must Suffer," 165–95.

61. Polhill, *Acts*, 263.

62. Tannehill, *Narrative Unity*, 2:141.

63. Tyson, "The Gentile Mission and the Authority of Scripture in Acts," 628; see also 629 where Tyson argues that "Luke omitted quotations and allusions to scripture in the Cornelius episode."

64. See Donald Juel, *Messianic Exegesis: Christological Interpretation of the Old Testament in Early Christianity* (Philadelphia: Fortress, 1988).

65. So Tannehill, *Narrative Unity*, 2:141.

66. Tannehill, *Narrative Unity*, 2:141–42.

67. Matson, *Household Conversion Narratives*, 113.

68. Philip Esler, "Glossalalia and the Admission of Gentiles into the Early Christian Community," *BTB* 22 (1992): 136.

69. Matson, *Household Conversion Narratives*, 113.

70. See Barrett, *Acts*, 1:536.

71. Krodel, *Acts*, 202.

72. Johnson, *Acts*, 197.

73. Barrett, *Acts*, 1:538.

74. Johnson, *Acts*, 200.

75. Contrary to most modern commentators on Acts 11:1–18, who dismiss these verses as merely summary of the preceding events, we see in the variations in this retelling a clue to Luke's understanding of these conversion stories.

76. See BDAG for texts.

77. Matson, *Household Conversion Narratives*, 120.

78. For more on the significance of this change, see Parsons, " 'Nothing Defiled AND Unclean': The Conjunction's Function in Acts 11:14."

79. Johnson, *Acts*, 198.

80. Funk, *Poetics*, 155.

81. Witherup, "Cornelius," 57.

82. John H. Elliott, "Temple Versus Household in Luke-Acts: A Contrast in Social Institutions," in *The Social World of Luke-Acts* (ed. Jerome Neyrey; Peabody, Mass.: Hendrickson, 1991), 211–41, quoting 213; cf. Matson, *Household Conversion Narratives*, 128–34.

83. Krodel, *Acts*, 204.

84. Clements, "The Old Testament Background of Acts 10:34–35," 213.

Epilogue

The three perspectives pursued in this book—Luke as storyteller, interpreter, and evangelist—are obviously interrelated. When serving as an interpreter of tradition or evangelist for the Good News, Luke deploys all of his rhetorical arsenal. That is to say, the *message* of Luke's writings—the "what"—is intricately interwoven with the *medium* of that message—the "how."

Thus, when we consider Luke as a storyteller, we are never far removed from his concerns as an interpreter or evangelist. By choosing to deal with specific examples of Luke's prowess as storyteller, interpreter, and evangelist, it might appear at first glance that I have failed to give the reader a sense of Luke and Acts "as a whole." My conviction, however, has been that one can move quite easily from the specific to the general, from the particular to the panoramic, and from the individual "events that have been fulfilled among us" to a deeper apprehension of the Truth in which we "have been instructed" (Luke 1:4). Therefore, it is my hope that this work, by considering these three angles of vision and the clarity each one provides for understanding Luke and Acts, will contribute to the overall appreciation for Luke's literary and theological accomplishments.

Bibliography

Secondary Literature

Aletti, J. N. *L'art de raconter Jésus Christ: L'écriture narrative de l'évangile de Luc*. Paris: Seuil, 1989.

Alexander, Loveday. "The Preface to Acts and the Historians." Pages 73–103 in *History, Literature, and Society in the Book of Acts*. Edited by Ben Witherington III. Cambridge: Cambridge University Press, 1996.

———. *The Preface to Luke's Gospel: Literary Convention and Social Context in Luke 1.1–4 and Acts 1.1*. Society for New Testament Studies Monograph Series 78. Cambridge: Cambridge University, 1993.

———. "Luke's Preface in the Context of Greek Preface-writing." *Novum Testamentum* 28 (1986): 48–74.

Alexander, Philip S. "Geography and the Bible (Early Jewish)." Pages 977–88 in vol. 2 of *The Anchor Bible Dictionary*. Edited by David Noel Freedman. 6 vols. New York: Doubleday, 1992.

Alter, Robert. *The Art of Biblical Narrative*. San Francisco: HarperCollins, 1981.

Armstrong, A. MacC. "The Methods of the Greek Physiognomists." *Greece and Rome* 5 (1958): 52–56.

Arndt, W. F. *The Gospel According to St. Luke*. Bible Commentary. Saint Louis, Mo.: Concordia, 1956.

Arterbury, Andrew E. "The Ancient Custom of Hospitality, The Greek Novels, and Acts 10:1–11:18." *Perspectives in Religious Studies* 29 (2002): 53–72.

———. *Entertaining Angels: Early Christian Hospitality in its Mediterranean Setting*. New Testament Monographs 8. Sheffield: Sheffield Phoenix Press, 2005.

Bailey, Kenneth. *Poet and Peasant.* Grand Rapids: Eerdmans, 1976.

Baldwin, C. S. *Medieval Rhetoric and Poetic (to 1400) Interpreted from Representative Works.* New York: Macmillan, 1928.

Barré, Michael L. "Qumran and the Weakness of Paul." *Catholic Biblical Quarterly* 42 (1980): 216–27.

Barrett, C. K. *A Critical and Exegetical Commentary on the Acts of the Apostles.* International Critical Commentary 30. Volume 1. Edinburgh: T&T Clark, 1994.

———. "Acts and the Pauline Corpus." *Expository Times* 78 (1976–77): 2–5.

Bassler, J. . "Luke and Paul on Impartiality." *Biblica* 66 (1985): 546–52.

Bauckham, Richard. "For Whom Were Gospels Written?" Pages 9–48 in *The Gospel for All Christians: Rethinking the Gospel Audiences.* Edited by Richard Bauckham. Grand Rapids: Eerdmans, 1998.

Bauer, J. "POLLOI." *Novum Testamentum* 4 (1960): 263–66.

Beavis, Mary Ann. "Ancient Slavery as an Interpretive Context for the New Testament Servant Parables with Special Reference to the Unjust Steward (Luke 16:1–8)." *Journal of Biblical Literature* 111 (1992): 37–54.

———. "Parable and Fable: Synoptic Parables and Greco-Roman Fables Compared." *Catholic Biblical Quarterly* 52 (1990): 473–98.

Bede, The Venerable. *Commentary on the Acts of the Apostles.* Translated by Lawrence T. Martin. Kalamazoo: Cistercian, 1989.

Berger, K. "Materialen zu Form und Überlieferungsgeschichte neutestamentlicher Gleichnisse." *Novum Testamentum* 15 (1973): 33–36.

———. "Hellinistische Gattungen im Neuen Testament." *ANRW* 25.2:1031–32. Part 2, *Principat,* 33.1. Edited by H. Temporini and W. Haase. NewYork: de Gruyter, 1989.

Betz, Hans D. *Galatians: A Commentary on Paul's Letter to the Churches in Galatia.* Hermeneia. Philadelphia: Fortress, 1979.

Black, Clifton C. "The Rhetorical Form of the Hellenistic Jewish and Early Christian Sermon: A Response to Lawrence Wills." *Harvard Theological Review* 81 (1988): 1–8.

Blomberg, Craig. *Interpreting the Parables.* Downer's Grove: InterVarsity, 1990.

———. "Midrash, Chiasmus, and the Outline of Luke's Central Section." Pages 240–44 in *Studies in Midrash and Historiography.* Edited by R. T. France and David Wenham. Gospel Perspectives 3. Sheffield: JSOT, 1983.

Boccaccini, Gabriele. *Middle Judaism: Jewish Thought, 300 B.C.E.–200 C.E.* Minneapolis: Fortress, 1991.

Bock, Darrell L. *Luke 1:1–9:50*. Baker Exegetical Commentary on the New Testament 3. Grand Rapids: Baker, 1994.

———. *Proclamation from Prophecy and Pattern: Lucan Old Testament Christology*. Journal for the Study of the New Testament: Supplement Series 12. Sheffield: JSOT, 1987.

Bonner, S. F. *Education in Ancient Rome*. Berkeley: University of California Press, 1977.

Boorstin, Daniel J. *The Discoverers*. New York: Random House, 1983.

Borgen, Peder. "From Paul to Luke: Observations Toward Clarification of the Theology of Luke-Acts." *Catholic Biblical Quarterly* 31 (1969): 168–82.

Boring, M. Eugene. "Mark 1:1–15 and the Beginning of the Gospel." *Semeia* 52 (1990): 43–81.

Botha, J. E. "Style in the New Testament: The Need for Serious Reconsideration." *Journal for the Study of the New Testament* 43 (1991): 71–87.

Bovon, François. *Das Evangelium nach Lukas*, vol. 1: *Lk 1,1–9,50*. Evangelisch-katholischer Kommentar zum Neuen Testament 3/1. Neukirchen-Vluyn: Neukirchener Verlag, 1989.

Braun, Willi. *Feasting and Social Rhetoric in Luke 14*. Society for New Testament Studies Monograph Series 85. Cambridge: Cambridge University Press, 1995.

Brawley, Robert. "Abrahamic Covenant Traditions and the Characterization of God in Luke-Acts." Pages 109–32 in *The Unity of Luke-Acts*. Edited by J. Verheyden. Bibliotheca ephemeridum theologicarum lovaniensium 142. Leuvan: Leuven University Press, 1999.

Broughton, T. R .S. "The Roman Army." Pages 5:427–45 in *The Beginnings of Christianity*. 5 vols. Edited by Foakes F. J. Jackson and Kirsopp Lake. Grand Rapids: Eerdmans. Repr., 1979.

Brown, H. Stephen. "Paul's Hearing at Caesarea: A Preliminary Comparison with Legal Literature of the Roman Period." *Society of Biblical Literature Seminar Papers* 35 (1996): 319–32.

Brown, Schuyler. "The Role of the Prologues in Determining the Purpose of Luke-Acts." Pages 99–111 in *Perspectives on Luke-Acts*. Edited by Charles H. Talbert. Danville, Va.: Association of Baptist Professors, 1978.

Bruce, F. F. "Is the Paul of Acts the Real Paul?" *Bulletin of the John Rylands University Library of Manchester* 58 (1976): 282–305.

Burridge, Richard A. "Biography." Pages 371–92 in *Handbook of Classical Rhetoric in the Hellenistic Period 330 B.C.–A.D. 400*. Edited by Stanley E. Porter. Leiden: Brill, 1997.

Cadbury, Henry. "Four Features of Lucan Style." Pages 87–102 in *Studies in Luke-Acts*. Edited by Leander E. Keck and J. Louis Martyn. Nashville: Abingdon, 1966.

———. *The Making of Luke-Acts*. London: S.P.C.K., 1958.

———. "Luke and the Horse-Doctors." *Journal of Biblical Literature* 52 (1933): 55–65.

———. "Commentary on the Preface of Luke." Pages 489–510 in Appendix C in vol. 2 of *The Beginnings of Christianity*. Part I. *The Acts of the Apostles*. Edited by F. J. Foakes-Jackson and Kirsopp Lake. London: Macmillan, 1933.

———. *The Style and Literary Method of Luke*. Cambridge, Mass.: Harvard University Press, 1920.

Callan, Terrence. "The Preface of Luke-Acts and Historiography." *New Testament Studies* 31 (1985): 576–81.

Calvin, John. *Commentary on a Harmony of the Evangelists, Matthew, Mark, and Luke*. 3 vols. Grand Rapids: Eerdmans, 1949.

Campbell, D. A. *The Rhetoric of Righteousness in Romans 3:21–26*. Journal for the Study of the New Testament: Supplement Series 65. Sheffield: JSOT, 1992.

Carter, *Matthew: Storyteller, Interpreter, and Evangelist*. Peabody, Mass.: Hendrickson, 1996.

Childs, Brevard S. *Myth and Reality in the Old Testament*. Studies in Biblical Theology 27. Naperville, Ill.: Alec R. Allenson, 1960.

Clark, D. L. *Rhetoric in Graeco-Roman Education*. New York: Columbia University Press, 1957.

Clarke, Albert C. *The Acts of the Apostles: A Critical Edition with Introduction and Notes on Selected Passages*. Oxford: Clarendon, 1933.

Clements, Ronald E. "The Old Testament Background of Acts 10:34–35." Pages 203–16 in *With Steadfast Purpose: Essays in Honor of Henry Jackson Flanders, Jr.* Edited by Naymond H. Keathley. Waco, Tex.: Baylor University Press, 1990.

Conrad, Edgar W. *Reading Isaiah*. Overtures to Biblical Theology. Minneapolis: Fortress, 1991.

Conzelmann, Hans. *Acts of the Apostles*. Translated by James Limburg, et al. Hermeneia. Philadelphia: Fortress, 1987.

———. *The Theology of St. Luke*. Translated by Geoffrey Buswell. New York: Harper, 1961.

Cosby, M. R. "Paul's Persuasive Language in Romans 5." Pages 209–26 in *Persuasive Artistry: Studies in New Testament Rhetoric in Honor of George A. Kennedy*. Edited by E. F. Watson. Journal for the Study of the New Testament: Supplement Series 50. Sheffield: JSOT, 1991.

Crossan, John Dominic. *In Parables: The Challenge of the Historical Jesus.* New York: Harper & Row, 1973.

Crouch, Frank. "The Persuasive Moment: Rhetorical Resolutions in Paul's Defense before Agrippa." *Society of Biblical Literature Seminar Papers* 35 (1996): 332–42.

Culy, Martin M. "Jesus—Friend of God, Friend of His Followers: Echoes of Friendship in the Fourth Gospel." PhD diss., Baylor University, 2002.

Culpepper, R. Alan. *Luke. The New Interpreter's Bible* 9. Pages 3–490. Edited by Leander E. Keck. Nashville: Abingdon, 1997.

———. *John, Son of Zebedee: The Life of a Legend.* Studies on Personalities of the New Testament. Columbia: University of South Carolina Press, 1994.

Cuvillier, E. "*Parabole* dans la Tradition Synoptique." *Etudes théologiques et religieuses* 66 (1991): 25–44.

Dahl, Nils Alstrup. "The Story of Abraham in Luke-Acts." Pages 66–86 in *Jesus in the Memory of the Early Church: Essays.* Minneapolis: Augsburg, 1976.

Danker, Frederick W. *Jesus and the New Age: A Commentary on St. Luke's Gospel.* Rev. and exp. ed. Philadelphia: Fortress, 1988.

Davies, W. D. *The Gospel and the Land: Early Christianity and Jewish Territorial Doctrine.* Berkeley: University of California Press, 1974.

Delebecque, E. "Les deux prologues des Actes des Apotres." *Revue thomiste* 80 (1980): 628–34.

Derrett, J. D. M. "The Friend at Midnight: Asian Ideas in the Gospel of St. Luke." Pages 78–87 in *Donum Gentilicium: New Testament Studies in Honour of David Daube.* Edited by E. Bammel, et al. Oxford: Clarendon, 1978.

Dilke, O. A. W. "Cartography in the Byzantine Empire." Pages 258–75 in *Cartography in Prehistoric, Ancient, and Medieval Europe and the Mediterranean.* Volume 1 of *History of Cartography.* Edited by J. B. Harley and David Woodward. Chicago. University of Chicago Press, 1987.

Dillman, Rainer. "Das Lukasevangelium als Tendenzschrift: Leserlenkung und Leseintention in Lk 1,1–4." *Biblische Zeitschrift* 38 (1994): 87–93.

Dillon, Richard J. "Previewing Luke's Project from His Prologue (Luke 1:1–4)." *Catholic Biblical Quarterly* 43 (1981): 205–27.

Dittenberger, W., ed. *Orientis Graecae Inscriptiones Selectae.* 2 vols. Leipzig: S. Hirzel, 1903–1905. Repr., Hildesheim: Olms, 1960.

Dodd, C. H. *Parables of the Kingdom.* London: Nisbet, 1935. Repr., New York: Scribner, 1961.

Dubois, J. D. "Le prologue de Luc (Lc 1:1–4): [écriture et prédication]." *Etudes théoligiques et religieuses* 52 (1977): 542–47.

Du Plessis, I. I. "Once More: The Purpose of Luke's Prologue (Lk I:1–4)." *Novum Testamentum* 16 (1974): 259–71.

Dupont, Jacques. "Conversion in the Acts of the Apostles." Pages 61–84 in *The Salvation of the Gentiles.* New York: Paulist, 1979.

Ehrman, Bart D. "The Cup, the Bread, and the Salvific Effect of Jesus' Death in Luke-Acts." *Society of Biblical Literature Seminar Papers* 30 (1991): 576–91.

Eisenstadt, S. N. and L. Roniger. *Patrons, Clients and Friends: Interpersonal Relations and the Structure of Trust in Society.* Themes in the Social Sciences. Cambridge: Cambridge University, 1984.

Elliott, John H. "Temple Versus Household in Luke-Acts: A Contrast in Social Institutions." Pages 211–41 in *The Social World of Luke-Acts.* Edited by Jerome Neyrey. Peabody, Mass.: Hendrickson, 1991.

Engberg-Pedersen, Troels. *Paul and the Stoics.* Edinburgh: T&T Clark, 2000.

Enslin, Morton S. "Once Again, Luke and Paul." *Zeitschrift für die Neutestamentliche Wissenschaft und die Kunde der älteren Kirche* 61 (1970): 268–71.

———. "'Luke' and Paul." *Journal of the American Oriental Society* 58 (1938): 81–91.

Esler, Philip. "Glossalalia and the Admission of Gentiles into the Early Christian Community." *Biblical Theology Bulletin* 22 (1992): 136–42.

Evans, Elizabeth C. *Physiognomics in the Ancient World.* Transactions of the American Philosophical Society 59. Philadelphia: The American Philosophical Society, 1969.

Farmer, William R. "Notes on a Literary and Form-Critical Analysis of Some of the Synoptic Material Peculiar to Luke." *New Testament Studies* 8 (1961/62): 301–16.

Finn, Thomas M. *From Death to Rebirth: Ritual and Conversion in Antiquity.* New York: Paulist, 1997.

Fiore, Benjamin. "The Theory and Practice of Friendship in Cicero." Pages 59–76 in *Greco-Roman Perspectives on Friendship.* Edited by J. T. Fitzgerald. Society of Biblical Literature Resources for Biblical Study 34. Atlanta: Scholars Press, 1997.

Fitzgerald, J. T., ed. *Greco-Roman Perspectives on Friendship.* Society of Biblical Literature Resources for Biblical Study 34. Atlanta: Scholars Press, 1997.

———. "Introduction." Pages 1–12 in *Greco-Roman Perspectives on Friendship.* Edited by J. T. Fitzgerald. Society of Biblical Literature Resources for Biblical Study 34. Atlanta: Scholars Press, 1997.

Fitzmyer, Joseph A. *The Acts of the Apostles*. Anchor Bible 31. New York: Doubleday, 1998.

———. *The Gospel According to Luke: Introduction, Translation, and Notes*. Anchor Bible 28. Garden City, N.Y.: Doubleday, 1981.

———. *The Gospel According to Luke X–XXIV.* Anchor Bible 28A. Garden City, N.Y.: Doubleday, 1985.

———. *Luke the Theologian: Aspects of His Teaching*. New York: Paulist, 1989.

Focke, F. "Synkrisis." *Hermes* 58 (1923): 327–68.

Ford, J. Massyngbaerde. "The Physical Features of the Antichrist." *Journal for the Study of the Pseudepigrapha* 14 (1996): 23–41.

Fraisse, J.-C. *Philia: La Notion d'Amitié dans la Philosphie Antique*. Bibliothèque d'Histoire de la Philosophie. Paris: Librairie Philosophique J. Vrin, 1974.

Funk, Robert. *Poetics of Biblical Narrative*. Sonoma: Polebridge, 1988.

———. *Parables and Presence*. Philadelphia: Fortress, 1982.

———. "The Apostolic *Parousia:* Form and Significance." Pages 249–68 in *Christian History and Interpretation: Studies Presented to John Knox*. Edited by W. R. Farmer. Cambridge: Cambridge University, 1967.

Gamble, Harry. *The New Testament Canon: Its Making and Meaning*. Guides to Biblical Scholarship. Philadelphia: Fortress, 1985.

Garland, David. *Reading Matthew: A Literary and Theological Commentary on the First Gospel.* New York: Crossroad, 1995.

Garland, Robert. *The Eye of the Beholder: Deformity and Disability in the Greco-Roman World.* Ithaca, N.Y.: Cornell University Press, 1995.

Gaventa, Beverly Roberts. *From Darkness to Light: Aspects of Conversion in the New Testament.* Overtures to Biblical Theology 20. Philadelphia: Fortress, 1986.

Gleason, Maud W. *Making Men: Sophists and Self-Presentation in Ancient Rome.* Princeton, Princeton University Press, 1995.

Goulder, Michael. *Luke: A New Paradigm.* 2 vols. Journal for the Study of the New Testament: Supplement Series 20. Sheffield: Sheffield Academic Press, 1989.

Gräbe, P. J. "Δύναμις as a Pneumatological Concept in the Main Pauline Letters." *Biblische Zeitschrift* 36 (1992): 228–29.

Grass. Joseph A. "Emmaus Revisited (Luke 24:13–35 and Acts 8:26–40)." *Catholic Biblical Quarterly* 26 (1964): 463–67.

Green, Joel B. *The Gospel of Luke.* New International Commentary on the New Testament. Grand Rapids: Eerdmans, 1997.

———. "The Problem of a Beginning: Israel's Scriptures in Luke 1–2." *Bulletin for Biblical Research* 4 (1994): 61–85.

————. "To Turn from Darkness to Light. (Acts 26:18): Conversion in the Narrative of Luke-Acts." Pages 103–18, 271–74 in *Conversion in the Wesleyan Tradition*. Nashville: Abingdon, 2001.

Guerra, A. *Romans and the Apologetic Tradition: The Purpose, Genre and Audience of Paul's Letter*. Society for New Testament Studies Monograph Series 81. Cambridge: Cambridge University Press, 1995.

Güttgemanns, Erhardt. "In welchem Sinne ist Lukas 'Historiker'? Die Beziehungen von Luk 1,1–4 und Papias zur antiken Rhetorik." *Linguistica Biblica* 54 (1983): 9–26.

Haacker, K. "Mut zum Bitten. Eine Auslegung von Lukas 11,5–8." *Theologische Beiträge* 17 (1986): 1–6.

Haenchen, Ernst. *The Acts of the Apostles: A Commentary*. Translated by Bernard Noble, et al. Philadelphia: Westminster, 1971.

————. "Das 'Wir' in der Apostelgeschichte und das Itinerar." *Zeitschrift für Theologie und Kirche* 58 (1961): 329–66.

Hamm, M. Dennis. "Acts 3:1–10: The Healing of the Temple Beggar as Lucan Theology." *Biblica* 67 (1986): 305–19.

————. "Acts 3:12–26: Peter's Speech and the Healing of the Man Born Lame." *Perspectives in Religious Studies* 11 (1984): 199–217.

————. "This Sign of Healing. Acts 3:1–10: A Study in Lucan Theology." PhD diss., St. Louis University, 1975.

Harley, J. B. and David Woodward, eds. *Cartography in Prehistoric, Ancient, and Medieval Europe and the Mediterranean*. Vol. 1 of *The History of Cartography*. Chicago: University of Chicago Press, 1987.

Harnack, Adolf von. *Luke the Physician: The Author of the Third Gospel and the Acts of the Apostles*. Translated by J. R. Wilkinson. New York: Putnam, 1909.   .

Hedrick, Charles. *Parables as Poetic Fictions: The Creative Voice of Jesus*. Peabody, Mass.: Hendrickson, 1994.

Hemer, Colin J. *The Book of Acts in the Setting of Hellenistic History*. Wissenschaftliche Untersuchungen zum Neuen Testament 49. Tübingen: J. C. B. Mohr, 1989.

Hengel, Martin. *Judaism and Hellenism: Studies in Their Encounter in Palestine During the Early Hellenistic Period*. Translated by John Bowden. Philadelphia: Fortress, 1974.

Hillard, T., A. Nobbs, and B. Winter. "Acts and The Pauline Corpus I: Ancient Literary Parallels." Pages 183–214 in *The Book of Acts in Its Ancient Literary Setting*. Edited by Bruce W. Winter and Andrew D. Clarke. Vol. 1 of *The Book of Acts in Its First Century Setting*. Edited by Bruce W. Winter. Grand Rapids: Eerdmans, 1993.

Hobart, William K. *The Medical Language of St. Luke*. Dublin: Hodges, Figgis, 1882. Repr., Grand Rapids: Baker, 1954.

Hock, Ronald F. "The Rhetoric of Romance." Pages 445–66 in *Handbook of Classical Rhetoric in the Hellenistic Period 330 B.C.–A.D. 400*. Edited by Stanley E. Porter. Leiden: Brill, 1997.

Hock, Ronald F. and E. N. O'Neil, eds. *The Chreia in Ancient Rhetoric: Volume I. The Progymnasmata*. Society of Biblical Literature Texts and Translations 27. Atlanta: Scholars Press, 1986.

Hogan, Derek. "The Forensic Speeches in Acts in Their Literary Environment." PhD diss., Baylor University, 2006.

———. "Paul's Defense: A Comparison of the Forensic Speeches in Acts, *Callirhoe*, and *Leucippe and Clitophon*." *Perspectives in Religious Studies* 29 (2002): 73–87.

Honoré, A. M. "A Statistical Study of the Synoptic Problem." *Novum Testamentum* 10 (1968): 95–147.

Hooker, Morna. *Jesus and the Servant: The Influence of the Servant Concept of Deutero-Isaiah in the New Testament*. London: SPCK, 1959.

Hornik, Heidi J. and Mikeal C. Parsons. *Illuminating Luke: The Infancy Narrative in Italian Renaissance Painting*. Harrisburg, Pa.: Trinity, 2003.

House, C. "Defilement by Association: Some Insights from the Usage of *koinos/koinoō* in Acts 10 and 11." *Andrews University Seminary Studies* 21 (1983): 143–53.

Hubbard, B. J. "Commissioning Stories in Luke-Acts: A Study of Their Antecedents, Form and Content." *Semeia* 8 (1977): 103–26.

Hughes, F. W. *Early Christian Rhetoric and 2 Thessalonians*. Journal for the Study of the New Testament: Supplement Series 30. Sheffield: JSOT, 1989.

Irwin, W. H. "Fear of God, the Analogy of Friendship and Ben Sira's Theodicy." *Biblica* 76 (1995): 551–59.

Jeremias, Joachim. *The Parables of Jesus*. 2d rev. ed. Translated by S. H. Hooke. New York: Charles Scribner's Sons, 1972.

Jervell, Jacob. *Luke and the People of God*. Minneapolis, Minn.: Augsburg, 1972.

Jewett, Robert. *The Thessalonian Correspondence: Pauline Rhetoric and Millenarian Piety*. Foundations and Facets: New Testament. Philadelphia: Fortress, 1986.

Johnson, A. F. "Assurance for Man: The Fallacy of Translating *Anaideia* by 'Persistence' in Luke 11:5–8." *Journal of the Evangelical Theological Society* 22 (1979): 123–31.

Johnson, Luke Timothy. *The Acts of the Apostles*. Sacra pagina 5. Collegeville, Minn.: Liturgical, 1992.

———. *The Gospel of Luke*. Sacra pagina 3. Collegeville, Minn.: Liturgical, 1991.

————. "On Finding the Lukan Community: A Cautious Cautionary Essay." Pages 87–100 in *Society of Biblical Literature Seminar Papers.* Edited by Paul J. Achtemeier. Missoula: Scholars Press, 1979.

Jolivet, Ira, Jr. "The Structure and Argumentative Strategy of Romans." PhD diss., Baylor University, 1994.

Juel, Donald. *Luke-Acts: The Promise of History.* Atlanta: John Knox, 1983.

————. *Messianic Exegesis: Christological Interpretation of the Old Testament in Early Christianity.* Philadelphia: Fortress, 1988.

Kennedy, George A. *The Art of Rhetoric in the Roman World.* Princeton: Princeton University Press, 1972.

————. *Classical Rhetoric and Its Christian and Secular Tradition from Ancient to Modern Times.* Chapel Hill: University of North Carolina Press, 1980.

————. *A New History of Classical Rhetoric.* Princeton: Princeton University Press, 1994.

————. *New Testament Interpretation through Rhetorical Criticism.* Chapel Hill: University of North Carolina Press, 1980.

————. "The Speeches in Acts." Pages 114–40 in *New Testament Interpretation through Rhetorical Criticism.* Chapel Hill: University of North Carolina Press, 1984.

Kennedy, George A., ed. *Progymnasmata: Greek Textbooks of Prose Composition Introductory to the Study of Rhetoric.* Fort Collins, Colo.: Chez l'auteur, 1999.

Kern, Philip H. *Rhetoric and Galatians: Assessing an Approach to Paul's Epistle.* Society of New Testament Studies Monograph 101. Cambridge: Cambridge University Press, 1998.

Klein, Günther. "Lukas 1,1–4 als theologisches Programm." Pages 193–216 in *Zeit und Geschichte: Dankesgabe an Rudolf Bultmann zum 80. Geburtstag.* Edited by Erich Dinkler. Tübingen: J. C. B. Mohr, 1964.

Knox, John. "Acts and the Pauline Letter Corpus." Pages 279–87 in *Studies in Luke-Acts: Essays Presented in Honor of Paul Schubert.* Edited by L. E. Keck and J. L. Martyn. Nashville: Abingdon, 1966.

Knox, Wilfred L. *The Acts of the Apostles.* Cambridge: Cambridge University Press, 1948.

Konstan, D. *Friendship in the Classical World.* Key Themes in Ancient History. Cambridge: Cambridge University Press, 1997.

Krodel, Gerhard. *Acts.* Augsburg Commentaries on the New Testament. Minneapolis: Augsburg, 1986.

Kümmel, Werner Georg. *Introduction to the New Testament.* Translated by Howard Clark Kee. Revised and enlarged English edition. Nashville: Abingdon, 1973.

Kürzinger, J. "Lk 1,3: . . . ἀκριβῶς καθεξῆς σοι γράψαι." *Biblische Zeitschrift* 18 (1974): 249–55.

Lentz, J. C. *Luke's Portrait of Paul.* Society for New Testament Studies Monograph Series 77. Cambridge: Cambridge University Press, 1993.

Levinsohn, Stephen H. *Textual Connections in Acts.* Society of Bibilical Literature Monograph Series 31. Atlanta: Scholars Press, 1987.

Levison, J. R. "Did the Spirit Inspire Rhetoric? An Exploration of George Kennedy's Definition of Early Christian Rhetoric." Pages 25–40 in *Persuasive Artistry: Studies in New Testament Rhetoric in Honor of George A. Kennedy.* Edited by E. F. Watson. Journal for the Study of the New Testament: Supplement Series 50. Sheffield: JSOT, 1991.

Long, W. R. "The Trial of Paul in the Book of Acts." PhD diss., Brown University, 1982.

Lüdemann, Gerd. *Early Christianity According to the Tradition in Acts: A Commentary.* Minneapolis: Fortress, 1989.

Mack, Burton L. *Rhetoric and the New Testament.* Guides to Biblical Scholarship. Minneapolis: Fortress, 1990.

Mack, Burton L. and Vernon K. Robbins. *Patterns of Persuasion in the Gospels.* Sonoma, Calif.: Polebridge, 1989.

Maddox, Robert. *The Purpose of Luke-Acts.* Studies of the New Testament and its World. Edinburgh: T&T Clark, 1982.

Malbon, Elizabeth Struthers. *Narrative Space and Mythic Meaning in Mark.* San Francisco: Harper & Row, 1986.

Malherbe, Abraham J. "A Physical Description of Paul." Pages 170–75 in *Christians Among Jews and Gentiles: Essays in Honor of Krister Stendahl on his Sixty-fifth Birthday.* Edited by George W. E. Nickelsburg with George W. MacRae. Philadelphia: Fortress, 1986.

Malina, Bruce J. "First-Century Personality: Dyadic, Not Individualistic." Pages 67–96 in *The Social World of Luke-Acts: Models for Interpretation.* Edited by Jerome H. Neyrey. Peabody, Mass.: Hendrickson, 1991.

———. *The New Testament World: Insights from Cultural Anthropology.* Rev. ed. Louisville: Westminster John Knox, 1993.

———. "Patron and Client: The Analogy Behind Synoptic Theology." *Forum* 4 (1988): 2–32.

Malina, Bruce J. and Jerome Neyrey. "Honor and Shame in Luke-Acts: Pivotal Values of the Mediterranean World." Pages 25–65 in *The Social World of Luke-Acts: Models for Interpretation.* Edited by Jerome H. Neyrey. Peabody, Mass.: Hendrickson, 1991.

———. *Portraits of Paul: An Archaeology of Ancient Personality.* Louisville: Westminster John Knox, 1996.

Marcus, Joel. *Mark 1–8.* Anchor Bible 27A. Garden City: Doubleday, 1999.

Marrou, Henri Irénée. *A History of Education in Antiquity.* London: Sheed & Ward, 1956.

Marrow, S. B. "Parrhesia and the New Testament." *Catholic Biblical Quarterly* 44 (1982): 431–46.

Marshall, I. Howard. "Acts and the 'Former Treatise.'" Pages 163–82 in *The Book of Acts in Its Ancient Literary Setting.* Edited by Bruce W. Winter and Andrew D. Clarke. Vol. 1 of *The Book of Acts in Its First Century Setting.* Edited by Bruce W. Winter. Grand Rapids: Eerdmans, 1993.

———. "Luke's View of Paul." *Southwest Journal of Theology* 33 (1990): 41–51.

———. "Luke and His 'Gospel.'" Pages 289–308 in *Das Evangelium und die Evangelien.* Wissenschaftliche Untersuchungen zum Neuen Testament 28. Edited by Peter Stuhlmacher. Tübingen: Mohr, 1983.

———. *Commentary on Luke.* New International Greek Testament Commentary. Grand Rapids: Eerdmans, 1978.

Martin, Clarice. "A Chamberlain's Journey and the Challenge of Interpretation for Liberation." *Semeia* 47 (1989): 105–35.

Martin, Dale B. *The Corinthian Body.* New Haven: Yale University Press, 1995.

Mathews, Thomas. *The Clash of the Gods: A Reinterpretation of Early Christian Art.* Rev. ed. Princeton: Princeton University Press, 1999.

Matson, David L. *Household Conversion Narratives in Acts: Pattern and Interpretation.* Journal for the Study of the New Testament: Supplement Series 123. Sheffield: Sheffield Academic Press, 1996.

Meier, John P. *The Vision of Matthew.* New York: Paulist, 1979.

Mesk, J. "Die Beispiele in Polemos Physiognomonk." *Wiener Studien* 50 (1932): 51–67.

Metzner, R. "In aller Freundschaft: ein frühchristlicher Fall freundschaftlicher Gemeinschaft (Phil 2.25–30)." *New Testament Studies* 48 (2002): 111–31.

Meynet, R. *L'Évangile selon saint Luc: Analyse rhétorique.* 2 vols. Paris: Cerf, 1988.

Michiels, R. "A conception lucanienne de la conversion." *Ephemerides theologicae lovanienses* 41 (1965): 42–78.

Millard, A. R. "Cartography in the Ancient Near East." Pages 107–16 in *Cartography in Prehistoric, Ancient, and Medieval Europe and the Mediterranean.* Volume 1 of *History of Cartography.* Edited by J. B. Harley and David Woodward. Chicago. University of Chicago Press, 1987.

Mitchell, Alan C. "'Greet the Friends by Name': New Testament Evidence for the Greco-Roman *Topos* on Friendship." Pages 225–62 in *Greco-Roman Perspectives on Friendship.* Edited by J. T. Fitzgerald. Society of Biblical Literature Resources for Biblical Study 34. Atlanta: Scholars Press, 1997.

————. "The Social Function of Friendship in Acts 2:44–47." *Journal of Biblical Literature* 111 (1992): 255–72.

Mitchell, Margaret. *Paul and the Rhetoric of Reconciliation: An Exegetical Investigation of the Language and Composition of 1 Corinthians.* Hermeneutische Untersuchungen zur Theologie 28. Tübingen: Mohr-Siebeck, 1991.

Moessner, David P. "The Meaning of καθεξῆς in the Lukan Prologue as the Key to the Distinctive Contribution of Luke's Narration among the 'Many.'" Pages 1513–28 in *The Four Gospels 1992. Festschrift Frans Neirynck.* Edited by F. Van Segbroeck, et al. Leuven: Leuven University Press, 1992.

————. "'The Christ Must Suffer,' The Church Must Suffer: Rethinking the Theology of the Cross in Luke-Acts." *Society of Biblical Literature Seminar Papers* 29 (1990): 165–95.

Moore, Stephen. "Are the Gospels Unified Narratives?" *Society of Biblical Literature Seminar Papers* 26 (1987): 443–58.

Morgenthaler, Robert. *Lukas und Quintilian. Rhetorik als Erzählkunst.* Zürich: Gotthelf Verlag, 1993.

————. *Die lukanische Geschichtsschreibung als Zeugnis.* 2 vols. Zurich: Zwingli, 1978.

Mueller, J. R. and S. E. Robinson. "Apocryphon of Ezekiel." Pages 492–95 in volume 1 of *The Old Testament Pseudepigrapha: Apocalyptic Literature and Testaments.* Edited by James H. Charlesworth. Garden City: Doubleday, 1983.

Mussner, F. "καθεξῆς im Lukasprolog." Pages 253–55 in *Jesus und Paulus: Festschrift für Werner Georg Kümmel zum 70. Geburtstag.* Edited by E. E. Ellis and E. Grässer. Göttingen: Vandenhoeck & Ruprecht.

Neyrey, Jerome. H. "The Forensic Defense Speech and Paul's Trial Speeches in Acts 22–26: Form and Function." Pages 210–24 in *Luke-Acts: New Perspectives from the Society of Biblical Literature Seminar.* Edited by C. H. Talbert. New York: Crossroad, 1984.

————. "The Symbolic Universe of Luke-Acts: 'They Turn the World Upside Down.'" Pages 271–304 in *The Social World of Luke-Acts: Models for Interpretation.* Edited by Jerome H. Neyrey. Peabody, Mass.: Hendrickson, 1991.

Neyrey, Jerome H., ed. *The Social World of Luke-Acts: Models for Interpretation*. Peabody, Mass.: Hendrickson, 1991.

Nock, Arthur Darby. *Conversion: The Old and New Religion from Alexander the Great to Augustine of Hippo*. London: Oxford University Press, 1933. Repr., Baltimore: John Hopkins University Press, 1998.

Nolland, John. *Luke 1–9:20*. Word Biblical Commentary 35A. Dallas: Word, 1989.

———. *Luke 9:21–18:34*. Word Biblical Commentary 35B. Dallas: Word, 1993.

O'Fearghail, Fearghus. "'Full of Spirit and Wisdom': Luke's Portrait of Stephen (6:1–8:1a) as a Man of Self-Mastery." Pages 97–114 in *Asceticism and the New Testament*. Edited by L. E. Vaage and Vincent L. Wimbush. New York: Routledge, 1999.

———. *The Introduction to Luke-Acts: A Study of the Role of Luke 1,1–4,44 in the Composition of Luke's Two-Volume Work*. Analecta biblica 126. Rome: Pontifical Biblical Institute, 1991.

Olyan, Saul M. "'Anyone Blind or Lame Shall Not Enter the House': On the Interpretation of Second Samuel 5:8b." *Catholic Biblical Quarterly* 60 (1998): 218–27.

O'Neil, Edward N. "Plutarch on Friendship." Pages 105–22 in *Greco-Roman Perspectives on Friendship*. Edited by J. T. Fitzgerald. Society of Biblical Literature Resources for Biblical Study 34. Atlanta: Scholars Press, 1997.

O'Reilly, Leo. *Word and Sign in The Acts of The Apostles: A Study in Lucan Theology*. Rome: Editrice Pontificia Università Gregoriana, 1987.

O'Toole, Robert. *The Christological Climax of Paul's Defense Speech in Acts 26*. Rome: Pontifical Biblical Institute, 1971.

Palmer, Darryl W. "Acts and the Ancient Historical Monograph." Pages 1–29 in *The Book of Acts in Its Ancient Literary Setting*. Edited by Bruce W. Winter and Andrew D. Clarke. Vol. 1 of *The Book of Acts in Its First Century Setting*. Edited by Bruce W. Winter. Grand Rapids: Eerdmans, 1993.

———. "The Literary Background of Acts 1.1–14." *New Testament Studies* 33 (1987): 427–38.

Parsons, Mikeal C. "Christian Origins and Narrative Openings: The Sense of a Beginning in Acts 1–5." *Review & Expositor* 87 (1990): 403–22.

———. "Acts." Pages 1–64 in *Acts and Pauline Writings*. Volume 7. Mercer Commentary on the Bible. Edited by Watson Mills, et al. Macon: Mercer University Press, 1997.

———. *The Departure of Jesus in Luke-Acts: The Ascension Narratives in Context*. Journal for the Study of the New Testament: Supplement Series 21. Sheffield: Sheffield Academic Press, 1987.

————. *Body and Character in Luke and Acts*. Grand Rapids: Baker, 2006.

————. " 'Nothing Defiled AND Unclean': The Conjunction's Function in Acts 11:14." *Perspectives in Religious Studies* 27 (2000): 263–74.

————. "The Place of Jerusalem on the Lukan Landscape: An Exercise in Symbolic Cartography." Pages 155–72 in *Literary Studies in Luke-Acts: Essays in Honor of Joseph B. Tyson*. Edited by Richard P. Thompson and Thomas E. Phillips. Macon: Mercer University Press, 1998.

————. Review of Philip H. Kern, *Rhetoric and Galatians: Assessing an Approach to Paul's Epistle*. *Religious Studies Review* 26 (2000): 268.

Parsons, Mikeal C., and Richard I. Pervo. *Rethinking the Unity of Luke and Acts*. Minneapolis: Fortress, 1993.

Penner, Todd. "Narrative as Persuasion: Epideitic Rhetoric and Scribal Amplification in the Stephen Episode in Acts." *Society of Biblical Literature Seminar Papers* 35 (1996): 352–67.

Pilch, J. J. and Bruce Malina, eds. *Biblical Social Values and Their Meaning: A Handbook*. Peabody, Mass.: Hendrickson, 1993.

Plummer, Alfred. *A Critical and Exegetical Commentary on the Gospel according to St. Luke*. 5th ed. *International Critical Commentary*. Edinburgh: T&T Clark, 1901.

Pogoloff, Stephen M. *Logos and Sophia: The Rhetorical Situation of 1 Corinthians*. Society of Biblical Literature Dissertation Series 134. Atlanta: Scholars Press, 1992.

Polhill, John. *Acts*. New American Commentary 26. Nashville: Broadman, 1992.

Porter, Stanley E. "Paul of Tarsus and His Letters." Pages 533–85 in *Handbook of Classical Rhetoric in the Hellenistic Period 330 B.C.–A.D. 400*. Edited by Stanley E. Porter. Leiden: Brill, 1997.

————. *The Plot of Acts: Essays in Literary Criticism*. Wissenschaftliche Untersuchungen zum Neuen Testament 15. Tübingen: Mohr-Siebeck, 1999.

Porter, Stanley E., ed. *Handbook of Classical Rhetoric in the Hellenistic Period 330 B.C.–A.D. 400*. Leiden: Brill, 1997.

Powell, Mark Allen. *What Are They Saying About Luke?* New York: Paulist, 1989.

Praeder, Susan Marie. "The Problem of First Person Narration in Acts." *Novum Testamentum* 29 (1987): 193–218.

Rabinowitz, Peter J. *Before Reading: Narrative Conventions and the Poetics of Interpretation*. Ithaca: Cornell University Press, 1987.

Rebenrich, Stefan. "Historical Prose." Pages 265–338 in *Handbook of Classical Rhetoric in the Hellenistic Period 330 B.C.–A.D. 400*. Edited by Stanley E. Porter. Leiden: Brill, 1997.

Robbins, Vernon K. *Exploring the Texture of the Texts: A Guide to Socio-Rhetorical Interpretation*. Philadelphia: Trinity, 1996.

———. "From Enthymeme to Theology in Luke 11:1–13." Pages 191–214 in *Literary Studies in Luke-Acts. Essays in Honor of Joseph B. Tyson*. Edited by Richard P. Thompson and Thomas E. Phillips. Macon, Ga.: Mercer University Press, 1998.

———. "Narrative in Ancient Rhetoric and Rhetoric in Ancient Narrative." *Society of Biblical Literature Seminar Papers* 35. Atlanta: Scholars Press, 1996.

———. "Prefaces in Greco-Roman Biography and Luke-Acts." *Perspectives in Religious Studies* 6 (1979): 94–108.

———. "Progymnastic Rhetorical Composition and Pre-Gospel Traditions: A New Approach." Pages 111–47 in *The Synoptic Gospels: Source Criticism and the New Literary Criticism*. Edited by Camille Focant. Bibliotheca ephemeridum theologicarum lovaniensium 110. Leuven: Leuven University Press, 1993.

———. "The Social Location of the Implied Author of Luke-Acts." Pages 305–32 in *The Social World of Luke-Acts: Models for Interpretation*. Edited by Jerome H. Neyrey. Peabody, Mass.: Hendrickson, 1991.

———. *The Tapestry of Early Christian Discourse: Rhetoric, Society, and Ideology*. London: Routledge, 1996.

———. "Using Rhetorical Discussions of the Chreia to Interpret the Pronouncement Stories." *Semeia* 64 (1994): vii–xvii.

———. "The Woman Who Touched Jesus' Garments: Socio-Rhetorical Analysis of the Synoptic Accounts." *New Testament Studies* 33 (1987): 502–15.

Roth, John. *The Blind, the Lame, and the Poor: Character Types in Luke-Acts*. Journal for the Study of the New Testament: Supplement Series 144. Sheffield: Sheffield Academic Press, 1999.

Saller, Richard. "Patronage and Friendship in Early Imperial Rome: Drawing the Distinction." Pages 49–62 in *Patronage in Ancient Society*. Edited by Andrew Wallace-Hadrill. London: Routledge, 1989.

———. *Personal Patronage Under the Early Empire*. Cambridge: Cambridge University Press, 1982.

Sanders, E. P. *Tendencies of the Synoptic Tradition*. Cambridge: Cambridge University Press, 1969.

Sandnes, Karl Olav. *Belly and Body in the Pauline Epistles*. Society for New Testament Studies Monograph Series 120. Cambridge: Cambridge University Press, 2002.

Satterthwaite, Philip E. "Acts against the Background of Classical Rhetoric." Pages 337–79 in *The Book of Acts in Its Ancient Literary Setting*. Edited by Bruce W. Winter and Andrew D. Clarke. Vol. 1 of *The*

Book of Acts in Its First Century Setting. Edited by Bruce W. Winter. Grand Rapids: Eerdmans, 1993.

Schneider, Gerhard. "Zur Bedeutung von καθεξῆς im lukanischen Doppelwerk." *Zeitschrift für die neutestamentliche Wissenschaft und die Kunde der älteren Kirche* 68 (1977): 128–31.

———. *Das Evangelium nach Lukas.* 2 vols. Ökumenischer Taschenbuch-Kommentar 3. Gütersloh: Mohn, 1977.

Schubert, Paul. "The Structure and Significance of Luke 24." Pages 165–86 in *Neutestamentliche Studien für Rudolf Bultmann zu seinem siebzigsten Geburtstag.* Edited by W. Eltester. Beihefte zur Zeitschrift für die Neutestamentliche Wissenschaft 21. Berlin: de Gruyter, 1957.

Schürmann, H. *Das Lukasevangelium.* 2 vols. Herders theologischer Kommentar zum Neuen Testament. Freiburg: Herder, 1969.

Scott, Bernard Brandon. *Hear Then the Parable: A Commentary on the Parables of Jesus.* Minneapolis: Fortress, 1989.

Scott, James M. "Luke's Geographical Horizon." Pages 483–544 in *The Book of Acts in Its First Century Setting.* Vol. 2. *Graeco-Roman Setting.* Edited by David W. J. Gill and Conrad Gempf. Grand Rapids: Eerdmans, 1994.

Sed, N. *La mystique cosmologique juive.* Ecole des Hautes Etudes en Science Sociales: Etudes Juives. Paris, 1981.

Segal, Alan F. *Rebecca's Children: Judaism and Christianity in the Roman World.* Cambridge: Harvard University Press, 1986.

Seim, Turid Karlesen. "Abraham, Ancestor or Archetype? A Comparison of Abraham-Language in 4 Maccabees and Luke-Acts." Pages 27–42 in *Antiquity and Humanity: Essays on Ancient Religion and Philosophy. Presentd to Hans Dieter Betz on His 70th Birthday.* Edited by Adela Yarbro Collins and Margaret M. Mitchell. Tübingen: Mohr Siebeck, 2001.

Shelton, J.-A. *As the Romans Did: A Sourcebook in Roman Social History.* 2d ed. New York: Oxofrd University Press, 1998.

Shuler, Philip. "The Rhetorical Character of Luke 1–2." Pages 173–89 in *Literary Studies in Luke-Acts.* Edited by Thomas Phillips and Richard Thompson. Macon, Ga.: Mercer University Press, 1998.

Siegert, F. "Lukas—ein Historiker, d.h. ein Rhetor? Freundschaftliche Entgegnung auf Erhardt Güttgemanns." *Linguistica Biblica* 55 (1984): 57–60.

Siker, J.S. *Disinheriting the Jews. Abraham in Early Christian Controversy.* Louisville: WestminsterJohnKnox, 1991.

Sloan, Robert. "'Signs and Wonders': A Rhetorical Clue to the Pentecost Discourse." *Evangelical Quarterly* 63 (1991): 225–40.

Smith, Catherine Delan. "Cartography in the Prehistoric Period in the Old World: Europe, the Middle East, and North Africa." Pages 54–101 in *Cartography in Prehistoric, Ancient, and Medieval Europe and the Mediterranean.* Volume 1 of *History of Cartography.* Edited by J. B. Harley and David Woodward. Chicago. University of Chicago Press, 1987.

Smith, Jonathan Z. *Map Is Not Territory: Studies in the History of Religions.* Studies in Judaism in Late Antiquity 23. Leiden: Brill, 1978.

Sneen, Donald J. "Exegesis of Luke 1:1–4 with Special Regard to Luke's Purpose as a Historian." *Expository Times* 83 (1971): 40–43.

Snodgrass, K. "*Anaideia* and the Friend at Midnight (Luke 11:8)." *Journal of Biblical Literature* 116 (1997): 505–13.

Soards, Marion L. *The Speeches in Acts: Their Content, Context, and Concerns.* Louisville: Westminster John Knox, 1994.

———. "The Speeches in Acts in Relation to Other Pertinent Ancient Literature." *Ephemerides theologicae lovanienses* 70 (1994): 65–90.

Spencer, F. Scott. *The Portrait of Philip in Acts: A Study of Roles and Relations.* Journal for the Study of the New Testament: Supplement Series 67. Sheffield: JSOT, 1992.

———. "The Ethiopian Eunuch and His Bible: A Social-Science Analysis." *Biblical Theology Bulletin* 22 (1992): 155–65.

———. *Journeying through Acts: A Literary-Cultural Reading.* Peabody, Mass.: Hendrickson, 2004.

Spilsbury, P. "God and Israel in Josephus: A Patron-Client Relationship." Pages 172–91 in *Understanding Josephus: Seven Perspectives.* Journal for the Study of the Pseudepigrapha: Supplement Series 32. Edited by Steve Mason. Sheffield: Sheffield Academic Press, 1998.

Stein, Robert H. "Luke 1:1–4 and Traditionsgeschichte." *Journal of the Evangelical Theological Society* 26 (1983): 421–30.

Stempvoort, P. A. van. "The Interpretation of the Ascension in Luke and Acts." *New Testament Studies* 5 (1959): 30–42.

Stendahl, Krister. *Paul Among the Jews and Gentiles.* Philadelphia: Fortress, 1976.

———. *The School of St. Matthew.* Acta seminarii neotestamentici upsaliensis 20. Lund: Gleerup, 1954.

Sterling, Gregory E. *Historiography and Self-Definition: Josephus, Luke-Acts, and Apologetic Historiography.* Novum Testamentum Supplements 64. Leiden: Brill, 1992.

Stolz, F. "Zeichen und Wunder: Die prophetische Legitimation und ihre Geschichte." *Zeitschrift für Theologie und Kirche* 69 (1972): 125–44.

Strauss, Mark L. *The Davidic messiah in Luke-Acts: The Promise and Its Fulfillment in Lukan Christology.* Journal for the Study of the New Testament: Supplement Series 110.

Streeter, B. H. *The Four Gospels: a Study of Origins, Treating of the Manuscript Tradition, Sources, Authorship, and Dates.* London: Macmillan, 1924.

Sundberg, A. C. "Canon Muratori: A Fourth-Century List." *Harvard Theological Review* 66 (1973): 1–41.

Talbert, Charles H. "Conversion in the Acts of the Apostles: Ancient Auditors' Perceptions." Pages 141–54 in *Literary Studies in Luke-Acts: Essays in Honor of Joseph B. Tyson.* Edited by Richard P. Thompson and Thomas E. Phillips. Macon: Mercer University Press, 1998.

———. *Literary Patterns, Theological Themes, and the Genre of Luke-Acts.* Society of Biblical Literature Monograph Series 20. Missoula, Mont.: Scholars Press, 1974.

———. *Reading Acts: A Literary and Theological Commentary on the Acts of the Apostles.* New York: Crossroad, 1997.

———. *Reading Luke: A Literary and Theological Commentary on the Third Gospel.* New York: Crossroad, 1982.

Tannehill, Robert. *Luke.* Abingdon Commentary on the New Testament. Nashville: Abingdon, 1996.

———. *The Narrative Unity of Luke-Acts.* 2 volumes. Philadelphia: Fortress, 1986.

Taylor, R. O. P. *Groundwork for the Gospels, With Some Collected Papers.* Oxford: Blackwell, 1946.

Terrien, Samuel. "The Omphalos Myth and Hebrew Religion." *Vetus Testamentum* 20 (1970): 313–38.

Thom, J. C. " 'Harmonious Equality': The *Topos* of Friendship in Neopythagorean Writings." Pages 77–103 in *Greco-Roman Perspectives on Friendship.* Edited by J. T. Fitzgerald. Society of Biblical Literature Resources for Biblical Study 34. Atlanta: Scholars Press, 1997.

Tiede, David. *Promise and History in Luke-Acts.* Philadelphia: Fortress, 1980.

Tolbert, Mary Ann. *Sowing the Gospel: Mark's World in Literary-Historical Perspective.* Minneapolis: Fortress, 1989.

Tyson, Joseph B. "The Gentile Mission and the Authority of Scripture in Acts." *New Testament Studies* 33 (1987): 619–31.

Unnik, W. C. van "Once More, St. Luke's Prologue." *Neotestamentliche* 7 (1963): 7–26.

Veltman, F. "The Defense Speeches of Paul in Acts." Pages 243–56 in *Perspectives on Luke-Acts.* Edited by C. H. Talbert. Perspectives in Religious Studies. Special Studies Series 5. Danville, Va.: Association of Baptist Professors of Religion, 1978.

Via, Dan O., Jr. *The Parables: Their Literary and Existential Dimension.* Philadelphia: Fortress, 1967.

Vielhauer, Philipp. "On The 'Paulinism' of Acts." Pages 33–50 in *Studies in Luke-Acts: Essays Presented in Honor of Paul Schubert*. Edited by L. E. Keck and J. L. Martyn. Nashville: Abingdon, 1966.

Vinson, Richard B. "A Comparative Study of Enthymemes in the Synoptic Gospels." Pages 119–41 in *Persuasive Artistry: Studies in New Testament Rhetoric in Honor of George A. Kennedy*. Edited by D. F. Watson. Journal for the Study of the New Testament: Supplement Series 50. Sheffield: Sheffield Academic Press, 1991.

Völkel, M. "Exegetische Erwägungen zum Verständnis des Begriffs καθεξῆς im lukanischen Prolog." *New Testament Studies* 20 (1973–1974): 289–99.

Voragine, Jacobus de. *The Golden Legend*. Translated by Granger Ryan and Helmut Ripperger. New York: Longmans, Green, 1941.

Walker, Jr., William O. "Acts and the Pauline Corpus Revisited: Peter's Speech at the Jerusalem Conference." Pages 77–86 in *Literary Studies in Luke-Acts: Essays in Honor of Joseph B. Tyson*. Edited by R. E. Thompson and T. E. Phillips. Macon, Ga.: Mercer University Press, 1998.

———. "Acts and The Pauline Corpus Reconsidered." *Journal for the Study of the New Testament* 24 (1985): 3–23.

Watson, Duane F. and Alan J. Hauser, eds. *Rhetorical Criticism of the Bible: A Comprehensive Bibliography with Notes on History and Method*. Biblical Interpretation Series 4. Leiden: Brill, 1994.

———. "Paul's Speech to the Ephesian Elders (Acts 20.17–38): Epideictic Rhetoric of Farewell." Pages 184–208 in *Persuasive Artistry: Studies in New Testament Rhetoric in Honor of George A. Kennedy*. Edited by D. F. Watson. Journal for the Study of the New Testament: Supplement Series 50. Sheffield: Sheffield Academic Press, 1990.

Wilkinson, John. *Health and Healing: Studies in New Testament Principles and Practice*. Edinburgh: Handsel, 1980.

Williams, David J. *Paul's Metaphors: Their Context and Character*. Peabody, Mass.: Hendrickson, 1999.

Wills, Jeffrey. *Repetition in Latin Poetry: Figures of Allusion*. Oxford: Clarendon, 1996.

Wilson, Stephen G. *Luke and the Law*. Society for New Testament Studies Monograph Series 50. Cambridge: Cambridge University, 1983.

Winter, Bruce W. and Andrew D. Clarke, eds. *The Book of Acts in Its Ancient Literary Setting*. Grand Rapids: Eerdmans, 1993.

———. "Official Proceedings and the Forensic Speeches in Acts 24–26." Pages 305–36 in *The Book of Acts in Its Ancient Literary Setting*. Edited by Bruce W. Winter and Andrew D. Clarke. Vol. 1 of *The*

Book of Acts in Its First Century Setting. Edited by Bruce W. Winter. Grand Rapids: Eerdmans, 1993.

———. "The Importance of the *Captatio Benevolentiae* in the Speeches of Tertullus and Paul in Acts 24:1–21." *Journal of Theological Studies* 42 (1991): 505–31.

Wintermute, O. S. "Jubilees." Pages 35–142 in *The Old Testament Pseudepigrapha*. 2 vols. Edited by James H. Charlesworth. Garden City, N.Y.: Doubleday & Co., 1985.

Witherington, Ben. *The Acts of the Apostles: A Socio-rhetorical Commentary*. Grand Rapids: Eerdmans, 1998.

Witherup, Ronald D. "Cornelius Over and Over and Over Again: 'Functional Redundancy' in the Acts of the Apostles." *Journal for the Study of the New Testament* 49 (1993): 45–66.

Woodward, David. "Medieval *Mappaemundi*." Pages 286–370 in *Cartography in Prehistoric, Ancient, and Medieval Europe and the Mediterranean*. Volume 1 of *History of Cartography*. Edited by J. B. Harley and David Woodward. Chicago. University of Chicago Press, 1987.

Wuellner, W. "The Rhetorical Genre of Jesus' Sermon in Luke 12.1–13.9." Pages 93–118 in *Persuasive Artistry: Studies in New Testament Rhetoric in Honor of George A. Kennedy*. Edited by D. F. Watson. Journal for the Study of the New Testament: Supplement Series 50. Sheffield: Sheffield Academic Press, 1990.

York, John O. *The Last Shall Be First: The Rhetoric of Reversal in Luke*. Journal for the Study of the New Testament: Supplement Series 46. Sheffield: Sheffield Academic Press, 1991.

Zafiropoulos, Christos A. *Ethics in Aesop's Fables: The Augusta Collection*. Mnemosyne, Supplements 216. Leiden: Brill, 2001.

Zweck, D. "The *Exordium* of the Areopagus Speech, Acts 17.22, 23." *New Testament Studies* (1989): 94–103.

Critical Editions and Translations

Baldwin, *Medieval Rhetoric and Poetic (to 1400) Interpreted from Representative Works*. New York: Macmillan, 1928.

Butts, James R. "The *Progymnasmata* of Theon: A New Text with Translation and Commentary." PhD diss., The Claremont Graduate School, 1986.

[Cicero]. *Ad Herennium*. Translated by Harry Caplan. Loeb Classical Library. Cambridge: Harvard University Press, 1964.

Felten, J., ed. *Nicolai Progymnasmata*. Rhetores Graeci 11. Leipzig: Teubner, 1913.

Förster, Richard, ed. *Scriptores Physiognomonic Graeci et Latini.* 2 vols. Lipsius: Teubner, 1893.

Heath, Malcolm. "Aphthonius Progymnasmata." No pages. Cited May 9, 2006. Online: http://www.leeds.ac.uk/classics/resources/rhetoric/prog-aph.htm.

John Chrysostom. *The Homilies on the Acts of the* Apostles. Oxford: John Henry Parker, 1851.

Nadeau, R. E. "The *Progymnasmata* of Aphthonius in Translation." *Speech Monographs* 19 (1952): 264–85.

Patillon, Michel and Giancarlo Bolognesi, eds. *Aelius Théon Progymnasmata.* Paris: Les Belles Lettres, 1997.

Plutarch. *Moralia.* Translated by F. C. Babbit. Volume 2. Loeb Classical Library. New York: G. P. Putnam, 1928.

Quintilian. *Institutio Oratoria.* Translated by H. E. Butler. New York: G. P. Putnam's Sons, 1920–1922.

Rabe, H., ed. *Ioannis Sardiani Commentarium in Aphthonii Progymnasmats.* Leipzig: Tebner, 1928.

————, ed. *Aphtonii Progymnasmata.* Rhetores Graeci 10. Leipzig: Teubner, 1926.

————, ed. *Hermogenes Opera.* Rhetores Graeci 10. Leipzig: Teubner, 1913.

Spengel, Leonard, ed. *Rhetores Graeci.* 2 vols. Leipzig: Teubner, 1854–1856.

Strabo. *Geography.* Translated by Horace Leondard Jones. Loeb Classical Library. Cambridge: Harvard University Press, 1917. Repr., 1989.

Index of Modern Authors

Index of Ancient Sources